International Marketing
An Annotated Bibliography

International Marketing
An Annotated Bibliography

S. Tamer Cavusgil

Tiger Li

Center for International Business Education and Research
The Eli Broad Graduate School of Management
Michigan State University

Bibliography Series

250 S. Wacker Drive • Chicago, Illinois 60606 • (312) 648-0536

016. 6588
C 383-1

Preface

Introduction

The AMA published two previous bibliographies on international marketing: Cavusgil and Nevin in 1983 and Goldstucker and de la Torre in 1972. Cavusgil and Nevin bibliography covered the decade prior to 1983. Since the latter review, rapid development has been witnessed in international business activity. With an annual growth rate of approximately 12%, the value of world trade has tripled and exceeded $3 trillion in 1990. In Asia, Japan has become an economic superpower next only to the United States. In Europe, 12 member countries of the European Community have decided to dismantle market barriers between them and form a unified market. Privatization is proceeding with rapid pace in the former East Bloc countries. In North America, the United States and Canada have initiated integration of their markets with a free-trade agreement which might soon include Mexico.

At the corporate level, substantial progress has occurred. Many companies have adopted a global marketing approach as their principal strategy. Instead of concentrating on one or two national markets, companies now attempt to market similar products in major markets of the world. International collaborative agreements, including strategic alliances and joint ventures, have been utilized extensively by firms to achieve entry and expansion advantages. Other creative forms of exporting, such as countertrade, technology transfer, and licensing have experienced a steady increase.

Has international marketing, as a body of knowledge that both reflects and guides cross-country marketing activities, experienced any growth paralleling the rapid development of global business? What progress, if any, has been accomplished within major research streams in the international marketing literature? Have any new perspectives or conceptual frameworks emerged in this field of inquiry?

With these questions in mind, we embarked on this project of compiling a new annotated bibliography. The project involved an extensive set of activities spanning one year, including planning, search for journals and articles, sifting through numerous publications, and final editing.

Objectives

This bibliography has five major objectives. First, we want to create an awareness of the growing body of literature in international marketing. We think that an up-to-date and a rather comprehensive reference book would greatly facilitate work in this field of study as well as stimulate future contributions to the literature. Considering the positive response from the marketing academics to the last bibliography by Cavusgil and Nevin (1983), this continuing effort would be worthwhile and beneficial to marketing researchers and practitioners.

Second, we wish to demonstrate one particular approach to the classification of international marketing literature. The suggested approach allows us to synthesize the vast literature into a meaningful framework which, in return, would facilitate the use and the dissemination of knowledge in an orderly and systematic manner. Our framework for classifying the existing literature is described in the next section.

Third, we hope to direct our readers' attention to the new research developments in international marketing, in particular the emergence of market globalization perspectives and interaction approach. The birth of these new research streams has not only expanded the scope of this field of study but also demonstrated that international marketing is on its way to becoming a better integrated and systematic discipline.

Fourth, we aim to direct the attention of scholars in international marketing to a variety of useful sources. The international marketing literature is scattered in a large number of journals and periodicals. Some very useful journals, particularly non-U.S. sources, may have escaped the attention of marketers. We believe that this book will assist readers in developing greater familiarity with the many sources of international marketing information. Further, we believe that readers will find some useful citations in this book which may have gone unnoticed. At the same time, we acknowledge that our coverage of journals is not entirely exhaustive.

Fifth, we want to facilitate assessments of the international marketing literature by readers. A quick review of this book will convince the readers that the contributions to various aspects of international marketing have not been balanced. On one hand, international marketing management continues to be the most prolific stream of literature and buyer behavior has made much progress in the last decade. On the other hand, there continues to be a scarcity of contributions to the topic of pricing decisions.

Framework for the Book

The vast literature in international marketing is organized in this book around the following themes or categories:

Review articles and conceptual contributions to international marketing. Here we classify into this category those articles that assess the state-of-the-art in international marketing or one of its subfields. A number of significant conceptual and theoretical articles in the field are also classified into this category.

Environmental aspects of international marketing. Articles examining the various impacts of economic, cultural, social, political, and legal factors on international marketing are included in this category.

Area-oriented and comparative studies. The writings in this category identify variations arising from differences in marketing systems in different countries, analyze similarities and differences of marketing problems and tasks in foreign countries, and provide an understanding of international marketing operations in a particular country or area.

Globalization issues in international marketing. This category contains three topics: internationalization process, market globalization, and strategic alliances and interaction approach. Internationalization process focuses on issues concerning attitudes and behavior of firms in the process of going international. Market globalization perspective deals with the issue of homogenization of customer needs and calls for firms to establish global strategy and develop global products. Strategic alliance and interaction perspectives focus on the emergence of international corporate linkages such as collaborative agreements, cooperative ventures, and strategic partnerships.

International marketing management. Articles classified into this section are concerned with the principal managerial decisions involved in international marketing. These decisions are found in the areas of entry and expansion strategies, foreign direct investment and joint ventures, licensing and technology transfer, export marketing and countertrade, channels of distribution and logistics, and so on. The reader will note that the contributions cited in this stream constitute the bulk of the bibliography.

Decision tools for international marketing. In this category we consider articles that deal with research methodology in international marketing, the findings of international marketing research, and buyer behavior in the international context. The reader will find that considerable progress has been achieved in these areas.

Illustrated in greater detail in the Table of Contents, this framework is a modified version of the same framework used in the previous bibliography. While it is neither totally comprehensive nor mutually exclusive, it does serve as a meaningful model by which we could classify the international marketing literature. In the cases where an article has multiple themes and may be placed in more than one category, the authors used their judgment in classifying it.

Criteria for Selection

We were guided by three broad criteria in selecting the articles for inclusion in this bibliography.

First, while attempting to expose the reader to a variety of sources in international marketing, we limited our search to those journals which are accessible in most North American libraries. We consulted approximately 30 journals in our search of the international marketing literature.

Second, we screened the literature for those articles which offered the greatest relevance to scholars and practitioners of international marketing. In sifting through the literature, we considered: (a) its potential usefulness to readers; (b) lasting contribution of the article as perceived by us; and (c) the total number of articles which competed for the limited space in that subsection. A number of the articles are included without abstracts because of space limitations. The total number of the articles contained in this bibliography is more than 600.

Third, we limited the coverage to those writings published during the period between January 1982 to October 1991. This was natural since the last international marketing bibliography by Cavusgil and Nevin covered the previous period and the writings in this book represent continuous efforts by researchers since then.

Along with these criteria, we were constrained by the publication guidelines of the AMA. The latter meant that we had to be rather selective in the process of identifying articles which were to be included in the bibliography. Admittedly, we left out some contributions that could have been included if it were not for space limitations.

Nevertheless, we feel that this bibliography is representative of the valuable contributions that have been made to the international marketing literature in the last decade and the users will find this book a rather handy and comprehensive reference manual. The authors are hopeful that future work will be facilitated and stimulated by this work.

Acknowledgements

We would like to express our appreciation to Professors Michael R. Czinkota, Georgetown University, and Robert Green, University of Texas at Austin, who, as past vice-presidents of the AMA's Global Division, first suggested that we embark upon this project. Together with Professor Jean J. Boddewyn of Baruch College, CUNY, they have also reviewed earlier versions of this bibliography. Their suggestions are sincerely appreciated.

In addition, we would like to acknowledge the AMA's Headquarters staff for their assistance. Finally, we thank Tamie Phetteplace of the Center for International Business Education and Research, the Eli Broad Graduate School of Management at Michigan State University for providing cheerful and competent secretarial assistance.

S. Tamer Cavusgil
Tiger Li
East Lansing, Michigan
December 1991

Table of Contents

Listing of the Journals Cited

Advances in International Marketing
Business Horizons
Business Marketing
California Management Review
Columbia Journal of World Business
European Journal of Marketing
Harvard Business Review
Industrial Marketing Management
Industrial Marketing and Purchasing
International Journal of Retailing
International Journal of Advertising
International Management
International Marketing Review
Journal of the Academy of Marketing Science
Journal of Advertising Research
Journal of Advertising
Journal of Business and Industrial Marketing
Journal of Business Research
Journal of Consumer Research
Journal of International Business Studies
Journal of Macromarketing
Journal of Marketing
Journal of Marketing Research
Journal of the Market Research Society
Long Range Planning
Management International Review
Public Relations Quarterly
Service Industries Journal
Singapore Marketing Review
Sloan Management Review

I. Review Articles and Conceptual Contributions to International Marketing

1.1.1

Aaby, Nils-Erik and Stanley F. Slater (1989), "Management Influences on Export Performance: A Review of the Empirical Literature 1978-88," *International Marketing Review*, 6(4), 7-26.

Literature in export performance is reviewed. Concerning firm characteristics, it is found that: (1) company size alone is not an important factor unless it is associated with factors such as financial strength or economy of scales; (2) export performance tends to be satisfactory when management is committed firmly to export; and (3) firms with better management systems and well-planned export activities are more successful. A company is unlikely to succeed if its management does not have an international vision, consistent export goals, favorable attitudes toward export, and the willingness to take risks. In addition, higher growth exporters place greater reliance on markets in developed countries than on those in less developed countries.

1.1.2

Albaum, Gerald and Robert A. Peterson (1984), "Empirical Research in International Marketing, 1976-1982," *Journal of International Business Studies*, 15(1), Spring-Summer, 161-173.

Empirical research in international marketing published from 1976 to 1982 is reviewed. The review focuses on what has been researched and how the research has been conducted. It is found that the "state of the art" in international marketing is still lagging behind that of domestic marketing research. Research in international marketing is fragmentary and not sufficiently programmatic to offer anything other than incomplete insights into the underlying phenomena of interest. 75% of the studies were concerned with either elements of the marketing mix or consumer behavior, and 31% of the studies involved the U.S. as a market area. Many of the studies utilized qualitative techniques; in particular, in-depth and unstructured interviews were frequently used. The authors propose that an information bank consisting of integrated empirical research findings on international marketing issues be established.

1.1.3

Amine, Lyn S. and S. Tamer Cavusgil (1983), "Exploring Strategic Aspects of Export Marketing," *International Marketing Review*, 1(2), Winter, 5-11.

This article examines the existing literature in international marketing and concludes that certain avenues of research are being actively pursued but much remains to be done. The authors highlight those areas where answers to policy questions are clearly beginning to emerge and identify other areas which have thus far received scant attention. The authors suggest that for research in exporting and international marketing to advance over-simplification of the issues be avoided at all costs. Piecemeal only yield, at best, a partial understanding. Far preferable would be the adoption of a systems approach which recognizes the interactive nature of the many macro- and micro-level variables.

1.1.4

Anderson, Erin and Hubert Gatignon (1986), "Modes of Foreign Entry: A Transaction Cost Analysis and Propositions," *Journal of International Business Studies*, 17(3), Fall, 1-26.

A transaction cost framework is proposed for investigating the entry mode decision. The theory is specifically concerned with maximizing long-term efficiency. The framework provides a theoretical basis for systematically interrelating the literature into propositions. It also provides propositions about interactions that resolve the apparently contradictory arguments advanced to date. The article illustrates the feasibility of clustering 17 entry modes into the degree of control the mode provides the entrant. It is concluded that the most appropriate entry mode is a function of the trade-off between control and the cost of resource commitment.

1.1.5

Atac, Osman A. (1986), "International Experience Theory and Global Strategy," *International Marketing Review*, 3(4), Winter, 52-61.

A full understanding of the economic development processes of the Newly Industrialized Countries is important both for the multinational corporations and the developing countries. This paper suggests a theoretical framework based on experience theory to explain how the NICs obtained their strategic comparative advantages in global markets. It is argued that the world social and economic environment of the post-World War II period was conducive for the realization of such advantages. Most recent changes, however, have important implications for the developing countries and the multinational corporations in the selection of global strategies.

1.1.6

Baliga, B.R. (1984), "World-Views and Multinational Corporations' Investments in the Less Developed Countries," *Columbia Journal of World Business*, 19(2), Summer, 80-84.

Three world-views appear to dominate multinational corporations' investments and operation decisions in less developed countries. The implications of these world-views are examined specifically with regard to their proclivity for conflict with the host governments. This article suggests that more comprehensive world-views are the appropriate starting point for business decisions.

1.1.7

Black, J. Stewart and Mark Mendenhall (1991), "The UCurve Adjustment Hypothesis Revisited: A Review and Theoretical Framework," *Journal of International Business Studies,* 22(2), 225-247.

Most of the scholarly research in the cross-cultural business field has been atheoretical and the subarea of cross cultural adjustment has been no different. Research on cross-cultural adjustment has been geared more toward a somewhat haphazard search for factors that influence cross-cultural adjustment, rather than toward theoretically explaining the adjustment process and why certain factors would be expected to influence adjustment. In the rare cases in which a theoretical perspective has been applied to cross-cultural research, the "U-Curve Theory" of Adjustment (UCT) has been one of the most consistently used. This paper systematically reviews the literature on UCT in an effort to determine the extent to which the empirical evidence either supports or refutes UCT and to examine the methodological rigor of the UCT empirical literature to determine the confidence that can be placed in the empirical findings.

1.1.8

Boddewyn, Jean J. and Marsha Baldwin Halbrich (1986), "Service Multinationals: Conceptualization, Measurement and Theory," *Journal of International Business Studies,* 17(3), Fall, 41-57.

The application of MNE definitions, measurements and theories to international service is still in its infancy, despite the considerable size and growth of this sector. The authors find although there are problems in defining, classifying, measuring, comparing and explaining service MNEs, they do not require special definitions and theories. They suggest delinking the concepts of multinational enterprise and foreign direct investment under certain conditions and qualifying the nature of ownership, internalization and location advantages in FDI theory as far as MNEs are concerned.

1.1.9

Boddewyn, Jean J. (1988), "Political Aspects of MNE Theory," *Journal of International Business Studies,* 19(3), Fall, 341-363.

Dunning's eclectic paradigm is expanded to include elements of firm internalization and location advantages. This expansion requires that various nonmarket forces be endogenized. Dunning's model is limited to the conditions necessary to explain foreign direct investment by MNEs. A complete explanation of MNE behavior requires that motivations and circumstances be considered as well. The analysis assumes traditional economic goals for the MNE—survival, profitability, and growth. What is missing is the consideration of true political goals like hegemony. An explicit integration of political elements into MNE theory may offer a better understanding of why certain MNEs have succeeded, while a purely economic analysis may not be able to account for their success.

1.1.10

Boddewyn, Jean J. (1985), "Theories of Foreign Direct Investment and Divestment: A Classificatory Note," *Management International Review*, 25(1), 57-65.

During the postwar period, a number of explanations have been offered for foreign direct investment instead of accepting the earlier rationale that firms invest abroad because it is profitable to do so. The authors suggest that the numerous theories can be reduced to a simpler classification that is more useful for understanding foreign investment and divestment and for detecting where current theories are weak. Existing theoretical models of foreign investment can be classified according to factors such as conditions, motivations, and precipitating circumstances. However, these categories are rather general so there can be overlaps. It is also necessary to recognize that in an organization specific factors influence investment and divestment decisions.

1.1.11

Buckley, Peter J. (1988), "The Limit of Explanation: Testing the Internalization Theory of the Multinational Enterprise," *Journal of International Business Studies,* 19(2), Summer, 181-193.

This paper explores the difficulties of testing the internalization approach in the modern theory of the multinational enterprise. The structure of the theory is elaborated and the conclusion drawn that testing cannot occur at the most general theoretical level but that the theory requires careful restricting assumptions to be placed on it to allow rigorous testing.

1.1.12

Buckley, Peter J. (1990), "Problems and Developments in the Core Theory of International Business," *Journal of International Business Studies,* 21(4), 657-665.

Two issues in core internalization theory are examined: (1) the relationship between internalization decisions and market structure, and (2) the relationship between internalization and competitive advantage. The first issue is analyzed with a reference to Hymer's contribution. The second issue is examined by contrasting the nature of these decisions with those building short-run competitive advantage. Avenues of development of the theory include the integration of nontraditional concepts and the reintegration of areas of research that have become divorced from core international business theory.

1.1.13

Buckley, Peter J. and Mark Casson (1988), "A Theory of Co-Operation in International Business ," *Management International Review,* 28(5), 19-38.

Cooperation can be analyzed from both economic and organizational perspectives. Equity joint ventures (JV) are attractive when the exploitation of internalization economics is constrained by scale economies in internalized facilities and by obstacles to merger. Some JVs provide a suitable context in which the parties can demonstrate mutual forbearance and thereby build up trust. An important role of JVs is to minimize the impact of quality uncertainty on collaborative research and training. JVs designed to cope with quality uncertainty are well adapted to help partners reciprocate. However, a degree of cynicism may be warranted in respect to claims advanced for certain types of JVs. For example, a JV may be merely a subterfuge, luring partners into risky commitments, a device to enhance collusion, or a pragmatic response to regulatory distortion.

1.1.14

Chakravarthy, Balaji S. and Howard V. Perlmutter (1985), "Strategic Planning for a Global Business," *Columbia Journal of World Business,* 20(2), Summer,3-10.

Strategic planning for the multinational corporation has become more complex in the last decade. The planning challenges for such corporations are the economic imperative, the political imperative, and strategic predispositions of the corporation. The planning challenge is to reconcile the differences among these forces. Four planning systems are described and illustrated with examples: (1) the top-down approach, (2) bottom-up planning, (3) portfolio planning, which uses both top-down and bottom-up approaches to suit its varying business contexts, and (4) dual structure planning.

1.1.15

Clark, Terry (1990), "International Marketing and National Character: A Review and Proposal for an Integrative Theory," *Journal of Marketing,* 54(4), October, 66-79.

People of each nation have a distinctive pattern of behavior and personality characteristics. This concept is examined in terms of its value and validity for use in international marketing. A marketing-relevant character concept with applicability to consumer and strategic decision making is proposed. The interpretive framework is developed in terms of Herskovits' five basic elements of culture: material culture, social institutions, belief systems, aesthetic systems, and language. The conceptualization developed is not without problems. Questions remain for three reasons: (1) This is a pioneering effort with little previous work to serve as a guide; (2) A marriage of methodologies that sometimes seem incompatible is suggested; (3)

Bringing together diverse literatures and weaving a common cloth of them is difficult.

1.1.16

Czinkota, Michael R. (1986), "International Trade and Business in the Late 1980s: An Integrated U.S. Perspective," *Journal of International Business Studies,* 17(1), Spring, 127-134.

The university community must recognize the concerns of both business executives and policymakers, and integrate them into the academic work in order to build a vision for international trade and business. Such an integration is attempted using the Delphi technique. Twenty-eight leaders in international business and trade were selected in the business, academic, and policy communities. Participants were asked to identify the major policy and business issues in international trade in the 1980s. After rank ordering these, the subjects were requested to elaborate on their views. The three most important issues identified were: (1) changes in the multilateral trade framework, (2) dealing with the international debt situation, and (3) development of the U.S. trade policy and trade law.

1.1.17

Dunning, John H. (1989), "The Study of International Business: A Plea for a More Interdisciplinary Approach," *Journal of International Business Studies,* 20(3), Fall, 411-436.

1.1.18

Dunning, John H. (1988), "The Eclectic Paradigm of International Production: A restatement and Some Possible Extensions," *Journal of International Business Studies,* 19(1), Spring, 1-31.

The author reviews some of the criticisms directed towards the eclectic paradigm of international production over the past decade, and restates its main tenets. He also considers a number of possible extensions of the paradigm and concludes by asserting that it remains "a robust general framework for explaining and analyzing not only the economic rationale of economic production but many organizational and impact issues in relation to MNE activity as well."

1.1.19

England, George W. (1983), "Some Methodological and Analytic Considerations in Cross-National Comparative Research," *Journal of International Business Studies,* 14(2), Fall, 49-59.

A methodological approach is presented to aid in the complex process of making inferences about the meaning and usefulness of observed national differences. By using data from an international study of "The Meaning of Working," three points are made: (1) it is important to use multiple methods of measurement for conceptual ideas or domains; (2) it is important to use intra-country reference group comparisons; and (3) it is important to use some form of relative position analysis in addition to score analysis.

1.1.20

Grosse, Robert (1985), "An Imperfect Competition Theory of The MNE," *Journal of International Business Studies,* 16(1), Spring, 57-80.

Multinational firm, as the central actor in international business, has been studied extensively across countries and within companies. No single theoretical structure can deal with all important aspects of these firms. Nonetheless, some explanatory tools such as the international product cycle transactions cost/internalization theory have shed substantial light on MNE activities. This presents an imperfect competition theory which explains six major MNE decisions with a simple model.

1.1.21

Horaguchi, Haruo and Brian Toyne (1990), "Setting the Record Straight: Hymer, Internalization Theory and Transaction Cost Economics," *Journal of International Business Studies,* 21(3), 487-494.

With the development of transaction cost theory, Hymer's works have become a matter of controversy. The Hymer controversy originated in the claims of McClain (1983) who said that the new theories of foreign direct investment (FDI) that emerged in the literature in the 1970s did not provide any distinct alternatives to what Hymer and Kindleberger had already proposed. These new theories are the eclectic theory and the theory of internalization. Both emphasize transaction cost market imperfections. When Hymer's dissertation and the writings on Coase are read together, it is clear the Hymer envisioned the international activities of a firm as being determined as much by tests of market power as by objective factors. Hymer viewed large multinational enterprises as consisting of widespread internal markets that cross industries and countries.

1.1.22

Huszagh, Sandra M., Richard J. Fox, and Ellen Day (1985), "Global Marketing: An Empirical Investigation," *Columbia Journal of World Business,* 20(4), Winter, 31-43.

This article reports the findings of an empirical investigation of the global marketing concept. The results indicate that some products clearly do not lend themselves to a global marketing approach. These products fail to pass simple tests of consistent acceptance in five similar countries. However, in the countries analyzed, the potential for global marketing does exist for several, specific product categories. These products exhibit consistent acceptance.

1.1.23

Jain, Subhash C. (1989), "Standardization of International Marketing Strategy: Some Research Hypotheses," *Journal of Marketing,* 53(1), January, 70-79.

International marketing standardization consists of two major aspects: process and program standardization. A framework for determining program standardization is presented. Program standardization is proposed to be a function of target market, market position, nature of product, environment, and organization factors. The framework is likely to be useful in directing future research efforts to key variables and relationships. It also has implications for domestic marketing decisions, international corporate management, and subsidiary management. The framework implies that corporate managers can influence certain variables to produce a climate where a greater degree of standardization would be feasible. These variables include establishing a geocentric orientation in the organization and providing opportunities for an ongoing parent-subsidiary dialogue.

1.1.24

Kim, Wi Saeng and Esmeralda O. Lyn (1990), "FDI Theories and the Performance of Foreign Multinationals Operating in the U.S.," *Journal of International Business Studies,* 21(1), 41-54.

A univariate analysis using unpaired t-test statistics shows that foreign firms operating in the US are less profitable than randomly selected US firms. These foreign-based multinational corporations spend more on research and development (R&D) and less on advertising than US firms, and they have higher debt levels combined with higher liquidity. Japanese firms exhibit more homogeneity than other foreign-owned firms and tend to be more R&D and advertising intensive. Western European firms are more efficient and more profitable, but they also have the lowest Tobin's q-ratio, signifying a lower growth rate. Canadian firms have the highest Tobin's q-ratio and high growth rate, but they have low profitability measures.

1.1.25

Kramer, Hugh E.(1989), "International Marketing: Methodological Excellence in Practice and Theory," *Management International Review,* 29(2), 59-65.

A review of the literature of the past ten years shows that international marketing has become a respected academic subdiscipline. International marketing involves at least three constructs: an intellectual or cognitive construct, an affective construct or philosophy directed by personal and cultural values, and a conative or behavioral construct. There are two different approaches to international marketing: one is related to the content of the discipline and the other concerns the process of developing a theory of international marketing. The first is a parametric approach and the latter an operational approach. Parametric approach is concerned with selection of the right data to be investigated, while operational approach focuses on selecting and manipulating the data in the right way.

1.1.26

Lancaster, Geoffrey and Inger Wesenlund (1984), " A Product Life Cycle Theory for International Trade: an Empirical Investigation," *European Journal of Marketing,* 18(6-7), 72-89.

By integrating product life cycle theory with international trade theories, the authors propose an international product life cycle perspective. According to their proposal, internationally many products follow a pattern which can be divided into four stages: (1) US export strength, (2) foreign production starts, (3) foreign production competitive in export markets, and (4) import competition. The authors also empirically tested their international product life cycle model by applying it to the textile industry.

1.1.27

Martinez, Jon I., and J. Carlos Jarillo (1989), " The Evolution of Research on Coordination Mechanisms in Multinational Corporations," *Journal of International Business Studies,* 20(3), Fall, 489-514.

The authors study the mechanisms of coordination used by multinational corporations through an exhaustive literature review. They find that as time has passed researchers have concentrated more on subtler and informal mechanisms abandoning their unidimensional focus on structural issues. They suggest that the increase in the study of those mechanisms may be due to the fact that MNCs are indeed making more use of them.

1.1.28

Morrison, Allen J. and Andrew C. Inkpen (1991), "An Analysis of Significant Contributions to the International Business Literature," *Journal of International Business Studies,* 22(1), 143-153.

Publications in international business for both authors and academic institutions are examined for the period 1980-1989. Nine publications with 659 articles are reviewed including Journal of International Business Studies, Columbia Journal of World Business, Harvard Business Review, Journal of Marketing, Academy of Management Journal, Academy of Management Review, Journal of Marketing Research, Journal of Finance, and American Economic Review. The publishing records at two key journals, Columbia Journal of World Business and Journal of International Business Studies, are reviewed to determine if certain universities show a greater propensity to publish in particular outlets.

1.1.29

Ohmae, Kenichi (1986), "Becoming a Triad Power: the New Global Corporation," *International Marketing Review,* 3(3), Autumn, 7-20.

Three major markets—"Triad" of Japan, Europe and United States—are emerging as the most important strategic battlefield for any company operating on a global scale. The author pinpoints four trends—increasing capital intensity, soaring R&D costs, converging worldwide consumer tastes and intensifying protectionism—which together make it imperative for a company to have an inside presence in all three Triad regions. The author also looks at the steps some companies have already taken toward becoming a Triad power.

1.1.30

Papadopoulos, Nicolas and Jean-Emile Denis (1988), "Inventory, Taxonomy and Assessment of Methods for International Market Selection," *International Marketing Review,* 5(3), Autumn, 38-51.

This research intends to assess the state-of-the-art on the subject of international market selection based on a comprehensive review and synthesis of the literature. It provides an inventory, taxonomy and brief review of the normative quantitative models that have been proposed in the literature, and compares them to current business practices in selecting foreign markets. This comparison reveals a theory-practice gap that is discussed in the context of the methodological and conceptual weaknesses of the models.

1.1.31

Perry, Anne C. (1990), "International Versus Domestic Marketing: Four Conceptual Perspectives," *European Journal of Marketing,* 24 (6), 41-54.

Four basic positions in the debate about international marketing versus domestic marketing are discussed. First, although there are differences in nature between foreign and domestic marketing, they are overcome when a dominant marketing system prevails abroad through its international efforts. Second, there are fundamental and sustained differences in nature between domestic and foreign marketing, based on differences in the physical, economic, political, social, and cultural environments. Third, national and international marketing are variations of a single marketing without borders, so that there are no differences in nature between the two on account of endogenous forces. Fourth, differences in local physical, economic, social, political, and cultural environments are being invalidated by the globalization of markets and other factors so that there are no differences of nature between domestic and international marketing on account of exogenous forces. The conceptualization of international marketing has mirrored the foreign endeavors of US, European, and Japanese marketers.

1.1.32

Porter, Michael E. (1990), "The Competitive Advantage of Nations," *Harvard Business Review,* 68(2), March-April, 73-93.

A nation's competitiveness depends on the capacity of its industry to innovate and upgrade. There are four broad attributes constituting a diamond of national advantages: factor conditions, demand conditions, related and supporting industries, and firm strategy, structure, and rivalry. Domestic rivalry and geographic concentration have great power to transform the diamond into a system. Government should play a role of catalyst and challenger. Company policies that will support the efforts of its leaders include: (1) creating pressure for innovation, (2) seeking the most capable competitors as motivators, (3) establishing early-warning systems, (4) improving the national diamond, (5) welcoming domestic rivalry, (6) globalizing to tap selective advantages in other nations, (7) using alliances only selectively, and (8) locating the home base to support competitive advantage.

1.1.33

Samli, Coskun and Wladyslaw Jermakowicz (1983), "The Stages of Marketing Evolution in East European Countries," *European Journal of Marketing,* 17(2), 26-33.

Because of the variations in their starting points, and the differences in their development patterns, the East European countries present a spectrum of centralization/decentralization which determines the conditions for markets and the distribution systems. The general direction for all of these countries has been one of decentralization. All East European countries, at different speeds and with varying success, have been moving from the authoritative stage toward the integrative stage. Consequently, the marketing and distribution systems have been going through a process of decentralization.

1.1.34

Sekaran, Uma (1983), "Methodological and Theoretical Issues and Advancements in Cross-Cultural Research," *Journal of International Business Studies,* 14(2), Fall, 61-73.

This article summarizes the issues and concerns of critics of cross-cultural research, and discusses how they are being addressed by researchers. Given the state of the art and the complexity of this field of research, the author recommends more inductive research and the pursuit of appropriate, but not overambitious sampling designs, so as to increase our understanding of cultures and encourage the building of richer theory bases. Taking an optimistic view of the field, the author predicts useful contributions by researchers which will enrich the art and science of cross-cultural management.

1.1.35

Terpstra, Vern (1987), "The Evolution of International Marketing," *International Marketing Review*, 4(2), Summer, 47-59.

A comparison between the pre- and post-1970 global environment is conducted in such areas as international finance and trade, commercial policy, and the academic side in order to determine some of the major global developments that have shaped international marketing practice. It is concluded that three major forces will affect international marketing for the remainder of the century: (1) continued integration of the world economy, (2) technological change, and (3) a more globalized competitive environment. In the future, international marketing will be constrained by developments in the international financial system and continued protectionist pressures. International marketers also will be challenged by the continued globalization of competition and markets. Successful marketers will respond by formulating global strategies, sharpening their skills, and seeking alliances to meet specific needs in their programs.

1.1.36

Thomas, Michael J. and Luis Araujo (1985), "Theories of Export Behaviour: A Critical Analysis," *European Journal of Marketing*, 19(2), 42-52.

After reviewing theories of export behavior, the authors conclude that: (1) Export behavior and foreign market entry decisions can be interpreted as innovation adoption behavior. (2) The export development process is determined by the interaction between the firm and the individual characteristics of managers. (3) Exporter profiles can be used in defining identifiable characteristics of firms at different stages in the innovation adoption process. (4) Most studies reviewed lack a solid empirical base; thus, their conclusions must be regarded as tentative. (5) The studies cited suggest that government policy designed to stimulate exports should not be confined to macro-level inducements, but rather should be aimed at influencing decision makers in individual firms.

1.1.37

Toyne, Brian (1989), "International Exchange: A Foundation for Theory Building in International Business," *Journal of International Business Studies*, 20(1), Spring, 1-15.

There does not appear to be a consensus concerning what is the conceptual domain of international business. This article argues that this is due in part to an emphasis on the firm as the unit of analysis. It is further argued that a comprehensive, generative and theoretically integrative definition of international business could be established if exchange were made the unit of analysis. By using the political economy paradigm and the various concepts of exchange adopted by the social sciences, nine characteristics are identified and developed which uniquely define the conceptual domain of international business.

1.1.38

Wood, Van R., Scott J. Vitell, and J. J. Boddewyn (1986), "Marketing and Economic Development: Review, Synthesis and Evaluation/Comment," *Journal of Macromarketing,* 6(1), 28-49.

A model is developed to review and synthesize research on marketing and development from the 1950s through the mid-1980s. The study shows the value of marketing to economic development. Marketing's benefits could include: (1) providing utility to consumers in less developed countries through savings of time and money in the buying process, (2) developing managers, entrepreneurs, and risk-takers in LDCs, (3) increasing the profit levels of LDC firms, and (4) enhancing the LDCs' gross national product. However, the government should cooperate with, rather than own, marketing institutions, and its policy and marketing activities should be coordinated with the country's stage of development. While praising the analysis as a whole, Boddewyn finds the definitions of "economic development" and "marketing" vague, and considers consumption and consumer behavior to be overemphasized.

II. Environmental Aspects of International Marketing

2.1 Economic Environment

2.1.1

Czinkota, Michael R. and Ilkka A. Ronkainen (1987), "Coping with Increased Trade Interdependence," *International Marketing Review,* 4(1), Spring, 9-15.

The issue of increased trade interdependence between nations is analyzed. Both domestic and international economic policy-making have to anticipate and accept the interlinkages between export and import flows. In setting economic goals, a long-term global orientation is needed to cope with these interdependencies to maintain the cohesiveness of the free-trade system.

2.1.2

El-Ansary, Adel I. (1986), "How Better Systems Could Feed the World," *International Marketing Review,* 3(1), Spring, 39-49.

This article defines food marketing system parameters, delineates the imperatives of marketing system reform, and recommends actionable managerial strategies for their reform.

2.1.3

Green, Robert T. and Trina L. Larsen (1987), "Environmental Shock and Export Opportunity," *International Marketing Review,* 4(4), Autumn, 30-42.

The impact of the oil shock of the 1970s on world export markets is examined. This sudden environmental change caused some nations to obtain sudden wealth and others to experience instant economic problems. The findings of the study illustrate the range of consequences for export markets that can occur, depending on the manner in which nations are affected by sudden change.

2.1.4

Gronhaug, Kjell and Tore Lorentzen (1983), "Exploring the Impact of Governmental Export Subsidies," *European Journal of Marketing,* 17(2), 5-12.

The purpose of this paper is to explore the impact of government export subsidies on the Norwegian export activities. The empirical findings supported the assumptions of cost barriers for specific export activities, and increased organizational export effectiveness due to learning. In addition the empirical data revealed the existence of conflict in allocations of means between the firms and the government authorities. This may reflect conflicting goals as well as perceived differences in usefulness of the various export activities. Variations in allocation of export activities across the firms studied besides unequal distribution of export subsidies across industries and various size-groups of firms were also observed.

2.1.5

Gutenberg, Jeffery S., Laurence W. Jacobs, and Charles F. Keown (1989), "The Marketing-Environmental Concept: A New Way to View International Marketing Strategy," *Singapore Marketing Review,* Vol.4, 55-61.

Problems and criticisms of the marketing concept are discussed, as well as the hierarchical view of the major philosophies of marketing management. The components of the marketing concept are brought together as a three-dimensional matrix and presented as the marketing-environmental concept. This matrix is offered as a new diagnostic planning tool for international marketing strategists.

2.1.6

Hill, John S. and Richard R. Still (1984), "Effects of Urbanization on Multinational Product Planning: Markets in Lesser-Developed Countries," *Columbia Journal of World Business,* 19(2), Summer, 62-67.

Differences in the relative urbanization of target markets in lesser-developed countries influence the product strategies used by multinational corporations. Products targeted to urban markets in lesser-developed countries need only minimal changes from those marketed in developed countries. Products targeted for both semi-urban and urban markets require more changes, and those targeted for national markets undergo further adaptions to accommodate the requirements of culturally-diverse rural populations.

2.1.7

Kennedy Jr., Charles R. (1984), "The External Environment-Strategic Planning Interface: U.S. Multinational Corporate Practices in the 1980s," *Journal of International Business Studies,* 15(2), Fall, 99-109.

This paper presents data collected by structured interviews concerning how external environmental analysis and strategic planning are related in major U.S.-based multinational corporations. The research was also undertaken to ascertain why and the extent to which firms have formally institutionalized the external environmental functions since the Iranian revolution.

2.1.8

Nielsen, Richard P. (1983), "Should a Country Move Toward International Strategic Market Planning?" *California Management Review,* 25(2), 34-44.

Arguments for and against country-international strategic market planning (CISMP) are presented. With CISMP, central government participates with privately owned and nationalized corporations in strategic international market planning; government aids businesses to improve or develop new foreign markets by providing corporate loans, financial subsidies for research and development, diplomatic assistance in foreign markets, and tariff protection in domestic markets. Countries that have implemented CISMP include France, Japan, and Sweden. While CISMP may be a logical extension of multinational corporate strategic planning, government may not be capable of intervening effectively in international markets, and economic losses may be more severe when CISMP strategies fail. Marketing efforts may be more efficiently coordinated with CISMP than with traditional classical and neoclassical economic models, however, CISMP may result in decreased individual and corporate freedom, and increased social control of economic activity.

2.1.9

Olsen, Janeen E. and Kent L. Granzin (1990), "Economic Development and Channel Structure: A Multinational Study," *Journal of Macromarketing,* 10(2), Fall, 61-77.

A model of multidimensional relationship between economic development and channel structure is conceptualized in terms of eight domains of development and three elements of channel structure. The domains include agriculture, communications and transportation, culture, demographic, income and savings, science and technology, health, and trade. The three elements of channel structure are wholesaler size, retailer size, and channel length. An empirical test of the conceptualization is performed using secondary data on economic development and primary data on the structure of the channel for cereal grains. The results indicate that all eight domains are related to at least one of the three elements of channel structure.

2.1.10

O'Sullivan, Patrick (1985), "Determinants and Impact of Private Foreign Direct Investment in Host Countries," *Management International Review,* 25(4), 28-35.

2.1.11

Piercy, Nigel (1984), "The Corporate Environment for Marketing Management and Marketing Budgeting," *International Marketing Review,* 1(3), Spring/Summer, 14-32.

The author introduces and makes use of the idea of the corporate environment—the organizational forces and conditions surrounding the marketing decision maker. This corporate environment includes such elements as organizational climate, organizational power and politics, and the use and manipulation of information within organizations.

2.1.12

Pollio, Gerald and Charles H. Riemenschneider (1988), "The Coming Third World Investment Revival," *Harvard Business Review,* 66(2), 114-124.

The economic factors that characterized the 1970s have changed, and a new wave of foreign direct investment is imminent. Now that real interest rates are higher, bank loans are harder to come by, and projections of commodities prices are dismally low, the Third World is willing to adjust its policies to share potential risk as well as profit. Investors, as always, want to leverage their wealth. And some, recognizing the opportunities in the Third World, are already beginning to develop contractual arrangements to fit the new economic times.

2.1.13

Poynter, Thomas A. (1986), "Managing Government Intervention: A Strategy for Defending the Subsidiary," *Columbia Journal of World Business,* 21(4), Winter, 55-65.

Most governments intervene in foreign-owned subsidiaries by restricting ownership, limiting financial and technological flows, and by costly requirements for local sourcing and exporting. This paper proposes a strategy for managing such unwanted government intervention. The basis for this strategy is that governments discriminate among firms on the basis of the firms' bargaining power. Implementation issues of this strategy are also considered explicitly. The host nation, MNE strategy, and the existing organization all play a role in implementing the subsidiary's specific defense strategy.

2.1.14

Robles, Fernando (1986), "Understanding Foreign Trade Zones," *International Marketing Review,* 3(2), Summer, 44-54.

This article reviews the emerging use of foreign trade zones in the United States and presents a competitive analysis framework to segment markets, determine levels of marketing effort, and develop differential marketing strategies for zone services. Using a two-dimensional model of potential use and competitive position, the proposed framework permits foreign trade zone services and market segments to be analyzed in a single model where differential marketing strategies can be readily identified. The case of a recently formed trade zone is used to illustrate the application of the proposed framework.

2.1.15

Seringhaus, F.H. Rolf (1986), "The Impact of Government Export Marketing Assistance," *International Marketing Review,* 3(2), Summer, 55-66.

The major focus is on the methodological and measurement issues that appear to have a confounding effect and may account for broad equivocality of the findings in many of the studies. An evaluation paradigm is developed and applied to the research reviewed. The article concludes with a synthesis of the issues and provides specific directions for future research.

2.1.16

Terpstra, Vern (1985), "The Changing Environment of International Marketing," *International Marketing Review*, 2(3), Autumn, 7-16.

Contemporary changes of the global marketplace are evaluated. The author offers observations and insights in the area of dynamic world geography and internationalization of business. Numerous examples are given for the arguments and a number of implications are offered.

2.1.17

Yu Chwo-Ming J. and Kiyohiko Ito (1988), "Oligopolistic Reaction and Foreign Direct Investment: the Case of the U.S. Tire and Textiles," *Journal of International Business Studies*, 19(3), Fall, 449-460.

This paper tests the impact of oligopolistic reaction and some firm-related and host country-related factors on FDI activities in the U.S. tire and textile industries. The results reveal that in an oligopolistic industry, firms' motivation of FDI is based on the behavior of rivals as well as host country-related and firm-related factors.

2.2 Cultural and Social Environment

2.2.1

Adler, Nancy J. (1983), "A Typology of Management Studies Involving Culture," *Journal of International Business Studies*, 14(2), Fall, 29-47.

As a methodological review, this paper delineates six approaches to researching cross-cultural management issues: parochial, ethnocentric, polycentric, comparative, geocentric, and synergistic. For each approach, assumptions are discussed concerning the similarity and difference across cultures and the extent to which management phenomena are or are not universal. The primary types of management questions which can be addressed using each approach are clarified.

2.2.2

Adler, Nancy J. and John L. Graham (1989), "Cross-Cultural Interaction: The International Comparison Fallacy?," *Journal of International Business Studies*, 20(3), Fall, 515-537.

Using a negotiation simulation, the behaviors of four culturally distinct groups—190 Americans, 72 Japanese, 100 Canadian Francophones, and 100 Canadian Anglophones—are compared across intracultural and cross-cultural situations. Negotiators in each of the four groups made changes. US negotiators were more satisfied in cross-cultural interactions. The Japanese were more attracted to US negotiators than to their fellow Japanese, even though their profits were reduced when bargaining with Americans. Francophone Canadians behaved much more cooperatively with Anglophone Canadians. The Anglophone Canadians spent more time and achieved lower joint profits in cross-cultural interactions.

2.2.3

Elbashier, A. M. and J.R. Nicholls (1983), "Export Marketing in the Middle East: the Importance of Cultural Differences," *European Journal of Marketing*, 17(1), 68-81.

The research focuses on the following objectives: (1) to investigate the perceptions of company export executives regarding the importance of cultural differences in the Arab world, and their perceptions of the most important differences impacting on their businesses, and (2) to understand the nature of the marketing problems created by these cultural factors. The findings show that the overall perception among managers interviewed regarding the importance of cultural factors in international marketing was very high; at the same time economic factors and political factors were regarded as even more important in the Arab world. Although cultural awareness was high, companies did not adopt a systematic approach to analyzing cultural differences as advocated in the marketing literature, relying primarily on personal observation and experience. Use of consumer market research was modest.

2.2.4

Graham, John L. (1985), "The Influence of Culture on the Process of Business Negotiations: an Exploratory Study," *Journal of International Business Studies*, 16(1), Spring, 81-96.

The process of business negotiations in the United States, Japan, and Brazil is compared. Three dyads from each country were videotaped during buyer-seller negotiation simulation. Both verbal behaviors and nonverbal behaviors were observed and recorded. Observed differences provide the basis for hypothesized differences which might be tested in future work.

2.2.5

Hofstede, Geert (1983), "The Cultural Relativity of Organizational Practices and Theories," *Journal of International Business Studies*, 14(2), Fall, 75-89.

This article summarizes the author's recently published findings about differences in people's work-related values among 50 countries. In view of these differences, ethnocentric management theories have become untenable. This concept is illustrated for the fields of leadership, organization, and motivation.

2.2.6

Johnstone, Harvey, Erdener Kaynak, and Richard M. Sparkman, Jr. (1987), "A Cross-Cultural/Cross-National Study of the Information Content of Television Advertisements," *International Journal of Advertising*, 6(3), 223-236.

A research was conducted to investigate cross-cultural and cross-national differences in marketing communications. Television commercials were selected from six different channels—three in Maine and three in the Maritime region of Canada. The commercials were selected randomly on each day of the week, and bilingual judges were asked to use fourteen criteria to determine whether an advertisement was informative or noninformative. Results indicated that 68.2 percent of ads were informative on at least one cue level and 25.7 percent were informative on two or more cues. The data also indicate that French-Canadian TV commercials contain more information than US TV commercials.

2.2.7

Kelley, Lane, Arthur Whatley and Reginald Worthley (1987), "Assessing the Effects of Culture on Managerial Attitudes: A Three-Culture Test," *Journal of International Business Studies*, 18(2), Summer, 17-31.

This study intends to isolate the influence of culture. Japanese, Chinese and Mexican managers, their ethnic-American counterparts, and Anglo-Americans are used to test the model. Results indicate unique persistent cultural characteristics with the cultural effect varying among the three groups of managers.

2.2.8

Kogut, Bruce (1988), "The Effect of National Culture on the Choice of Entry Mode," *Journal of International Business Studies*, 19(3), Fall, 411-432.

Characteristics of national cultures have frequently been claimed to influence the selection of entry modes. This article investigates this claim by developing a theoretical argument for why culture should influence the choice of entry.

2.2.9

Lane, Henry W. and Paul W. Beamish (1990), "Cross-Cultural Cooperative Behavior in Joint Ventures in LDCs," *Management International Review*, 30(3), 87-102.

North American behavioral patterns and cultural influences that may be barriers to increased global effectiveness are discussed. These influences on the process of establishing and managing joint ventures in less developed countries are examined.

Developing a business in the Third World is a long-term investment. An unwillingness to spend the requisite amount of time in a country may be indicative of an unrealistic superiority complex. Identifying and selecting a partner is perhaps the most important consideration in establishing a cooperative venture. Good local partners are more apt to have access to competent local managers than are foreign firms. The use of local managers is recommended to ensure that the foreign parent acquires the necessary knowledge of the local economy, culture, and politics.

2.2.10

Maddox, Robert C. and Douglas Short (1988), "The Cultural Integrator," *Business Horizons,* 31(6), November-December, 57-59.

Failure to analyze a situation when a firm introduces a new product can result in a failure of the introduction if the impact on and reaction by different elements of a society are not considered. As more and more companies operate across cultures, the cost of making mistakes is rising. Thus, there is a need for a new function within these organizations to deal with intercultural problems. This function would integrate a company's practices with the culture of the host country, allowing for the firm's effective operation. Another traditional method of dealing with the need for integration culturally is to hire managers who are technically and managerially competent. A basic deficiency is the lack of cultural expertise. Yet another method involves positioning a cultural integrator at each foreign location. While there is no best way to select such an integrator, the individual chosen must be proficient in both conceptual and human skills.

2.2.11

O'Shaughnessy, Nicholas J. (1985), "Strategy and US Cultural Bias," *European Journal of Marketing,* 19(4), 23-32.

New models for strategic analysis have proliferated in recent years. Theory and practice have suggested that these structures can be used like any other item of US culture. However, it is hypothesized: (1) that strategic analysis models rest on a set of premises that are biased toward expectations of managers in the US, (2) that they may be more unwieldy when applied to other western nations, and (3) that they may have only limited application for developing nations. The US displays a strong orientation in favor of change; assumptions of flux and fluidity are part of the culture. In many cultures, by contrast, a variety of factors is likely to make strategic planning different from that in the US or account for the total absence of such planning. These factors include a high degree of political and social instability, lack of information, and attitudes.

2.2.12

Reeder, John A. (1987), "When West Meets East: Cultural Aspects of Doing

Business in Asia," *Business Horizons,* 30(1), 69-74.

Westerners who contemplate doing business with Asians should become familiar with the cultural differences so as to avoid miscommunications and misunderstandings. Most importantly, the Western businessperson should remember that pride and dignity are very culturally protected in Asia, with "saving face" of utmost concern. As a result, frankness should be avoided. In addition, Westerners in Asia should: (1) conduct themselves with dignity, (2) avoid public displays of strong emotion, (3) invest in the time needed to establish interpersonal trust, (4) show sincerity and a preference for personal and long-term relationships, (5) demonstrate patience both in short-term dealings and for long-term prospects, (6) display a persistent firmness, combined with flexibility and the willingness to explore all possible alternatives, (7) consult with an Asian intermediary to become acquainted with local customs.

2.2.13

Rosenberg, Larry J. (1986), "Deciphering the Japanese Cultural Code," *International Marketing Review,* 3(3), Autumn, 47-57.

Neglecting Japanese cultural factors limits marketing success and leads to failure. Key Japanese anthropological concepts are explained, for the purpose of revealing how they create opportunities or problems for Western firms. Implications are discussed with emphasis on how sensitivity to Japanese values can be integrated with marketing planning.

2.2.14

Samiee, Saeed and Adam Mayo (1990), "Barriers to Trade with Japan: A Socio-Cultural Perspective," *European Journal of Marketing,* 24(12), 48-66.

The relationship between cultural elements and barriers to trade with Japan is examined. Understanding the social and cultural influences is the first step in revealing the hidden barriers to trade. It is demonstrated that visible barriers cannot be directly influenced by exporters. However, the persistent effort and pressure of firms and governments have been successful in reducing or eliminating most of the barriers. Invisible barriers, which are influenced by cultural elements, may be overcome by marketers with patience and persistence to become familiar with the market.

2.2.15

Tansuhaj, Patriya, James W. Gentry, Joby John, L. Lee Manzer and Bong Jin Cho (1991), "A Cross-national Examination of Innovation Resistance," *International Marketing Review,* 8(3), 7-20.

In this five-country study, the cultural values of fatalism, traditionalism, and religious commitment were found to explain cross-cultural variation in innovation resistance in Senegal and in the United States, but not in India, South Korea, and Thailand. Even though the results were different for every country, fatalism was generally associated with less willingness to try new non-technical products and with higher levels of perceived product risk. Differences were found to be related to entertainment and media innovations as opposed to technical or fashion-oriented innovations. The results do not support the contention that a global, standardized marketing strategy may appropriate for the introduction of new products in foreign markets.

2.2.16

Tse, David K., Kam-hon Lee, Ilan Vertinsky, and Donald A. Wehrung (1988), "Does Culture Matter? A Cross-Cutural Study of Executives' Choice, Decisiveness, and Risk Adjustment in International Marketing," *Journal of Marketing,* 52(4), October, 81-95.

The authors investigate whether a manager's home culture significantly influences his or her international marketing decisions. They also examine whether the impact of home culture diminishes in an open economy with intense exposure to international markets, giving way to a process of "globalization." Decision making in four simulated international marketing situations was studied with executives from the People's Republic of China, Hong Kong, and Canada. The findings confirm that home culture has predictable, significant effects on the decision making of the executives from these countries. Chinese executives from Hong Kong were influenced by a combination of Western and Chinese cultural norms.

2.2.17

Yau, Oliver H. M.(1988), "Chinese Cultural Values: Their Dimensions and Marketing Implications," *European Journal of Marketing,* 22(5), 44-57.

Kluckhohn and Strodbeck classify Chinese cultural values into five orientations. The man-to-nature orientation shows that the Chinese usually attribute failure of products or services to fate rather than to the company from whom the product was purchased, or even the manufacturer. The importance of the man-to-himself philosophy emphasizes the value of abasement in salesforce management. A look at the relational aspect shows off-duty personal behavior is highly important to the firm's image and its effectiveness. Firms also need to keep in mind the informal channels of communication in Chinese society, the brand loyalty, the small social circles, and the importance of the extended family. The time orientation reemphasizes the values of past-time orientation and continuity that tend to make the Chinese so brand loyal.

2.3 Political and Legal Environment

2.3.1

Banker, Pravin (1983), "You're the Best Judge of Foreign Risks," *Harvard Business Review,* 61(2), March-April, 156-165.

Despite the prominence of exposure management, many companies still lack sophisticated strategies for coping with the unpredictable environments they face in international markets. In this article, a financial expert gives readers the benefit of his years of international experience. His practical guide to exposure techniques shows where many that are considered sacred fall down and where more innovative methods might do a better job.

2.3.2

Brewer, Thomas L. (1983), "The Instability of Governments and the Instability of Controls on Funds Transfers by Multinational Enterprises: Implications for Political Risk Analysis," *Journal of International Business Studies,* 24(3), Winter, 147-157.

This article represents a departure from previous empirical political risk studies: it explicitly focuses on the association between specific governmental policy changes and other forms of political instability. A cross-national study of 115 countries finds positive but weak relationships between policy instability and other indicators of political instability. The findings indicate the need to reconsider common assumptions about political risk.

2.3.3

Chase, Carmen D., James L. Kuhle, Carl H. Walther (1988), "The Relevance of Political Risk in Direct Foreign Investment," *Management International Review,* 28(3), 31-38.

In order to investigate the relevance of political risk in direct foreign investment and to evaluate the usefulness of political stability indexes in measuring such risk, data from 46 developed and less developed countries were examined. Direct foreign investment return and a political risk rating were calculated for each country. A technique of random portfolio diversification was then used to examine the political risk premium as part of the total direct foreign investment return. This process generated five new portfolios of countries, each of which was examined using regression analysis to measure the relationship between excess political risk and risk premium during the 13-year period from 1972 to 1984. The results showed no consistent positive relationship between political risk and political risk premium. In other words, direct foreign investors received no compensation for investing in countries rated less stable than in countries rated more stable.

2.3.4

Encarnation, Dennis J. and Sushil Vachani (1985), "Foreign Ownership: When Hosts Change the Rules," *Harvard Business Review,* 63(5), 152-160.

Legislation that requires multinational corporations to dilute their equity in overseas subsidiaries will never be welcome on the fortieth floor. At best it heralds shared ownership and perhaps control; at worst it can mean a reluctant departure from the country. Yet the consequences of such legistaltion are often surprisingly favorable, as this study makes clear. New product lines and markets, risk diversification, and higher earnings are among the benefits MNCs operating in India enjoyed in the wake of that country 's "hostile" equity laws. They did so, in large part, because their managers were prepared to be flexible and imaginative in responding to the government's demands.

2.3.5

Friedmann, Roberto and Jonghoon Kim (1988), "Political Risk and International Marketing," *Columbia Journal of World Business,* 23(4), Winter, 63-74.

This paper presents different definitions of political risk, highlights political risk events that have been noted as relevant, discusses the different approaches used in theoretical frameworks explaining political risk, and reviews the difficulties found in political risk assessment techniques. With that background, the paper discusses the role of political risk in international marketing and suggests several research questions with the purpose of stimulating further research in the area.

2.3.6

Ghadar, Fariborz (1982), " Political Risk and the Erosion of Control: the Case of the Oil Industry," *Columbia Journal of World Business,* 17(3), Fall, 47-51.
The increasing nationalization of multinational oil companies (MNOCs) is examined. As the MNOC loses control over its operations, political risk increases, profits decline and the oil company is nationalized. Since this sequence of events is predictable, the author recommends firms to take steps to increase their means of control and to consider these actions in strategic planning.

2.3.7

Gillespie, Kate (1989), "Political Risk Implications for Exporters, Contractors and Foreign Licensors: The Iranian Experience," *Management International Review,* 29(2), 41-52.

The emphasis on FDI may leave exporters, contractors, and foreign licensors with the impression that political risk is of little or no concern to them. The assumptions behind this belief are examined and US corporate losses in Iran are assessed in order to illustrate empirically the implications of political risk to exporters, contractors, and foreign licensors. The analysis reveals that the most common issue was not expropriation of FDI but the failure of Iranian parties to pay for products or services received. The award to R. J. Reynolds Tobacco Co. of over $36 million in payment for cigarettes delivered far exceeded most expropriation awards.

2.3.8

Guisinger, Stephen (1989), "Total Protection: A New Measure of the Impact of Government Interventions on Investment Profitability," *Journal of International Business Studies,* 20(2), Summer, 280-295.

Two new measures are proposed: total protection and an internationalized version of the marginal effective rate of taxation. These measures incorporate all government interventions in a single, easily understood common denominator readily applicable to empirical research.

2.3.9

Jones, Randall J. Jr. (1984), "Empirical Models of Political Risks in U.S. Oil Production Operations in Venezuela," *Journal of International Business Studies,* 15(1), Spring/Summer, 81-95.

In nine of the years between 1961 and 1978, Venezuelan regimes took actions adverse to the profitability of U.S. oil companies' local production operations. In this study two time-series discriminant models were developed for classifying each of the 18 years according to the occurrence of such action. In the first model, adverse government action was found more likely to occur following years of economic decline and periods when U.S. companies earned high profits from petroleum investments in Venezuela. In the second model, government action tended to occur after periods of relative deprivation experienced by Venezuelans.

2.3.10

Kennedy, Charles R., Jr. (1988), "Political Risk Management: A Portfolio Planning Model," *Business Horizons,* 31(6), November-December, 26-33.

The author offers a decision matrix that integrates political risk concepts with portfolio planning tools. The Boston Consulting Group's market growth/relative market share matrix is used as a foundation. When assessing a firm's political risk, general managers first must perform a general country analysis and assess the particular risk to the firm. In general, five political risk strategies are available: (1) Adapt, by conforming to government policies and wishes and maintaining a high public profile in civic activities, (2) Politick, by acting informally behind the scenes, (3) Withdraw from or avoid the country, (4) Restructure through a sharing strategy such as joint venture formation, and (5) Restructure with a serve strategy involving the sale of equity and its replacement by management-service contracts.

2.3.11

Mascarenhas, Briance and Clifford Atherton (1983), "Problems in Political Risk Assessment," *Management International Review,* 23(2), 22-32.

2.3.12

McElarth, Roger (1988), "Environmental Issues and the Strategies of the International Trade Union Movement," *Columbia Journal of World Business,* 23(3), Fall, 63-68.

In recent years, numerous catastrophic accidents (Bhopal, Sandoz, Chernobyl) have clearly demonstrated the international dimension of environmental issues. This paper examines the initiatives taken by the international trade union movement with respect to environment issues and seeks to identify the strategies supporting these initiatives.

2.3.13

Nigh, Douglas (1985), "The Effect of Political Events on United States Direct Foreign Investment: a Pooled Time-Series Cross-sectional Analysis," *Journal of International Business Studies,* 16(1), Spring, 1-17.

The effect of political events on the manufacturing direct investment (MDFI) decisions of U.S. multinational corporations is examined. The relationship between political events and MDFI is investigated through regression analysis of pooled time-series and cross-sectional data and through various tests of the homogeneity of the relationship across groups of countries.

2.3.14

Nigh, Douglas and Karen D. Smith (1989), "The New US Joint Ventures in the USSR: Assessment and Management of Political Risk," *Columbia Journal of World Business,* 24(2), Summer, 39-44.

The management of political risk by the first US companies entering joint ventures in the USSR is examined. Thirteen companies were identified as having signed joint venture agreements with the USSR; nine participated in the study. Executives were interviewed by telephone about their company's joint venture in the USSR. These firms perceived a political risk linked with their joint venture in the USSR but considered it to be at a manageable level. They attempted to reduce their political risk by putting little capital at risk or by shifting the risk to lenders or the USSR partner. These multinational firms also structured joint venture agreements so that they were assured of receiving hard currency for their participation in the joint venture, in most cases by selling their products to the US-USSR joint ventures or by generating joint venture exports that were readily exchanged for hard currency.

2.3.15

Poynter, Thomas A. (1982), "Government Intervention in Less Developed Countries: the Experience of Multinational Companies," *Journal of International Business Studies*, 13(1), Spring/Summer, 9-25.

It is a fact of international business that governments intervene in the operations of foreign direct investors. These government actions create a high level of uncertainty in international planning and are very costly to the foreign investor. It appears, however, that not all firms experience the same degree of intervention. Within almost all nations, the government appears to intervene in some foreign companies more than in others. At one extreme some firms are forced out of the nation, while at the other extreme firms tend to grow and prosper. The purpose of this paper is to explain these different experiences of foreign firms, and then to address the question: How can foreign firms reduce the amount of intervention they experience? The conclusions are based on the intervention histories of more than 100 firms.

2.3.16

Rice, Gillian and Essam Mahmoud (1986), "A Managerial Procedure for Political Risk Forecasting," *Management International Review*, 26(4), 12-21.

Research in political risk shows that managers think political instability is a major factor in the foreign investment decision. Political risk is the probability of not maintaining a viable business operation in an overseas country due to significant changes in the political environment. No one political risk forecasting technique is accurate for all political risk forecasting situations; political risk forecasting should be examined from the viewpoint of the individual firm. A procedure to assist firms in selecting a forecasting technique for a specific problem involves the following steps: problem definition, identification of lead time, identification of data pattern, accuracy of the method, cost of using the method, cost analysis, and subjective and environmental factors.

2.3.17

Schmidt, David A. (1986), "Analyzing Political Risk," *Business Horizons*, 29(4), July-August, 43-50.

Maintaining a direct investment position abroad requires the development of a political risk policy in which restrictive policies by host governments are more important than political events or rhetoric. Risk depends on the characteristics of the foreign asset—who owns it, what technology it uses, and to what economic sector it belongs. A framework for analysis classifies risks as: (1) transfer risk, (2) operational risk, and (3) ownership-control risk. Conglomerate investments are most at risk; vertical and horizontal investments are less likely to be subjected to restraints. The most important attribute of any foreign investment operation is the sector of economic activity in which it engages. Ownership and technology represent mitigating factors. Host governments are more apt to aim policy measures at primary and service-sector operations, with industrial manufacturing operations at a lower priority. The higher the level of technology, the less likely the operation is to be constrained.

2.3.18

Sethi, S. Prakash and K. A. N. Luther (1986), "Political Risk Analysis and Direct Foreign Investment: Some Problems of Definition and Measurement," *California Management Review,* 28(2), 57-68.

A framework for political risk analysis is presented which recognizes the multidimensional nature of political risk. According to the framework, multinational firms face political risks due to political, economic, and sociocultural sources in both home and host countries. These risks are managed through a variety of international, home country, and host country containment strategies. Political risk analysis must be guided by the containment strategies that a firm has adopted so that it achieves a relevant focus. Broad measures of political risk based on secondary data will be of limited use since data quality will be inconsistent. Such data cannot substitute for experience and familiarity with host country environments. Global/regional political risk scales must be based on comparable input-output data for included countries and supplemented with current country-specific information.

2.3.19

Shreeve, Thomas W. (1984), "Be Prepared for Political Changes Abroad," *Harvard Business Review,* 62(4), July-August, 111-118.

While top managers increasingly recognize the importance of political change, they have been unable to satisfactorily monitor it. It's not for want of trying. Most large international companies have made a bow in the direction of political analysis, and some have gone to the trouble of setting up elaborate systems. But few programs work as well as their planners hope. The major reason they don't, according to the author, is that executives have been concerned with the theoretical methodology for analyzing data rather than the practical importance of the process for gathering and diseminating information throughout the company. In a detailed study of seven multinationals, the author has found that none has a generic solution to the problem of how to monitor political developments. He points out the advantages and disadvantages of each system and shows how companies can learn to set up effective political risk assessment functions in their own organization.

2.3.20

Simon, Jeffrey D. (1982), "Political Risk Assessment: Past Trends and Future Prospects," *Columbia Journal of World Business,* 17(3), Fall, 62-71.

There is little consensus as to what constitutes "political risk," nor an accepted methodology for assessing overseas developments. Not knowing where to turn when political judgments must be made, most corporations adopt the subjective, sporadic analyses of overseas staff or independent consultants. The author views past political risk research and develops a framework for identifying and anticipating different types of political risk.

2.3.21

Stoever, William A. (1985), "The Stages of Developing Country Policy Toward Foreign Investment," *Columbia Journal of World Business,* 20(3), Fall, 3-11.

When and how much can a less-developed country change its policies to obtain more benefits without driving foreign investment away? This article proposes a series of economic growth stages which a developing country's policy might typically experience as its desirability as an investment site increases.

2.3.22

Tallman, Stephen B. (1988), "Home Country Political Risk and Foreign Direct Investment in the United States," *Journal of International Business Studies,* 19(2), Summer, 219-234.

The proposition that home country political risk factors influence outward foreign direct investment is investigated. Results indicate that investment activity from the ICs in the U.S. is dependent on home country economic and political conditions.

2.4 Other Environmental Issues

2.4.1

Globerman Steven (1988), "Government Policies Toward Foreign Direct Investment: Has a New Era Dawned?" *Columbia Journal of World Business,* 23(3), 41-48.

A strong worldwide trend is documented towards liberalization of government legislation restricting inward foreign direct investment. The article identifies and evaluates alternative explanations of this trend. Recent government behavior appears to reflect both cyclical and secular influences including developments in the international trade environment.

2.4.2

Maronick, Thomas J. (1988), "European Patent Laws and Decisions: Implications for Multinational Marketing Strategy," *International Marketing Review,* 5(2), Summer, 31-40.

2.4.3

Onkvisit, Sak and John J. Shaw (1988), "Marketing Barriers in International Trade," *Business Horizons,* 31(3), May-June, 64-72.

Many governments distort trade and welfare arrangements using a combination of tariff and nontariff methods to gain economic and political advantages. There are five major categories of nontariff barriers. First, government participation in trade can range from simple guidance to state trading to subsidies. Second, customs and entry procedures barriers involve classification, valuation, inspection, documentation, license, and health and safety regulations. Third, product requirements may apply to product standards, testing, specifications, packaging, labeling, and marking. Fourth, quotas, also known as quantitative control, can be absolute or voluntary. Fifth, financial regulation can take the form of exchange controls, multiple exchange rates, prior import deposits and credit restrictions, and profit remittance restrictions.

III. Area-Oriented and Comparative Studies

3.1 North America

3.1.1

Bello, Daniel C. and Nicholas C. Williamson (1985), "The American Export Trading Company: Designing A New International Marketing Institution," *Journal of Marketing,* 49(4), Fall, 60-69.

This article analyzes the relationship between basic operating characteristics and the mix of export services provided by export management companies, the closest existing American institution to trading companies. The findings suggest that the operating decisions regarding both the type of product exported and the supplier represented have fundamental implications for the export services that American trading companies must be able to provide.

3.1.2

Buatsi, Seth N. (1986), "Organizational Adaptation to International Marketing," *International Marketing Review,* 3(4), Winter, 17-26.

The nature and extent of organizational adaptation of international marketing involvement are investigated. The domestic and international marketing strategies of firms are compared. The results demonstrate significant differences between the domestic and international marketing operations of firms, including the product market strategies and the commitment of human resources.

3.1.3

Capon, Noel, Chris Christodoulou, John U. Farley and James M. Hulbert (1987), "A Comparative Analysis of the Strategy and Structure of United States and Australian Corporations," *Journal of International Business Studies,* 18(1), Spring, 51-74.

3.1.4

Collins, J. Markham (1990), "A Market Performance Comparison of U.S. Firms Active in Domestic, Developed and Developing Countries," *Journal of International Business Studies,* 21(2), 271-287.

While the positive benefits of international portfolio diversification are well documented in the literature, the case of direct foreign investment (DFI) diversification is less clear. DFI may benefit investors through superior cash flows or lower risk relative to strictly domestic firms. Three groups of US firms are examined: firms without significant international operations, firms with international operations in developed countries, and firms with international operations in developing countries. Risk-return performance analysis is performed on the three groups. The findings reveal that, while developing country DFI results in inferior performance, there are no statistically significant differences in market performance among the three. The results indicate that US multinationals do not benefit their stockholders by diversifying into developing countries.

3.1.5

Cornwell, T. Bettina (1989), "Foreign-Trade Zones in the United States: A Longitudinal Management Perspective," *International Marketing Review*, 6(6), 42-52.

Issues related to U.S. foreign-trade zones as perceived by the zone managers are examined. A longitudinal study of foreign-trade zone managers was conducted. The results of the two surveys and an extensive dialogue with foreign-trade zone managers suggest a continuing lack of awareness and understanding of the benefits of zone operations on the part of potential zone users. Implications are discussed from a marketing management perspective.

3.1.6

Douglas, Susan P. and C. Samuel Craig (1983), "Examining Performance of U.S. Multinationals in Foreign Markets," *Journal of International Business Studies*, 14(3), Winter, 51-62.

In the U.S. a basic tenet of business philosophy is that profitability is related to market share. The generality of this finding in markets outside the U.S. is examined by the authors based on a sample of product business drawn from the PIMS (Profit Impact of Marketing Strategy) data base. All businesses belong to firms whose corporate headquarters are located in the U.S. The relation between seven marketing mix variables and market share and ROI (return on investment) is compared. In general, the relationship between market share and ROI appears to hold in European and other foreign markets. The marketing mix variables associated with these measures of performance, however, as well as the strength of the relationship, vary by market area.

3.1.7

Globerman, Steven (1984), "The Consistency of Canada's Foreign Investment Review Process—A Temporal Analysis," *Journal of International Business Studies*, 15(1), Spring/Summer, 119-129.

Since its inception, Canada's Foreign Investment Agency has been criticized for applying its criteria for screening reviewable foreign direct investments in an inconsistent manner. This paper evaluates the consistency of FIRA's review process over time, using published data on the disposition of reviewable proposals. The critical notion underlying the test is that discrete and significant changes in acceptance rates for reviewable proposals may indicate unanticipated changes in FIRA's de facto screening criteria. Significant discrete changes can be identified in the acceptance rates for reviewable proposals over the period 1974-82.

3.1.8

Hook Jr., Ralph C. and Michael R. Czinkota (1988), "Export Activities and Prospects of Hawaiian Firms," *International Marketing Review,* 5(4), Winter, 51-57.

3.1.9

Kotabe, Masaaki (1989), "Assessing the Shift in Global Market Share of U.S. Multinationals," *International Marketing Review,* 6(5), 20-35.

Based on the U.S. Department of Commerce's survey data of U.S. direct investment abroad for 1977 and 1985, this study examines the shift in global market share of U.S. multinational manufacturing firms for the 1977-1985 period. Consolidated global market shares of U.S. multinationals for 26 industries are estimated for 1977 and 1985. The shift in their global market share is analyzed from a perspective of three alternative, if not independent, strategic thrusts: namely, home market orientation, export orientation, and foreign production orientation. Contrary to the commonly stated claim that the competitiveness of U.S. manufacturing firms has been declining, findings of this study indicate that, on average, U.S. manufacturing multinationals have maintained global market share on a consolidated basis fairly well.

3.1.10

Li, Jiatao and Stephen Guisinger (1991), "Comparative Business Failures of Foreign-controlled Firms in the United States," *Journal of International Business Studies,* 22(2), 209-224.

The comparative business failures of foreign-owned or controlled firms and domestically owned firms are investigated. Original data are collected regarding foreign-controlled firms in the U.S. that filed for bankruptcy protection and were involuntarily liquidated or ceased operations mainly due to poor financial performance during the 1978-1988 period. The findings show that foreign-controlled firms fail less often than domestically owned firms. New U.S. affiliates of foreign companies are found to suffer a higher failure rate than more established affiliates. Modes of entry, forms of foreign ownership, and national culture are also found to have effects on the failures of foreign controlled firms in the United States.

3.1.11

Norburn, David, Sue Birley, Mark Dunn, and Adrian Payne (1990), "A Four Nation

Study of the Relationship Between Marketing Effectiveness, Corporate Culture, Corporate Values, and Market Orientation," *Journal of International Business Studies,* 21(3), 451-468.

This research explores the ways in which senior executives in the UK, the US, Australia, and New Zealand characterized their firm's marketing effectiveness. Corporate culture and beliefs are explored. At the international management level, contributions to theoretical development have emanated from three different perspectives: contextual, behavioral, and environmental. The results give support to those theorists who advance cultural specificity as the main moderator of top managerial attitudes. However, they also emphasize that the best predictor of marketing effectiveness is similar in all four nations—the primacy of the importance of people and quality. Across each of the four categories, variations in managerial attitudes, beliefs, and values are observed, suggesting that national culture shapes individual behaviors into kaleidoscopic formats, each different in subtle patterning.

3.1.12

Reed, John S. (1989), "Dawn of the Post-World War II Era," *Columbia Journal of World Business,* 24(4), Winter, 5-9.

3.1.13

Ronstadt, Robert and Robert J. Kramer (1982), "Getting the Most Out of Innovation Abroad," *Harvard Business Review,* 60(2), March-April, 94-99.

The authors of this article explore the weakness of American companies' international innovation efforts and offer guidance for making better use of existing resources. Their analysis is based on interviews with more than 50 U.S., European, and Japanese managers of multinationals. It is also based on a mail survey of 240 corporations around the world and on data covering 100 foreign-based R&D investments.

3.1.14

Rugman, Alan M. (1986), "The Role of Multinational Enterprises in U.S.-Canadian Economics Relations," *Columbia Journal of World Business,* 21(2), Summer, 15-27.

The role of Multinational Enterprises in the Canadian economy is analyzed. The author demonstrates that the U.S. and Canadian multinationals rely upon different sources of strength for their success. These country specific and firm specific advantages are outlined. Policy recommendations which take these advantages into account are made.

3.1.15

Rugman, Alan M. and Roderick Tilley (1987), "Canada's Reversal from Importer to Exporter of Foreign Direct Investment," *Management International Review,* 27(3),13-25.

3.1.16

Sanderson, Susan Walsh and Robert H. Hayes (1990), "Mexico—Opening Ahead of Eastern Europe," *Harvard Business Review,* 68(5), September-October, 32-42.

Although Eastern Europe has tremendous potential, Mexico is North America's regional opportunity. Mexico has begun to emerge from decades of state intervention, antagonism toward its neighbors, and resistance to foreign investment. Mexico has almost 90 million increasingly literate and motivated people. Many US companies have recognized the benefits of establishing maquiladora assembly facilities along the Mexico-US border. Since 1988, global corporations have invested some $80.8 billion in Mexico. The US share of this investment has been about 63%. Mexico's $80 billion-plus in debt still represents about $1,000 per capita, but Hungary's per capita foreign debt is more than twice as great. The ratio for the US is over $2,000 per person, and it is increasing by almost 20% per year. To encourage growth in the sophistication and competitiveness of its companies, Mexico has instituted its own version of Japan's Deming Award for outstanding achievement in quality, customer responsiveness, and quality of work life.

3.1.17

Seringhaus, F. H. Rolf and Guenther Botschen (1991), "Cross-National Comparison of Export Promotion Services: The Views of Canadian and Austrian Companies," *Journal of International Business Studies,"* 22(1), 115-133.

Export promotion systems and services in Canada and Austria are contrasted and evaluated. While the Canadian system is government-based, the Austrian system is mainly operated by private sectors. A survey of stratified samples of exporters in Canada and Austria shows significant differences in perceived usefulness of services. Compared with Canadian firms, Austrian companies appear more inclined to use export support and more willing to acquire exporting know-how externally.

3.1.18

Shipley, David D. (1985), "Marketing Objectives in UK and US Manufacturing Companies," *European Journal of Marketing,* 19(3), 48-56.

Marketing heads of US and UK manufacturing firms were interviewed in 1979 and 1980 to study the nature of marketing objectives. The analysis of objectives focuses on their time-relatedness, flexibility, and consistency with each other. Objectives in export and domestic markets are also compared. The findings show much similarity between the countries, with most firms specifying profit variables as their principal objective in both markets. The widespread use of multiple objectives, along with the types of objectives, probably creates conflict and hampers effectiveness. Most firms set annual objectives but not longer-range goals, and this practice may impair effective marketing planning and control. Most do not reconsider priorities over time; this rigidity of policy can also have serious detrimental effects.

3.2 Europe and Other Developed Areas

3.2.1

Barker, A. Tansu (1987), "Consumerism in New Zealand," *International Marketing Review,* 4(3), Summer, 63-74.

The attitudes and perceptions of New Zealanders toward current consumerism issues are outlined and compared with four other countries. Many of the opinions expressed are critical of the existing practices of business and appear to be common in the other four countries. The theory of consumer product life cycle suggesting the development of national consumer movements was not supported by the data obtained in New Zealand.

3.2.2

Collins, Robert S., Roger W. Schmenner, and D. Clay Whybark (1990), "Pan-European Manufacturing: The Yellow Brick Road to 1992," *Business Horizons,* 33(3), May-June, 15-22.

3.2.3

Darling, John R.(1987), "A Longitudinal Analysis of the Competitive Profile of Products and Associated Marketing Practices of Selected European and Non-European Countries," *European Journal of Marketing,* 21(3), 17-29.

A 1985 longitudinal analysis of the general attitudes of consumers in Finland toward the products of the UK, France, Germany, Japan, and the US followed up similar studies conducted in 1975 and 1980. For this study, "attitude" refers to ideas, feelings, emotions, and connotations associated with products from an identifiable country. The findings of the analysis derive from the clear-cut support of the three hypotheses that were tested. The Finnish consumer's knowledge of a product's country of origin is sufficient to provoke differing images of (1) product attributes or qualities, (2) nonproduct aspects of marketing mixes that are commonly associated with products, and (3) satisfaction derived from acquisition of goods with made-in labels from various countries. It was found that Finnish consumers seemed to have the most positive attitudinal response to products and marketing activities of Germany and Japan.

3.2.4

Delachaux, Francois B. (1990), "The Effects of 1992 on European Business," *Business Horizons,* 33(1), January-Feburary, 33-36.

The goal of the Treaty of Rome is to create an economic community that would bring about improvements in the lives of its inhabitants. Through mergers, acquisitions, and other agreements, companies are trying to reach the size needed to be able to serve the new European market. Things remaining to be done before the 1992 deadline include: (1) establishment of a European central bank, (2) modification of the rules governing mergers and acquisitions, and (3) normalization of rules and regulations applicable to products. Things already accomplished include: (1) Eight out of the 12 countries have declared they will guarantee the free movement of capital by 1990; (2) Road transportation is in the process of becoming free and regulations are being standardized; (3) Progress has been made toward a unique license for banking. Industrial businesses that have not yet begun to adapt to the new conditions may eventually find themselves unable to survive.

3.2.5

Foxall, Gordon (1984), "Co-operative Marketing in European Agriculture: Organizational Structure and Market performance," *International Marketing Review,* 1(3), Spring/Summer, 42-57.

This paper is concerned with the contribution of co-operative organizational structure and behavior to the variations in co-operative market shares found in European agriculture. It is argued that there is a clear relationship between organizational factors and the market position of the co-operative sector in each country and that this has implications for the encouragement of co-operative organization which is an aim of UK public policy.

3.2.6

Friberg, Eric G. (1989), "1992: Moves Europeans Are Making," *Harvard Business Review,* 67(3), May-June, 85-89.

European managers are preparing for the challenges of European unification in 1992. Their preparations include: (1) Reduce overcapacity and high fixed costs. Electrolux is one company that has dealt aggressively with the problem, closing or focusing every factory it has acquired over the past ten years. (2) Build scale. The fragmented structure of many European industires makes it difficult to conduct world-class R&D. Unilever, Lufthansa, and Deutsche Bank are taking the necessary steps to achieve global scale. The same goal is at the heart of Europe's largest business deal: the $18 billion merger between Sweden's ASEA and Switzerland's Brown Boveri will restructure the Continent's electrical engineering and equipment industry. (3) Recognize international competition. If large companies want to compete on equal terms with global rivals, they must expand their reach through acquisitions of, strategic alliances with, and equity participation in overseas companies. (4) Work to homogenize local tastes.

3.2.7

Grant, Robert M. (1987), "Multinationality and Performance Among British Manufacturing Companies," *Journal of International Business Studies,* 18(3), Fall, 79-89.

3.2.8

Hogberg, Bengt and Clas Wahlbin (1984), "East-West Industrial Cooperation: the Swedish Case," *Journal of International Business Studies,* 15(1), Spring/ Summer, 63-79.

Although industrial cooperation is an important means for the East to acquire Western technology, most of the Swedish companies interviewed are rather reluctant to engage in such cooperation. They often cooperate in order to protect a market or to promote exports of other products, and the partners seldom strive toward a common goal. This increases the risk of problems during the implementation of the agreements; problems of quality, delivery failures from the East, and management and coordination are especially frequent; the latter two are strongly associated with unsuccessful results. Complicated agreements involving several partners have a tendency to fail. The differences between the two economic and political systems manifest themselves in management styles, freedom to act, and make it difficult to integrate operations. East-West industrial cooperation, therefore, seldom leads to an intensive integration where the partners specialize and supplement each other.

3.2.9

Jacqueme, Joyce (1990), "Target 1992: Europe's New Frontier," *International Management,* 45(7), August, 50-53.

Portugal is struggling to keep up with the rapid pace of European development. The country faces a formidable range of challenges. The most critical are infrastructure and education. There will be many individual and corporate losers as Portugal confronts the challenge of full competition in an open EC market. The country as a whole, however, should emerge as a winner.

3.2.10

Kaikati, Jack G. (1989), "Europe 1992—Mind Your Strategic P's and Q's," *Sloan Management Review,* 31(1), Fall, 85-92.

Business executives should start mapping corporate strategy for dealing with Europe 1992. An important place to begin charting a corporate strategy is to monitor

European developments, lobby decision makers, and prepare to face giant Euro-firms. To aid in this process, the US Department of Commerce has set up a special office called Single Internal Market: 1992 Information Service. However, US firms should not rely on importing directly to the European Community (EC), especially since the introduction of three EC directives on forklifts, meat, and television programming. Joint ventures and strategic alliances are probably more productive ways of gaining a foothold in Europe. In addition, direct investment can be made in Europe that would take advantage of cost savings, although local content regulations and tough rules of origin should be considered in selecting a host country.

3.2.11

Magee, John F. (1989), "1992: Moves Americans Must Take," *Harvard Business Review,* 67(3), May-June, 78-84.

Europe is determined to achieve economic unity and to compete on at least equal terms with the economic giants of America and Asia. Preparing for 1992 the author examines the dangers and opportunities for four kinds of companies: (1) American-based multinationals need pan-European strategies. Improved transport, the reduction of regulatory barriers, and newly legalized alliances make local focus a dangerous approach. (2) Businesses with one European subsidiary have four choices: expand, ally, rationalize, or get out. (3) Companies that export to Europe have two concerns: strengthened European competition and increased European protectionism. (4) Companies that do no business with Europe are not out of danger. Increased European competitiveness can mean trouble for complacent business.

3.2.12

Stewart, D. B. (1983), "Competition in the UK Automobile Markets: An Empirical Study," *European Journal of Marketing,* 17(1), 14-25.

The strategies of the MNEs operating in the UK are examined. By segmenting the product offerings in this market it is possible to assess the effectiveness of the product policies of competing producers over the period 1978-80. Particular attention is paid to the competitiveness of the domestic producers.

3.2.13

Yip, George S. (1991), "A Performance Comparison of Continental and National Business in Europe," *International Marketing Review,* 8(2), 31-39.

Most observers expect Europe 1992 to enhance the performance of European businesses as they expand from a national to a continental scope. But there is little direct evidence to date of the potential gain in profitability at the business level. Using the PIMS Program database of 89 European continental businesses and 253 European Single-country businesses, this study attempts to provide evidence in this direction. The author finds that, in contrast to North America, European continental businesses were much less profitable than national businesses over the period 1972-1987. This performance gap indicates the potential gain from the unified European market.

3.3 South America

3.3.1

Christensen, Carl H., Angela da Rocha, and Rosane Kerbel Gertner (1987), "An Empirical Investigation of the Factors Influencing Exporting Success of Brazilian Firms," *Journal of International Business Studies,* 18(3), Fall, 61-77.

The authors interviewed 152 Brazilian companies that were exporting in 1978 and again 6 years later in 1984 to determine the factors that were correlated with the continuance of exporting. Firm characteristics, export management practices, and manager perceptions were each found to be correlated with exporting success thus supporting the basic contention that it is possible to predict export performance.

3.3.2

Greer, Thomas V. and Michael J. Chattalas (1989), "The Role of the Promotion Fund of the International Coffee Agreement," *International Marketing Review,* 6(3), 47-61.

3.3.3

Moxon, Richard W. (1987), "International Competition in High Technology: the Brazilian Aircraft Industry," *International Marketing Review,* 4(2), Spring, 7-20.

This paper reviews the growth of the Brazilian aircraft industry, and evaluates the strategic choices and government policies that have influenced its development. Brazil's goals of military independence, technological development and improvement of its balance of payments have influenced the development path chosen and the requirements for success. Brazil's attempts to overcome the barriers to achieving technological competence, cost competitiveness, market acceptance and financial sustainability are described. It is argued that the government has played a crucial role in providing financial resources and a protected domestic market, but that it has allowed the key enterprise, Embraer, to maintain an emphasis on commercial viability and international competitiveness.

3.3.4

Wells, Christopher (1988), "Brazilian Multinationals," *Columbia Journal of World Business,* 23(4), Winter, 13-23.

Brazilian companies, driven by the need to export, are using their advanced management and technical skills to successfully run subsidiaries abroad.

3.4 Developed Areas in Asia

3.4.1

Campbell, Nigel (1987), "Japanese Business Strategy in China," *Long Range Planning*, 20(5), October, 69-73.

A survey was conducted involving 115 foreign companies in Beijing, China. The intention of the survey was to record the foreign communities' opinions about the Chinese business environment. Of the companies surveyed, 60 were Japanese, 25 were from the US, and 30 were European. The survey identified five main differences of the Japanese approach to doing business in China: approaches to strategy, investment, technology transfer, trading, and building local relationships. It appears that the Japanese regard China as a long-term investment and are prepared to accept low initial profits. The Japanese also prefer trading rather than investing in equity joint ventures, and they are more adept at using Chinese cultural practices to their benefit. Attention to detail and local understanding marks the differences between the Japanese approach to business in China and that of its competitors.

3.4.2

Doyle, P., J.Sauners, and V. Wong (1986), "Japanese Marketing Strategies in the UK: a Comparative Study," *Journal of International Business Studies,* 17(1), Spring, 27-46.

Hypotheses about Japanese marketing are examined using a matched sample of British companies and their major Japanese competitors. Japanese subsidiaries in Britain are shown to be much more market-oriented, more single-minded in their pursuit of market share and more alert to strategic opportunities than their British counterparts. Organizationally, however, their subsidiaries are more like successful British companies than the Japanese stereotype.

3.4.3

Ghoshal, Sumantra (1988), "Environmental Scanning in Korean Firms: Organizational Isomorphism in Action," *Journal of International Business Studies,* 19(1), Spring, 69-86.

This paper reports some of the findings of a study on environmental scanning practices in six large Korean firms and compares the results with those of previous studies on scanning conducted in the United States.

3.4.4

Johansson, Johny K. (1986), "Japanese Marketing Failures," *International Marketing Review*, 3(3), Autumn, 33-46.

Six Japanese marketing cases are evaluated in depth. It is known how the "success" interpretation which so often is promulgated by the firms and press alike in fact hides serious mistakes and results which in other countries would be interpreted as "failures."

3.4.5

Kiel, Geoffrey C. and Carol Ann Howard (1984), "The Pacific Rim—Vision or Reality," *European Journal of Marketing*, 18(4), 5-23.

For many marketing managers, the Pacific Rim raises several questions and challenges. This paper intends to supply answers for those questions which include: What is the Pacific Rim and what is its real importance both in terms of economic growth and market potential? To what extent does the Pacific Rim rival the European Community as a major world trading bloc? What are the implications of these developments in the Pacific Rim for international marketing strategy? These questions have special relevance in the European Community given the criticism by some commentators that many EC politicians and businessmen have largely ignored developments in the Pacific.

3.4.6

Kimura, Yui (1989), "Firm-Specific Strategic Advantages and Foreign Direct Investment Behavior of Firms: The Case of Japanese Semiconductor Firms," *Journal of International Business Studies*, 20(2), Summer, 296-314.

This research examines the effects of firm-specific strategic advantages on the FDI behavior of Japanese semiconductor firms. It investigates the strategic advantages necessary for undertaking FDI in this industry, and shows that these advantages are systematically associated with the variation on FDI behavior. The author identifies technological innovation, a broad product line, and vertical linkages with downstream businesses as sources of such strategic advantages.

3.4.7

Kotabe, Masaaki (1985), "The Roles of Japanese Industrial Policy for Export Success: A Theoretical Perspective," *Columbia Journal of World Business*, 20(3), Fall, 59-64.

Because of Japan's export success and the U.S.'s decline in the international trade arena, the Japanese style of industrial policymaking has become a major issue in regard to the revitalization of U.S. competitiveness. Concerning whether or not a country should move toward international strategic planning, this article offers a theoretical framework for industrial policy, drawing from international trade and commercial policy theories, with an emphasis on the Japanese experience.

3.4.8

Kotabe, Masaaki (1984), "Changing Roles of the Sogo Shoshas, the Manufacturing Firms, and the MITI in the Context of the Japanese 'Trade or Die' Mentality," *Columbia Journal of World Business,* 19(3), Fall, 33-42.

This article explores the relationship between the Japanese government, the general trading companies and the manufacturing companies within the Japanese "trade-oriented" economy. Central to the discussion is Kojima's distinction between "trade-oriented" and "anti-trade-oriented" policy. The changing role of the MITI is discussed in relation to the issues of protectionism and Japanese multinational business transactions.

3.4.9

Kotabe, Masaaki, Dale F. Duhan, David K. Smith Jr., and Dale R. Wilson (1991), "The Perceived Veracity of PIMS Strategy Principles in Japan: An Empirical Inquiry," *Journal of Marketing,* 55(1), January, 26-41.

Japanese executives' perceptions of the veracity of different profit impact of market strategy (PIMS) principles are examined. Questionnaires were sent to Japanese executives in Japan. The result shows that most of the PIMS principles found in the US were perceived by Japanese executives to apply in Japan. Japanese executives perceived a firm's market position to be the most important influence on firm performance. Finally, Japanese and US executives differed in their views on the level of veracity of strategy issues.

3.4.10

Kumar, Krishna and Kee Young Kim (1984), "The Korean Manufacturing Multinationals," *Journal of International Business Studies,* 15(1), Spring/ Summer, 45-61.

The authors discuss the development of the overseas manufacturing direct investment by Korean firms and the relationship between parent firms and overseas affiliates. Three main issues are discussed: the ownership-specific assets, location-specific factors, and government policies are the important sets of variables that help to explain the internationalization of the Korean firms in the manufacturing sector, the nature of technology transfer by Korean multinationals to their subsidiaries, and the benefits as a result of its overseas investment to Korea.

3.4.11

Lazer, William (1985), "Different Perceptions of Japanese Marketing," *Interna-*

tional Marketing Review, 2(3), Autumn, 31-38.

This article explores differences in perceptions of Japanese market protection, superpower status, government assistance, Westernization, competition, organization, consumers and decisions.

3.4.12

Lazer, William, Shoji Murata, and Hiroshi Kosaka (1985), "Japanese Marketing: Towards a Better Understanding," *Journal of Marketing,* 49(2), Spring, 69-81.

Japanese companies are recognized as world class marketers. Yet, sources of information in English about the development of Japanese marketing and marketing management decisions, strategies, and operations are relatively sparse. This article, the result of Japanese/American collaboration based on the deliberations of a Japanese study team, is designed to help fill this gap. Four main topics are addressed: stages in the growth of the marketing discipline, the nature of government/marketing relationships, marketing decisions and strategies, and selected practices. Fundamental sociocultural concepts underlying Japanese marketing approaches are discussed, and care is taken to highlight conceptual and operational differences from American marketing.

3.4.13

Levy, Brian (1988), "Korean and Taiwanese Firms as International Competitors: the Challenges Ahead," *Columbia Journal of World Business,* 23(1), 43-51.

The divergent strategic orientations of national Korean and Taiwanese firms are analyzed. Korean firms focus on high volume, high productivity manufacture of standardized products; Taiwanese firms, smaller than their Korean counterparts, emphasize flexibility and rapid response in market niches for nonstandardized products. The paper traces the origins of these divergent strategic orientations; it summarizes the results of field interviews with Korean and Taiwanese manufacturers of footwear, of keyboards for personal computers, and of assembled personal computers; it explores the implications of the observed differences for the national firms, and for their international competitors.

3.4.14

Magaziner, Ira C. and Mark Patinkin (1989), "Fast Heat: How Korea Won the Microwave War," *Harvard Business Review,* 67(1), January-February, 83-92.

3.4.15

Roehl, Thomas and J. Frederick Truitt (1987), "Japanese Industrial Policy in Aircraft Manufacturing," *International Marketing Review,* 4(2), Spring, 21-32.

3.4.16

Ryans, Adrian B. (1988), "Strategic Market Entry Factors and Market Share Achievement in Japan," *Journal of International Business Studies,* 19(3), Fall, 389-409.

The literature on market share change is reviewed to identify situational and marketing strategy factors associated with market share achievement. Then the author tests certain hypotheses suggested by this and related literature. The results indicate that a few key situational and marketing strategy variables account for a large proportion of the variation in achieved market share in Japan.

3.4.17

Suzuki, Sadahiko and Richard W. Wright (1985), "Financial Structure and Bankruptcy Risk in Japanese Companies," *Journal of International Business Studies,* 16(1), Spring, 97-110.

3.4.18

Wong, Veronica, John Saunders, and Peter Doyle (1987), "Japanese Marketing Strategies in the United Kingdom," *Long Range Planning,* 20(6), December, 54-63

This article reports results from interviews with marketing management of 15 Japanese firms operating in the UK and 15 of their UK competitors. Audio/hi-fi, machine tool, and miscellaneous industries were surveyed. The Japanese firms were managed mostly by local employees similar in age, background, and experience to those of their UK competitors. Results show that the Japanese subsidiaries were: (1) much more oriented to long-term market share than to short-term profits, (2) more responsive to strategic openings, and (3) more ambitious. Although there were not many organizational differences between the two groups, the Japanese firms tended to have product- or market-based divisions and to have ongoing, informal procedures for planning and control.

3.5 Eastern Europe

3.5.1

Adler, Nancy J., Nigel Campbell, and Andre Laurent (1989), "In Search of Appropriate Methodology: From Outside the People's Republic of China Looking in," *Journal of International Business Studies,* 20(1),Spring, 61-74.

3.5.2

Artisien, Patrick F.R. and Peter J. Buckley (1985), "Joint Ventures in Yugoslavia:

Opportunities and Constraints,'' *Journal of International Business Studies,* 16(1), Spring, 111-135.

This research examines the opportunities and constraints facing Western multinational companies which invest in joint ventures in Yugoslav industry. The empirical evidence drawn from a sample of 42 West European and North American companies addresses itself to the formation and success of joint ventures, the route to foreign direct investment in Yugoslavia and motives and preferences for joint ventures to other forms of industrial cooperation.

3.5.3

Beamish, Paul W. and Hui Y. Wang (1989), ''Investing in China via Joint Ventures,'' *Management International Review,* 29 (1), 57-64.

3.5.4

Fonfara, Krzysztof and Marylyn Collins (1990), ''The Internationalization of Business in Poland,'' *International Marketing Review,* 7(4), 86-99.

In 1981, Poland announced an economic reform program with the aim of moving toward a market-oriented economic system. However, there are few indications to suggest that the economic reform measures have been put effectively into practice. The contradiction between the central government's export priorities and the lack of export motivation on the part of companies has resulted in a failure of export policy. Macroeconomic and microeconomic conditions interact in creating a formidable barrier to the internationalization of Polish enterprises. To create a genuine climate of internationalization, it would be necessary to : (1) create conditions for competition in the home market, (2) demonopolize the economic system, (3) provide the financial motivation for firms to develop risky overseas operations, (4) develop a modern system of managerial education, and (5) create a professional infrastructure supporting overseas operations.

3.5.5

Frankenstein, John and C.N. Chao (1988), ''Decision-Making in the Chinese Foreign Trade Administration: a Preliminary Survey,'' *Columbia Journal of World Business,* 23(3), 35-40.

Personal interviews with Chinese foreign trade decision-makers in several locations in China revealed Chinese perceptions of important variables in what ''makes the deal.'' The availability of foreign exchange together with price and other immediate cost factors appear to be key issues. In the complexities of the Chinese administrative maze, the end-user emerged as a key decision-maker in choosing a foreign vendor, but local and central authorities were also important. The survey showed that a certain degree of decentralization has occurred in China.

3.5.6

Gardner, H. Stephen (1988), "Restructuring the Soviet Foreign Trade System," *Columbia Journal of World Business,* 23(2), Summer, 7-11.

The recent reforms of the Soviet foreign trade system to reorganize the administrative hierarchy have given domestic enterprises more access to the foreign market, allowed the formation of joint ventures, significantly changed the price and incentive systems.

3.5.7

Holton, Richard H. (1985), "Marketing and the Modernization of China," *California Management Review,* 27(4), 33-45.

Since 1978, there has been a move toward economic modernization in the Peoples' Republic of China. Previously, marketing decisions had been highly centralized within the government bureaucracy, so enterprise managers had little or no influence over policies. However, with economic readjustment, China has become more market-oriented. It now permits trade with foreign firms and the establishment of some small-scale private enterprises. In addition, marketing decision making is more decentralized. Managers in enterprises exempted from centralized planning are discovering the entire marketing mix, including product policy, pricing policy, advertising and promotion policies, and channels policy. Marketing in China is inhibited by the strong regionalism of the nation and China's primitive transportation system. China's successful move into international markets will require that enterprise managers be able to determine the products and product attributes desired by consumers.

3.5.8

Holzman, Franklyn D. (1983), "Systemic Bases of the Unconventional International Trade Practices of Centrally-Planned Economics," *Columbia Journal of World Business,* 18(4), Winter, 4-9.

The foreign trade behavior of centrally-planned economics differs from that of capitalist market economies. CPEs don't use tariffs or explicit quotas, their exchange rates are not functional, intra-bloc trade is rigidly bilaterally balanced, currencies are inconvertible, and so forth. It is argued here that international trade is an extension of domestic trade. The domestic economic institutions and mechanisms of CPEs are sketched briefly and, on this basis, their observed unconventional foreign trade practices are explained.

3.5.9

Jacobs, Everett M. (1986), "New Developments in Soviet Advertising and Marketing Theory," *International Journal of Advertising,* 5(3), 243-246.

This article compares theories of advertising and marketing in Soviet and Western countries and describes how theory in the USSR has progressed in recent years. The work of Demidov and Kardashidi is given particular attention. Soviet advertising practice has been affected adversely by the central planners' aim of controlling advertising and consumption, so that demand is not stimulated beyond what is thought to be desirable. However, without abandoning their traditional product orientation, Soviet marketing theorists have developed the notion that consumer interests should be more important in product development. Moreover, in sharp contrast to prior Soviet practice, market segmentation is examined as a means to increase the effectiveness of advertising. However, the omission of the important geographical and national group variables from this segmentation strategy suggests that political considerations will remain paramount in any changes in theory or practice.

3.5.10

Jacobson, David (1990), "First Steps Are Critical for U.S. Marketers in East Germany," *Business Marketing,* 75(10), October, 43.

Americans interested in buying an East German company must be cautious of their selections. Important sources of information include the Overseas Private Investment Corp. and the US Department of Commerce's Eastern European Business Information. In addition, a marketer must ensure that its purchase is protected against nebulous ownership laws. Other problems include inadequate roads and poor communications equipment. The most successful ventures will occur in such industries as construction and environmental cleanup, which contribute to an improved infrastructure. Until the East German economy stabilizes and more sophisticated customer decision-making processes evolve, face-to-face selling and personal relationships will remain important.

3.5.11

Kiser III, John W. (1982), "Tapping Eastern Bloc Technology," *Harvard Business Review,* 60(2), March-April, 85-93.

Although Americans tend to see the COMECON countries as technologically backward, some large U.S. companies have acquired licenses for highly useful processes and products from those markets. This author points out some of the difficulties of buying technology from the Communist world and shows U.S. companies how to take advantage of the opportunities.

3.5.12

Larson, Milton R. (1988), "Exporting Private Enterprise to Developing Communist Countries: A Case Study on China," *Columbia Journal of World Business,* 23(1), 79-90.

The prospect for successful direct foregoing investment in China has been enhanced by sustained governmental effort to legislate market incentives into its command economy. As is true generally for developing nations, domestic governmental and foreign investor goals conflict over such basic issues as expropriation of profit. This article offers an overview of China's evolving commercial and legal climate for foreign investment and provides guidance in reducing China's foreign investment tax incentives to an understandable form.

3.5.13

Lazer, William (1986), "Soviet Marketing Issues, A Content Analysis of Pravda," *Journal of Business Research,* 14(2), April, 117-131.

The author conducted a content analysis of marketing and marketing related items published in Pravda, the newspaper of the Central Committee of the Soviet Communist Party, from 1977 to 1981. The analysis suggests that (1) marketing management in the USSR is in the rudimentary stage of development; (2) the supply of desired products and services and the demand are in great disequilibrium; (3) product quality is lacking; and (4) bureaucratic conflicts hinder the development of more efficient distribution systems.

3.5.14

Lee, Kam-Hon and Thamis Wing-Chun Lo (1988), "American Businesspeople's Perceptions of Marketing and Negotiating in the People's Republic of China," *International Marketing Review,* 5(2), Summer, 41-51.

3.5.15

McGuinness, Norman (1991), "Selling Machinery to China: Chinese Perceptions of Strategies and Relationships," *Journal of International Business Studies,* 22(2), 187-207.

The impact of marketing strategies and customer relationships on Chinese purchasers is examined. Data was collected from textile manufacture, food processing, flour milling, and grain oil production. The findings suggest that the most important factors in winning sales in China are product quality, promotional efforts, and service. Competitors whose quality levels are not of the highest may have to exert more than average promotional and service efforts to capture sales. An entry strategy of being first, ahead of other Western competitors, also seems to have paid handsome dividends. Cutting prices and offering special terms does not necessarily influence preferences. The Chinese managers seem to demand mainly that prices be in keeping with the quality offered, and there be some flexibility on matters such as technology transfer and countertrade.

3.5.16

Naor, Jacob (1985), "Marketing in a Resource-Short Socialist Environment: Romania," *International Marketing Review*, 2(2), Summer, 31-41.

Resource shortages appear to have had a significant impact on the development of marketing thought and practice in Romania. This paper examines the impact of resource shortages on marketing as well as the ability of the system to meet its planned goals. It appears that resource shortages have not been instrumental in bringing about a more widespread acceptance of western-style marketing practices in Romania.

3.5.17

Naor, Jacob (1986), "Towards A Socialist Marketing Concept—The Case of Romania," *Journal of Marketing*, 50(1), January, 28-39.

Interest in marketing appears to be increasing in all East bloc countries, and Romania is no exception. The context within which marketing activities currently take place there is presented, and a socialist Romanian version of the marketing concept is proposed. Examples of the application of the concept, both in Romania and in two other socialist countries with less central planning, are provided. Except for a portion still in the experimental stage, the Romanian model appears to fit well the marketing reality of the three socialist countries examined.

3.5.18

Pye, Lucian W. (1986), "The China Trade: Making the Deal," *Harvard Business Review*, 64(4), 74-90.

As host, the Chinese control the pace and form of negotiations. They want to establish and build a cooperative relationship that will eventually work in their favor. At the heart of the cultural give-and-take is the common Chinese attempt to get the other side to exaggerate its capabilities so that the Chinese can then keep going back to the well of cooperation for more help. Successful American companies have learned the rules of the Chinese game and are thus not forced to show their hand. They understand the power of Chinese delaying tactics and even use some of their own. They learn to hold back and not become over enthusiastic. The Chinese place much value on loyalty; when foreign executives handle things well, they can establish a personal relationship with the Chinese that can withstand the strongest shift in the political winds.

3.5.19

Ross, Madelyn C. (1986), "China and the United States' Export Controls System," *Columbia Journal of World Business*, 21(1), Spring, 27-33.

Technology transfers between the United States and China are governed by a complex export controls system that operates on both a bilateral and multilateral level. The system has changed rapidly during the 1980s, reflecting the warming trend in United States-China relations and the constant pressure of technological advances. Yet, many argue that it is not changing fast enough. Each step forward seems to create new problems and complications of its own.

3.5.20

Samli, A. Coskun (1986), "Changing Marketing Systems in Eastern Europe: What Western Marketers Should Know," *International Marketing Review,* 3(4), Winter, 7-16.

East European marketing progress has followed a series of economic reforms in different countries of the region. Changing marketing systems in these countries can be depicted as a move away from an authoritative to an integrative macro system. Most of the countries are at different points on this particular spectrum. Marketing reforms are more specifically related to both economic and managerial decentralization. Most marketing decisions are beginning to be made at the enterprise level rather than at the central governmental level. U.S. and other Western practitioners must understand these changes so that they can expand their business with this potentially large market.

3.5.21

Sasseen, Jane, Michael Farr, Tammi Gutner, and Karoly Ravasz (1990), "The Grim Reality: East Germany, Poland, Hungary, Czechoslovakia, Romania, Bulgaria," *International Management,* 45(3), April, 24-38.

For the struggling East bloc countries, the chances of successfully returning to health are far from equal. Much of the early money spent by Western firms will go into building the basic structures needed to operate. The biggest challenge will be rebuilding the human capital to provide badly needed management expertise. East Germany, with a strong industrial tradition and West German support, is the likeliest to succeed and the only truly safe route for Western investment in Eastern Europe. Poland's overbearing debt and lack of management expertise counter its skilled and very cheap labor force, and its privatization effort. Hungary's head start in economic reform may yet stumble under its heavy debt. Czechoslovakia, a once-model economy, awaits legislation to start its economic overhaul. Both Bulgaria and Romania are plagued with political instability and risk falling even farther behind the other Eastern European nations.

3.5.22

Sherr, Alan B. (1988), "Joint Ventures in the USSR: Soviet and Western Interests with Considerations for Negotiations,'' *Columbia Journal of World Business,* 23(2), Summer, 25-41.

3.5.23

Stewart, Sally and Nigel Campbell (1986), ''Advertising in Mainland China: A Preliminary Study,'' *International Journal of Advertising,* 5(4), 317-323.

Advertising in China is increasing rapidly, but little information has been published on who the major advertisers are. This article reports findings of a research on advertisements that appeared during a selected week in October 1985. Television commercials were videotaped, radio advertising recorded, billboards noted, and newspaper advertisements in the two major dailies clipped. Little advertising by foreign firms was found and, of that, virtually all was by Japanese companies. For example, 12 out of 14 of the foreign advertisements, among a total of 114 billboard ads checked, were Japanese. Industrial product advertising accounted for more than 25 percent of all the TV and radio ads analyzed. Averaged over the week, there were about 6-7 minutes of TV and 12-13 minutes of radio advertising daily, while advertising occupied about 20 percent of the total space in the two newspapers.

3.5.24

Terpstra, Vern (1988), ''The Chinese Look to World Markets,'' *International Marketing Review,* 5(2), Summer, 7-19.

Since its formation in 1949, the People's Republic of China has generally followed a policy of independent national development. The PRC played a small role in international trade. In the mid-1980s, with one quarter of the world' population, China accounted for only about one per cent of world trade. In 1979, with the end of the Cultural Revolution and the beginning of Deng's program of the Four Modernizations, China began opening to the world economy. It is searching for Western technology and equipment to accelerate its economic development. In order to pay for these Western imports, China must export to earn the necessary foreign exchange. Thus, because of its change in policy, China is becoming more active in international marketing.

3.5.25

Thorelli, Hans B. (1985), ''Market Socialism in the People's Republic of China,'' *International Marketing Review,* 2(2), Summer, 7-14.

This paper describes the recent economic experiments in China, and analyzes current and potential developments as approximating a society of market Socialism, a hybrid variety of socio-economic system never truly tested anywhere else. Implications to Western companies interested in doing business in the PRC are briefly discussed.

3.5.26

Vlachoutsicos, Charalambos A. (1988), "Doing Business with the Soviets: What, Who and How?" *Columbia Journal of World Business,* 23(2), 67-79.

Prevalent thinking in the American business world has it that the Soviets are interested first and foremost in high technology projects. The article demonstrates that this assumption is no longer valid. Gorbachev's economic reforms have opened a vast range of new opportunities for American companies in the Soviet market. Opportunities lie in many other areas besides high technology. Experience with the recent Soviet economic reforms underlines the need for fresh attitudes in the American business world about doing business with Soviets in less traditional areas of trade.

3.5.27

Webber, Alan M. (1989), "The Case of the China Diary," *Harvard Business Review,* 67(6), November-December, 14-15.

3.6 Developing Areas

3.6.1

Amine, Lyn S. and S. Tamer Cavusgil (1983), "Mass Media Advertising in a Developing Country: The Case of Morocco," *International Journal of Advertising,* 2(4), October-December, 317-330.

Mass media advertising systems and practices in Morocco were examined. Most local advertising agencies were small and television represented the only advertising medium which was capable of reaching a national audience. Outdoor advertising and point-of-sale advertising were not widely used. Five case studies of advertising campaigns conducted by 4 multinational firms and one local company were analyzed to assess the determinants of advertising effectiveness in Morocco. Successful campaigns were found to be those for local products and well-established foreign products, while campaigns for new foreign products failed. The primary determinants of advertising success in Morocco were found to be knowledge of the local environment, and the ability to appeal to Moroccan consumers in their own symbolic and linguistic terms.

3.6.2

Chidomere, Rowland C. (1986), "Environmental Factors and Distribution of Household Appliances in Nigeria," *International Marketing Review,* 3(4), Winter, 44-51.

This study assesses the relationship between the size of household appliance distribution in Nigeria, and the economic, technological, and socio-cultural environment. It also examines how the existing relationship could explain the marketing practices.

3.6.3

Goldman, Arieh (1982), "Adoption of Supermarket Shopping in a Developing Country: the Selective Adoption Phenomenon," *European Journal of Marketing*, 16(1), 17-26.

The purpose of this study was to gain insights into some of the issues involved in the introduction of the supermarket into a developing country-Israel. The question studied here is how the appearance of supermarkets affected the food shopping patterns of urban consumers. The study reveals that in spite of the generally easy accesibility of the supermarkets to the study respondents many of them continue to buy some of their food needs in the traditional stores. While a very high proportion of the sample have adopted supermarket shopping in the sense that they regularly purchase there some food items, only a small proportion of these supermarket shopping "adopters" are purchasing there all of their food needs.

3.6.4

Howard, Donald G. and Michael A. Mayo (1988), "Developing a Defensive Product Management Philosophy for Third World Markets," *International Marketing Review*, 5(1), Spring, 31-40.

As the controversy which surrounded the marketing of Nestle's infant formula in developing countries relaxes its decade-long hold on the news media and is consigned to the pages of marketing texts under the examples of how not to market, international marketers must ask themselves how a similar debacle can be avoided in the future. This paper suggests that the product management techniques commonly employed for markets in developed countries are inappropriate for markets in lesser-developed countries. To market successfully in LDCs, a firm must re-examine both its product offerings and its product management philosophy.

3.6.5

Lecraw, Donald J. (1983), "Performance of Transnational Corporations in Less Developed Countries," *Journal of International Business Studies*, 14(1), Spring/Summer, 15-33.

The determinants of the performance of a sample of 153 TNCs in six light manufacturing industries in the ASEAN countries are analyzed. Firm profitability increased as the firm's market share, advertising, and R&D intensity increased and as the market shares of the two largest firms in the industry and tariffs increased. Profitability decreased as the market share of the third largest firm in the industry increased, as import penetration increased, as the growth in the firm's sales increased, and as the number of home countries of the TNCs in the industry increased.

3.6.6

Lecraw, Donald J. (1984), "Bargaining Power, Ownership, and Profitability of Transnational Corporations in Developing Countries," *Journal of International Business Studies,* 15(1), Spring/Summer, 27-43.

As the bargaining power of the transnational corporations in the sample increased relative to the bargaining power of the host country, and as the desire of the TNCs for a high level of equity ownership increased, the percent equity ownership of the TNCs in their subsidiaries increased. The relationship between percent equity ownership and subsidiary success from the TNCs' viewpoint, however, was J-shaped. High and low levels of equity ownership were associated with high levels of success. Control of critical operational variables by the TNC was directly related to success.

3.6.7

Luqmani, Mushtaq, Ghazi M. Habib, and Sami Kassem (1988), "Marketing to LDC Governments," *International Marketing Review,* 5(1), Spring, 56-67.

A managerial framework is provided to examine and analyze factors that may influence government decision-making in LDCs. In order to successfully market to these buyers, a series of screens or hurdles have to be cleared. These include meeting eligibility, following procedures, establishing critical linkages, developing competitive offers, and exerting appropriate influence. Further, international firms can enhance their success and profits by taking a serious, long-term approach to these markets.

3.6.8

Mafi, Mohammad and Lawrence P. Carr (1990), "Guidelines for Marketing in Iran," *Industrial Marketing Management,* 19(2), May, 167-171.

Recent history has educated the Iranian people to be selective, and they no longer will compromise their values and cultural principles for a fast-paced economic improvement in their quality of life. A prescription for successful marketing in Iran involves developing (1) cultural competence, (2) product adaptation, (3) logistics and distribution, (4) promotion, (5) pricing, and (6) resources. The religious undertones that influence the government and culture must be understood; religion or politics should not be discussed unless the speaker is fully knowledgeable in those areas. In addition, all product instructions should be in Farsi, the Iranian language, and must not contain offensive material. Finally, an awareness of the product or service being offered must be developed, and promotion programs should be very clear and honest. With a willingness to barter, some excellent arrangements can be made.

3.6.9

Malhotra, Naresh K. (1986), "Why Developing Societies Need Marketing Technologies," *International Marketing Review*, 3(1), Spring, 61-73.

The author proposes a conceptual framework and a research methodology for transferring marketing technology to developing countries to address important societal problems. The methodology is described and illustrated with an empirical investigation. Guidelines for implementation of this methodology in developing countries are provided.

3.6.10

Miller, Fred and A. Hamdi Demirel (1988), "Efes Pilsen in the Turkish Beer Market: Marketing Consumer Goods in Developing Countries," *International Marketing Review*, 5(1), Spring, 7-19.

The Turkish beer market and the experience of Turkey's most successful brewer, Efes Pilsen, are examined. The article begins with a summary of relevant modern Turkish history and an overview of the beer market. Using the product life-cycle, it describes the development of the market and Efes' strategies for competing within it. It also assesses the impact of the government's 1984 decision to reclassify beer as an alcoholic beverage.

3.6.11

Mitchell, Ivor S. and Anthony I. Agenmonmen (1984), "Marketers' Attitudes Toward the Marketing Concept in Nigerian Business and Non-Business Operations," *Columbia Journal of World Business*, 19(3), Fall, 62-71.

This paper studies the contribution of the marketing concept to Nigerian businesses and consumers, its contribution to management and marketing operations, and its possible application to non-marketing activities. In their conclusion, the authors point out that although the marketing concept has been accepted in Nigeria, problems in relation to implementation still exist.

3.6.12

Okoroafo, Sam C. (1988), "Determinants of LDC Mandated Countertrade," *International Marketing Review*, 5(4), Winter, 16-24.

The increased use of government-imposed countertrade by developing nations to meet their economic goals has been of particular concern to international executives. Frequently, countertrade can be mandated by LDCs on transactions even with their long-time trading partners. Firms therefore need to anticipate actions of their LDC trading partners to be competitive in the global market place. Inadequate preparation can result in repercussions such as exclusion from specific deals, to exclusion from a particular country-market.

3.6.13

Sethi, Vikram, Lokesh Datta, Gordon Wise, and G.M. Naidu (1990), Passage to India: A Marketing Perspective," *International Marketing Review,* 7(1), 48-67.

There are several appealing aspects of the Indian market to international firms. First, India is the largest single market in the developing world, excluding the Peoples' Republic of China. Second, India's labor is abundant and cheaply available. Third, the country is ideally located both geographically and economically to serve Asia, Africa, the Middle East, and the Eastern bloc countries. Finally, a survey of 34 joint venture companies indicates high rates of return. Guidelines for export marketing to India include knowing the possibilities and limitations, understanding the market's composition and the market channels, and participating in international trade shows in India.

3.6.14

Sharan, Vyuptakesh (1985), "Internationalism of Third World Firms: an Indian Case Study," *International Marketing Review,* 2(2), Summer, 63-71.

The emergence of third world multinational corporations is a comparatively new phenomenon, providing scarce foreign exchange for less developed countries. This article explores some of the reasons behind the emergence of third world MNCs and in particular examines the successes and failures of Indian MNCs.

3.6.15

Smith, David K. Jr. (1989), "Creating Countertrade Opportunities in Financially Distressed Developing Countries: Framework and Nigerian Example," *International Marketing Review,* 6(5), 36-49.

This article addresses the question of how firms interested in identifying and exploiting business opportunities in less developed countries can use countertrade exchange mechanisms to accomplish their objectives. Key dimensions of this issue are illuminated using a business development model. To highlight critical interactions between countertrading and the business analysis model, the case of Nigeria is examined. Several issues suggested by the case analysis are generalized into do's and don'ts for prospective LDC countertrade.

3.6.16

Stoever, William A. (1989), "Why State Corporations in Developing Countries

Have Failed to Attract Foreign Investment," *International Marketing Review,* 6(3), 62-75.

This article discusses the behavioral and organizational reasons why the investment promotion materials of state-owned enterprises in some developing countries are very poor as marketing literature. It gives examples selected from nine LDCs' publications to illustrate specific ways in which they are inappropriate: by focusing on the enterprise's own concerns rather than the concerns of potential investors; by acting as a rule enforcer rather than a facilitator for foreign companies; by addressing the wrong audience or learning the wrong lessons from past experiences, etc. The appendix gives suggestions for how the same contents could be presented in more dynamic and attractive language.

3.6.17

Tang, Roger Y.W. (1988), "The Automobile Industry in Indonesia," *Columbia Journal of World Business,* 23(4), Winter, 25-35.

Major findings are summarized from an empirical study of the automobile industry in Indonesia by describing the importance of the automobile industry and the demand for and supply of automobiles in Indonesia. Market structure, distribution network and the role of Japanese multinational companies are explained.

3.6.18

Thorelli, Hans B., and Gerald Sentell (1982), "The Ecology of Consumer Markets in Less and More Developed Countries," *European Journal of Marketing,* 16(6), 54- 63.

This study compares the consumer market ecosystems of the LDCs, primarily represented by Thailand, and the more developed countries. The outstanding feature of the consumer buying process in the LDC is that it is often fraught with high risk. This is due to market structure problems as well as to characteristics of sellers and buyers themselves. Three major structural factors existing side by side frequently reinforce each other. They are the lack of quality control in local manufacturing, the equally striking lack of transportation and storage facilities suitable to the preservation of fresh foods, and the predatory practices of sellers. In Thailand, as in many other LDCs, chicanery is not unethical—it is a game.

3.6.19

Tuncalp, Secil (1988), "Strategy Planning in Export Marketing, The Case of Saudi Arabia," *Columbia Journal of World Business,* 23(3), Fall, 69-76.

A better understanding of the market characteristics is essential for exporters wanting to penetrate the lucrative Saudi market. This paper focuses on different aspects of export marketing including market research, segmentation and targeting, and planning of the Four Ps and offers some practical insights for strategy and tactics.

3.6.20

Weigel, Dale R. (1988), ''Investment in LDCs: the Debate Continues,'' *Columbia Journal of World Business,* 23(1), Spring, 5-9.

The issue of investment in LDCs is analyzed. The author finds that the sources and the nature of private direct investment in developing countries are changing. As a result, developing countries need to better coordinate their policies toward direct investment with their macroeconomic objectives and their natural advantages. They also need to engineer in-depth policy changes and put in place effective investment policies.

3.6.21

Wortzel, Lawrence H. (1983), ''Marketing to Firms in Developing Asian Countries,'' *Industrial Marketing Management,* 12(2), April, 113-123.

The marketing of capital goods and industrial components to firms in developing nations is discussed in reference to three stages of technological development. During the implementation stage, firms require total production packages to produce a limited line of products. Foreign suppliers must change their focus from the marketing of products to the marketing of technology, providing raw materials, equipment, and training. In the assimilation stage, firms focus on purchasing parts and components, some available in the local market, but most obtained from foreign suppliers. Product lines are extended to substitute for imported consumer goods. Industrial marketing activities must be directed toward identifying potential products and the items needed for their production. During the improvement stage, an emphasis on improving productivity and extending product lines brings about a renewed dependence on foreign sources of sophisticated components and equipment.

IV. Globalization Issues in International Marketing

4.1 Internationalization Process

4.1.1

Aggarwal, Raj and Tamir Agmon (1990), "The International Success of Developing Country Firms: Role of Government-Directed Comparative Advantage," *Management International Review*, 30(2), 163-180.

The concept of vertical dynamic comparative advantage is extended to model three stages of government-business relations in the process of firm internationalization that has accompanied the economic development of newly industrialized countries (NIC). India, Singapore, and the Republic of Korea represent different stages of the transition process from phase one of import substitution to phase two of export-based international business activities to phase three of foreign direct investment. In each case, the corporate sector took government-directed macroeconomic conditions as an input in developing its own long-term international strategy. In the model, the process of developing international business activities in NIC firms is shaped by two major factors—government policy and profit maximizing behavior by firms. The government may initiate the process and control its initial stages, but the role of government diminishes as the country and the corporate sector move successfully through the three stages.

4.1.2

Diamantopoulos, Adamantios (1988), "Identifying Differences Between High- and Low-Involvement Exporters," *International Marketing Review*, 5(2), Summer, 52-60.

The past 15 years have seen an ever-increasing interest in the empirical study of export behavior as evidenced by the growing amount of literature in the field. Partly responsible for this growing interest appears to be the realization that most of the normative literature on exporting has been based on the assumption that companies adopt a "rational" approach to exporting, an assumption that has been challenged in empirical studies. This paper supports Piercy who points out, "it seems that the great bulk of what has been written, said and taught about exporting is founded on the assumption that companies are internationally active, committed, problem-solving exporters. It has been shown that this assumption is descriptively false and indeed may be normatively questionable."

4.1.3

Dichtl, Erwin, Hans-Georg Koeglmayr, and Stefan Mueller (1990), "International Orientation as a Precondition for Export Success," *Journal of International Business Studies,* 21(1), 23-40.

Empirical evidence suggests that as many as one-third of the small and medium-sized West German firms with a primarily domestic focus could be turned into successful exporting firms. Problems can be found in the areas of: (1) language proficiency and the availability of qualified personnel, (2) distribution arrangements, service, and investments, and (3) market research and government information services. Some measures that could help correct these problems include: (1) more support from diplomatic and consular officers, (2) government assistance programs that would help small and medium-sized firms to participate in overseas fairs and trade shows, (3) greater attention to the information needs of potential exporters, and (4) stronger governmental efforts to raise the level of awareness about the importance of imports.

4.1.4

Green, Robert T. (1985), "Internationalization and Diversification of U.S. Trade: 1970 to 1981," *International Marketing Review,* 2(2), Summer, 53-62.

This paper presents the shifts which occurred in the nature of U.S. international trade between 1970 and 1981. It first considers the shifts in the countries to which this nation exports its products and the countries from which it obtains its imports. The paper then describes the changes which have occurred in the specific product categories which are exported and imported; which products have gained and lost the greatest share of U.S. exports and imports. The findings of the study imply that U.S. firms are becoming more internationalized in orientation and more diversified in the nature of their imports and exports.

4.1.5

Johanson, Jan and Jan-Erik Vahlne (1990), "The Mechanism of Internationaliza-tion," *International Marketing Review,* 7(4), 11-24.

In the Uppsala Internationalisation Model, the internationalization of the firm is seen as a process in which the enterprise gradually increases its international involvement. The firm is seen as a loosely coupled system in which different actors in the firm have different interests and ideas concerning the development of the firm. The model explains two patterns in the internationalization of the firm: (1) The firm's engagement in the specific country market develops according to an establishment chain and (2) Firms enter new markets with successively greater psychic distance. The model has been criticized as being too deterministic and as saying something important only about the early stages of internationalization. In comparison, the

Eclectic Paradigm predicts that production will be established where advantages can be enjoyed. This paradigm predicts the company will optimize rationally, while the Internationalization Model assumes that no optimization will occur.

4.1.6

Johnson, Chalmers (1983), "The 'Internationalization' of the Japanese Economy," *California Management Review*, 25(3), 5-26.

This article explores why and how Japan's economy was closed and examines the recent efforts to open it. During the 1950s, the Japanese government operated and perfected what is recognized today as a model of the state-guided capitalist developmental system. It worked well in Japan and led to the industrialization of Japan and to some of the highest rates of capital formation ever achieved by any economy. The "internationalization" of the Japanese economy actually involves the dismantling of the government-business relationship of the high-speed growth era from 1955 to 1973. Japanese government policy has been the main barrier to foreign penetration of the market rather than cultural differences, as is widely held. The internationalization of the Japanese economy is inevitable, as it has become essential to Japan's continued prosperity.

4.1.7

Joynt, Pat (1985), "A Strategy for Small Business Internationalization," *International Marketing Review*, 2(3), Autumn, 64-73.

A new Norwegian approach to assisting small companies to develop international operations is examined. The aim of the scheme is to mold groups of small companies with related products into separate entities which serve as vehicles for international market entry. An outside consultant is responsible for guiding and supporting each group's activities.

4.1.8

Juul, Monika and Peter G. P. Walters (1987), "The Internationalisation of Norwegian Firms—A Study of the U.K. Experience," *Management International Review*, 27(1), 58-66.

The authors formulate four propositions concerning the internationalization experience of Norwegian firms in the UK: (1) Foreign direct investment (FDI) in the UK will be preceded by export operations, and initial investment will focus on establishing corporate marketing and distribution facilities; (2) FDI in the UK will have taken place before investment in other non-Scandinavian overseas markets; (3) The nature of the product offered in the UK will evolve in an incremental manner, with the initial focus on a physical good being widened to include services, systems, and know-how; (4) The UK subsidiaries will have an important role in collecting, evaluating, and transmitting information on the UK operating environment back to the parent. Information was gathered from twelve Norwegian firms that had established marketing or manufacturing subsidiaries in the UK. There is clear evidence to support the first two propositions, but support for the last two is less conclusive.

4.1.9

Karafakioglu, Mehmet (1986), "Export Activities of Turkish Manufacturers," *International Marketing Review*, 3(4), Winter, 34-43.

Factors influential in directing Turkish manufacturers to exporting are discussed. The research shows that the majority of these companies started exports due to unexpected orders and entered this field as a result of domestic economic factors. Therefore, a different marketing strategy is not implemented for exports. However, as size and export volume increase, a change in attitudes is observed, supporting the findings of previous empirical studies that involvement in export marketing is a sequential and gradual process.

4.1.10

Keng, Kau Ah and Tan Soo Jiuan (1989), "Differences between Small and Medium Sized Exporting and Non-Exporting Firms: Nature or Nurture," *International Marketing Review*, 6(4), 27-40.

This article focuses on the relevant demographics, attitudes, behaviors, and concerns of small-medium sized exporting and non-exporting firms in Singapore in an attempt to determine whether measures can be developed to nurture non-exporters into exporters. The findings suggest that while basic differences in demographics exist between the two groups, the attitudinal and behavioral differences are acquired. Therefore, programs may be developed to nurture non-exporting firms to be export-oriented.

4.1.11

Millington, Andrew I. and Brian T. Bayliss (1990), "The Process of Internationalisation: UK Companies in the EC," *Management International Review*, 30(2), 151-161.

The authors investigate one of the stages in the process of internationalization—the formation of a manufacturing subsidiary or joint venture in an overseas market. The firms analyzed were taken from the Extel UK Quoted Companies List of more than 3,000 companies quoted on the UK Stock Exchange. The study involves 50 of the manufacturing transnational operation companies in the European Community and their parent companies. The results do not support a narrowly incremental view of the process of internationalization. A step-wise internationalization process is the exception rather than the rule. The analysis suggests that the dichotomy between planned and reactive, or opportunist, investments can be substantially explained by the international experience of the parent companies. The results support a life cycle model that is based on the international development of the firm rather than the market or product.

4.1.12

Perry, Anne C. (1990), "The Evolution of the U.S. International Trade Intermediary in the 1980s: A Dynamic Model," *Journal of International Business Studies,* 21(1), 133-153.

A model is proposed for use in analyzing that dynamic evolution of US international trade intermediaries (ITI). The model is based on Miles' (1980) model of organizational evolution, which focuses on the processes by which organizations manage the constraints imposed on them by the external environment. The basic model is changed to include: (1) transaction-cost analysis, (2) an expanded conceptual framework for operationalizing the decisions made by ITIs, (3) the concept of ask environment, and (4) a redefinition of strategy. The expanded conceptual framework clarifies the concepts of actor, process, structure, and function. The redefinition of strategy is based on Dunning's (1981) eclectic paradigm, which includes the concept of ownership or firm-specific advantages.

4.1.13

Reichel, Jurgen (1988), "The Internationalisation of Importing Companies," *European Journal of Marketing,* 22(10), 31-40.

Insight into the internationalization process of importing companies is provided by studying the buying function of six Swedish importers of foodstuffs. The study was based on 40 interviews with people in leading managerial positions in the companies. One of the factors in which the importer is especially interested, particularly if the importer deals with perishable goods, is the exporter's relationship to the channels of distribution. The widely held opinion that the activities of importers of consumer goods are international was confirmed. Two strategies for internationalization are: (1) incremental, in which firms buy their products from countries in the same geographical and cultural region, and (2) evolutionary, in which firms go outside their own region. The outside country chosen becomes a catalyst in awakening the interests of other importers to the possibilities of the whole region.

4.1.14

Sharma, D. Deo and Jan Johanson (1987), "Technical Consultancy in International-ization," *International Marketing Review,* 4(4), Autumn, 20-29.

Previous studies of the internationalization process of firms have focused on the internationalization of manufacturing firms. This article analyzes the internationali-zation of technical consultansy firms, a service industry. On the basis of two Swedish case studies the article concludes that the firms' networks of relationships with other firms has a critical role in the marketing internationalization of the firms.

4.1.15

Sullivan, Daniel and Alan Bauerschmidt (1990), "Incremental Internationalization: A Test of Johanson and Vahlne's Thesis," *Management International Review,* 30(1), 19-30.

Johanson and Vahlne (1977) theorized that the internationalization of the firm is an incremental process owing to the progressive reduction of psychic distance through managers' gradual accumulation of experiential knowledge of foreign markets. A study of forest products firms in Austria, Finland, Sweden, and West Germany failed to support this conceptualization. No significant differences in the appreciation of barriers and incentives to internationalization were found among the managers of firms at various stages of internationalization. A methodological shortcoming of Johanson and Vahlne and of the majority of the relevant literature is the concentration on Scandinavian industrial firms. The "by-nation" findings of the study suggest the possibility that nation-specific factors moderate the internationalization process.

4.1.16

Tansuhaj, Patriya S. and James W. Gentry (1987), "Firm Differences in Perceptions of the Facilitating Role of Foreign Trade Zones in Global Marketing Logistics," *Journal of International Business Studies,* 18(1), Spring, 19-33.

This article provides insight into the role that foreign trade zones play in the internationalization process of the firm. It investigates differences between users and non-users of foreign trade zones in terms of firm characteristics, the awareness of zone benefits, and the importance of the benefits to the firms surveyed.

4.1.17

Tung, Rosalie L. and Edwin L. Miller (1990), "Managing in the Twenty-First Century: The Need for Global Orientation," *Management International Review,* 30(1), 5-18.

US business is in the early stages of another "great leap forward" in the internationalization of the world's economic activity; this has great implications for top management. US managers and executives appear to be consistently ethnocentric in their approach to the practice of management, including their approach to management succession and the development and implementation of policies, practices, and procedures designed to support corporate management succession. If US corporations fail to integrate an international perspective into their human resource management policies and practices, their ability to compete successfully in the global marketplace will continue to be encumbered. Management and executive development programs that focus on live international business problems, foreign assignments, and repatriation of employees are examples of how human resources management can contribute to the globalization process.

4.1.18

Yip, George S., Pierre M. Loewe, and Michael Y. Yoshino (1988), "How to Take Your Company to the Global Market," *Columbia Journal of World Business,* 23(4), Winter, 37-47.

Deciding how to deal with the globalization of markets poses tough issues and choices for managers. There are both external business forces and internal organizational factors to consider. External business forces revolve around the interaction of industry drivers of globalization and the different ways in which a business can be global. Understanding this interaction is key to formulating the right global strategy. Internal organizational factors play a major role in determining how well a company can implement global strategy. This paper provides a systematic approach to developing and implementing a global strategy.

4.2 Market Globalization

4.2.1

Belli, Pedro (1991), "Globalizing the Rest of the World," *Harvard Business Review,* 69(4), July-August, 50-55.

The economies of industrialized nations have become increasingly intertwined through global trade and global products. However, globalization has largely left out two continents of the globe that encompass more than 60 countries and 20% of the world's population, namely Africa and Latin America. The declining protectionism represents an unprecedented opportunity. Nations in Latin America and Africa are not only more attractive places to do business but also offer new opportunities for direct investment and ownership. The issue facing marketers in the developed nations is whether to pursue this opportunity. The timing for addressing the issue is good, as the possibility of an expanded free-trade zone from Canada to Argentina becomes closer to being realized.

4.2.2

Kreutzer, Ralf Thomas (1988), "Marketing-Mix Standardization: An Integrated Approach in Global Marketing," *European Journal of Marketing,* 22(10), 19-30.

An analytical framework is provided as an aid for enterprises making the decision as to whether or not global marketing can support their firm in working out competitive advantages. The analysis is first concerned with whether marketing-mix standardization is important for the branch or the market of the organization in question. This step is geared toward strategic factors of success. The analysis is next concerned with finding out ways in which marketing-mix standardization can be practiced by one particular company. Segmentation as a concept is helpful in this context when considered in relation to standardization. In order to maximize the use of a global marketing concept and to detect the inevitable risks early enough, a determination must be made of the positive and negative effects of a standardization strategy on the customers and countries considered as well as the possible consequences to the firm itself.

4.2.3

Boddewyn, Jean J., Robin Soehl, and Jacques Picard (1986), "Standardization in International Marketing: Is Ted Levitt in Fact Right?" *Business Horizons,* 29(6), November-December, 69-75.

Levitt's article on the globalization of markets (1983) offers plausible ideas but lacks evidence. Few facts about the present state of international marketing standardization and adaptation have been available until recently. A survey of US marketing in the European Economic Community (EEC) reveals some findings that can be used to determine whether international companies can or will standardize. Results provide some support for Levitt's arguments, showing that product standardization was fairly high in 1983 and had been growing since 1973. However, there was less change than anticipated in 1973. While Levitt is good at hedging his bets, he has drawn attention to a new "marketing myopia" and has urged the recognition that business competition is increasingly global, requiring a new vision of how to compete through standardized and affordable quality.

4.2.4

Crespy, Charles T. (1986), "Global Marketing is the New Public Relations Challenge," *Public Relations Quarterly,* Vol.31, Summer, 5-8.

Advances in worldwide communications are making tastes and preferences more similar everywhere, yet government regulation of business practices, especially advertising, has become quite diverse. Multinational corporations need qualified personnel to run interference for global marketing campaigns, and that is what is presenting the global challenge to the public relations industry. Opportunities for PR professionals lie in representing corporate interests in two distinct areas: (1) relations with international firms and international public interest groups, and (2) relations with foreign governments. Each new world brand roll-out must be inextricably linked to a global PR campaign.

4.2.5

Daniels, John (1987), "Bridging National and Global Marketing Strategies Through Regional Operations," *International Marketing Review,* 4(3), Summer, 29-44.

Cross-national strategy as opposed to country-by-country strategy may take place on a regional or on a global basis. This paper examines the European regional office experience of 16 large U.S. firms in terms of (1) the types of responsibilities they handle and why, (2)the problems of removing control and/or duties from country subsidiaries, and (3) the relationship between a regional and global strategy and implementation. The companies' experiences have been quite diverse, thus highlighting multiple opportunities but they need to approach the development of regional operations cautiously. In spite of some problems, the future for European regional management seems bright.

4.2.6

Davidson, William H. and Philippe Haspeslagh (1982), ''Shaping a Global Product Organization,'' *Harvard Business Review,* 60(4), July-August, 125-132.

One of the most widely practiced organizational responses to problems in international operations by the late 1970s was the worldwide or global product structure. The idea of the system is simple—to meet the challenge posed by world markets, why not make the responsibilities for domestic product divisions worldwide in scope? The authors of this article make it plain that many companies have adopted these systems without thinking through the full impact of such changes on their organizations. Most fundamental, the simplicity of the idea masks the complexity of implementing it.

4.2.7

Douglas, Susan P. and C. Samuel Craig (1989), ''Evolution of Global Marketing Strategy: Scale, Scope and Synergy,'' *Columbia Journal of World Business,* 24(3), Fall, 47-59.

The development of effective international marketing strategy should take into consideration the extent of a firm's experience overseas and the stage in the evolution of its international development. There are three key phases in this evolution: (1) initial foreign market entry, (2) expansion of national markets, and (3) global rationalization. In the phase of initial entry, the main decisions relate to the choice of countries to enter, the timing of entry, and the mode of entry. For local market expansion, the key decisions center around the development of products, product lines, and product businesses that offer promise of market growth in each country. For global rationalization, the main decisions focus on improving the efficiency of operations worldwide and developing a global strategy.

4.2.8

Douglas, Susan P. and Yoram Wind (1987), ''The Myth of Globalization,'' *Columbia Journal of World Business,* 22(4), Winter, 19-29.

Considerable controversy has arisen in recent years concerning the most appropriate strategy in international markets. It has been cogently argued that a strategy of global products and brands is the key to success in international markets. This paper examines critically the key assumptions underlying this philosophy, and the conditions under which it is likely to be effective. Barriers to its implementation are highlighted. Based on this analysis, it is proposed that global standardization is merely one of a number of strategies which may be successful in international markets.

4.2.9

Dymsza, William (1984), "Trends in Multinational Business and Global Environment: A Perspective," *Journal of International Business Strategy,* Vol.15, Winter, 25-46.

MNCs have to make tradeoffs of the advantages of global integration of their business against pressures for adaption to national conditions and the demands of other important actors. Many MNCs will engage in more joint ventures, various contractual arrangements and countertrade. The recent rise of third world MNCs adds to competitive intensity.

4.2.10

Hamel, Gary and C.K. Prahalad (1985), "Do You Really Have a Global Strategy?" *Harvard Business Review,* 63(4), July-August, 139-148.

The Japanese competition attacked in the 1970s. U.S. and European companies were caught napping at first, but quickly responded. However, according to the authors, the corporate response to Japan's thrust has been half-hearted and without appreciation for its long-term objectives. Many companies have miscalculated both the timing and the workability of their strategies, in part because they don't understand what global strategy really is. So they continually fall behind and lose market share in most of the leading markets of the future. Through a detailed analysis of the tire and television markets, the authors show that only by thinking about strategy in a more analytic light can U.S. companies overtake the competitors.

4.2.11

Hout, Thomas, Michael E. Porter, and Eileen Rudden (1982), "How Global Companies Win Out," *Harvard Business Review,* 60(5), September-October, 98-108.

The power of global strategies is illustrated in this article by the histories of three companies that have what the authors think it takes to win the new competitive game. These case studies illustrate the risks, the fight, and the ultimate reward of competing globally. They should help managers decide whether a global strategy is appropriate for their companies.

4.2.12

Kacker, Madhav (1986), "Coming to Terms with Global Retailing," *International Marketing Review*, 3(1), Spring, 7-20.

The growth of mass retailing and the increasing homogeneity of foreign markets have established a basis for global retailing. Trends toward retailing globalization are evidenced by the growing foreign direct investment in retail operations and the international expansion of retail franchises. Under high competitiveness, retail operations in foreign markets will have to be innovative in order to survive. Restrictive political and economic environments in Europe will favor the US as the prime target for foreign direct retailing investment. Developing countries increasingly will provide attractive locations for franchise retailing and for retail buying operations that face supply constraints and high costs in domestic markets. There will be growth in the international marketing of private brands and labels for strong retailers with established names and reputations.

4.2.13

Kanter, Rosabeth Moss (1991), "Transcending Business Boundaries: 12,000 World Managers View Change," *Harvard Business Review*, 69(3), May-June, 151-164.

The findings of a World Leadership Survey conducted by Harvard Business Review are reported. More than 10,000 responses were received from 25 countries. The most important message from the survey is that change is everywhere—regardless of country and culture. However, the idea of a corporate global village where a common culture of management unifies the practice of business around the world is more dream than reality. The survey uncovers deep national differences that overwhelm age, sex, or industry distinctions among respondents. Germans appear the most cosmopolitan. Japanese report the strongest work ethic among top managers. Cultural alliances appear to unite the views of Italians and Spaniards with those of Mexicans, Brazilians, and Venezuelans.

4.2.14

Kashani, Kamran and John A. Quelch (1990), "Can Sales Promotion Go Global?" *Business Horizons*, 33(3), May-June, 37-43.

The forces challenging the traditional thinking about sales promotion among multinational corporations are explored. Sales promotions are increasingly becoming a headquarters concern because of an increase in cost, complexity, global branding, and transnational trade. Despite these factors, sales promotion remains primarily a local activity. There are important differences among countries with respect to economic development, market maturity, perceptions, regulations, and trade structure. To help clarify the respective roles of headquarters and country management, a framework is presented that takes into account a brand's geographic scope and communication on one hand and the different elements of sales promotion decision making on the other.

4.2.15

Kashani, Kamran (1989), "Beware the Pitfalls of Global Marketing," *Harvard Business Review*, 67(5), September-October, 91-98.

This is a case study of an European company's experience in globalization. In 1982, Henkel, West Germany's leading industrial and consumer adhesives producer, relaunched Pattex, an internationally accepted but stagnating contact adhesive. Despite doubts from country subsidiaries, the global relaunch was so successful that Henkel tried to duplicate it with Pritt 00 the company's number one glue-stick brand around the world. Though some research indicated that the Pritt plan might not work, management went alhead. The global strategy failed to improve Pritt's performance. The subsidiaries aided Pritt's decline by diverting funds from Pritt's promotion to other products. Henkel's experience illustrates two pitfalls of global marketing: insufficient use of research and poor follow-up. Other pitfalls include overstandardization, narrow vision, and inflexibility in implementation.

4.2.16

Kirkland, Richard I., Jr. (1988), "Entering A New Age of Bounderless Competition," *Fortune*, March 14, 40-48.

Policy makers must resist the temptation to see the growing good fortune of Asia and other developing countries as a diminution of their own. These countries will become major markets. North America, Japan and Europe are the major world markets, and to stay competitive, a company must have a significant presence in at least two of them and probably all three. In an ever more integrated global economy, the ability of any nation's industries to gain or protect world market shares will increasingly be determined by the efficiency with which companies make as well as manage their overseas investments. The growing irrelevance of borders for corportations will force policy-makers to rethink old approaches to regulation.

4.2.17

Kogut, Bruce (1984), "Normative Observations on the International Value-Added Chain and Strategic Groups," *Journal of International Business Studies*, 15(2), Fall, 151-167.

The formulation of strategy can be fruitfully viewed as placing bets on certain markets and on certain links of the value-added chain. The key to understanding a global strategy is to locate how competitive positions in one national market change the economics for entry into other countries and into other product lines. This article argues that global strategies succeed by creating certain economies along and between value-added chains and by designing marketing programs that adapt products to national needs and yet exploit these upstream economies. Two major conclusions are that a company can compete in different strategic groups across countries and that a hallmark feature of a global strategy is the creation of operation flexibility from uncertainty.

4.2.18

Korey, George (1986), "Multilateral Perspectives in International Marketing Dynamics," *European Journal of Marketing,* 20(7), 34-42.

In international marketing, problems must be viewed from several perspectives including technical, organizational, personal, international, and cultural. These perspectives are used in addition to normal economic, market, and political perspectives. The potential advantages of the global approach to marketing include: (1) larger volume of production, (2) proper use of new technological developments and research, (3) increased opportunities to balance differences in sales in various areas, (4) improved marketing methods from extended world contacts, (5) new ideas for the marketing staff from the influence of foreign designs and developments, and (6) the strengthened competitive position of the global multinational firm in the domestic market.

4.2.19

Kotabe, Masaaki (1990), "Corporate Product Policy and Innovative Behavior of European and Japanese Multinationals: An Empirical Investigation," *Journal of Marketing,* 54(2), April, 19-33.

In an empirical study, personal letters and questionnaires were sent to the chief executive officers of 250 foreign subsidiaries operating in the US; usable responses were received from 43 European and 28 Japanese subsidiaries. The findings indicate several major changes in the competitive environment that will have a substantial impact on the way US and foreign multinational companies should operate in global markets. Introduction of new products alone does not appear to ensure any measurable immunity from competitive threat in an environment of rapid technological turnover. The interaction of product and process innovations is a crucial determinant of the market performance of European and Japanese multinationals. A corporate policy of globally standardized products is associated with a higher level of product and process innovations than is corporate product policy allowing product adaptation.

4.2.20

Levitt, Theodore (1983), "The Globalization of Markets," *Harvard Business Review,* 61(3), May-June, 92-102.

According to the author well-managed companies have moved from emphasis on customizing items to offering globally standardized products that are advanced, junctional, reliable, and low-priced. Multinational companies that concentrated on idiosyncratic consumer preferences have become befuddled and unable to take in the forest because of the trees. Only global companies will achieve long-term success by concentrating on what everyone wants rather than worrying about the details of what everyone might like.

4.2.21

Martenson, Rita (1987), "Is Standardization of Marketing Feasible in Culture-Bound Industries? A European Case Study," *International Marketing Review,* 4(3), Summer, 7-17.

Global marketing is based on cross-cultural similarities instead of cross-cultural differences. For a company encountering markets with similar cultural values it is easy to standardize the marketing program. Typically, however, most markets have different cultural values. The global marketer therefore has to decide how to coordinate its marketing program in the best way possible. This case study shows how a global retailer has coordinated its marketing program in an industry which has resisted the forces of globalization more than most other industries.

4.2.22

Owen, Gordon M. W. (1991), "Competing for the Global Telecommunications Market," *Long Range Planning,* 24(1), February, 52-56.

In spite of its relative market maturity, the annual growth rates of telecommunication in the developed countries have been over 20%. The rapid development can be attributed to several factors, including deregulation of telecommunications services, technology changes, and computers and electronic information storage. Internationally structured companies especially have taken advantage of the reduction in costs of telecommunications. However, there is scope for further deregulation particularly in Japan and Europe.

4.2.23

Parry, John (1990), "Hunting Heads in the Global Village," *International Management,* 45(4), May, 52-54.

4.2.24

Porter, Michael E. (1986), "Changing Patterns of International Competition," *California Management Review,* 28(2), 9-40.

Multinational corporations need to adjust their strategies to the changing pattern of international competition that has been emerging since the late 1970s. Firms may be distinguished according to whether they operate in multi-domestic industries or in global industries. Firms in global industries cannot rely upon country-by-country competitive strategies. Instead, they must form linkages among the various activities in the value chain in order to achieve operational effectiveness. Globally competing firms must determine the optimal configuration of activities and coordination of activities. Countries of operation must be selected to serve as global platforms providing environments conducive to the development of comparative advantage and attractive local demand conditions.

4.2.25

Quelch, John A. and Edward J. Hoff (1986), "Customizing Global Marketing," *Harvard Business Review,* 64(3), 59-68.

Executives often view global marketing as an either/or proposition—either full standardization or local control. The authors argue that when a global approach can fall anywhere on a spectrum from tight worldwide coordination on programming details to loose agreement on a product idea, why the extreme view? In applying the global marketing concept and making it work, flexibility is essential. Managers need to tailor the approach they use to each element of the business system and marketing program. For example, a manufacturer might market the same product under different brand names in different countries or market the same brands using different product formulas.

4.2.26

Rosen, Barry Nathan (1990), "Global Products: When Do They Make Strategic Sense?" *Advances in International Marketing,* Vol.4, 57-71.

This article examines the origins, applicability and renewed interest in the global product concept. A set of questions and answers are offered which define the limits of the concept. While useful in guiding efforts to unify markets, it cannot be applied in every case. Particular problems are that a globalized product strategy may provide openings for competitions to exploit, ignore the advantages to serving small segments, promote overcapacity, and can lead to gray marketing. Guidelines are provided to help the marketer decide when global product strategies are appropriate.

4.2.27

Rau, Pradeep A. and John F. Preble (1987), "Standardization of Marketing Strategy by Multinationals," *International Marketing Review,* 4(3), Summer, 18-28.

This paper presents an analysis of the current debate on "global marketing" and the degree to which multinational firms can standardize their marketing practices across countries. World markets are getting increasingly homogenized but the authors contend that the framework and associated propositions generated in the paper could help multinational firms determine the degree of standardization that is possible in different markets.

4.2.28

Salmon, Walter J. and Andre Tordjman (1989), "The Internationalisation of Retailing," *International Journal of Retailing,* 4(2), 3-16.

The internationalization of retailing is not a new phenomenon, but it remains partial and marginal. In the evolution of strategies used in the internationalization of retailing, retailers first developed the investment strategy. More recently, they have made use of the multinational strategy and the global strategy. The multinational strategy involves the implantation of autonomous affiliates operating comparably to the parent company but adapted to the local market. The global strategy corresponds to a reproduction outside the national frontiers of the retailer of a formula that is known to be successful in the originating country. The homogenization of consumer groups around the world, the reduction in transportation costs, and improved circulation of information favor the continued acceleration of retail's internationalization.

4.2.29

Simmonds, Kenneth (1985), "Global Strategy: Achieving the Geocentric Ideal," *International Marketing Review,* 2(1), Spring, 8-17.

A geocentric approach to global strategic formation is presented. It describes the geographic adjustments that are the embodiment of both attack and defence under global competition, and the geographic units that multinationals adopt as their primary organizational units to identify and carry out these adjustments.

4.2.30

Sugiura, Hideo (1990), "How Honda Localizes Its Global Strategy," *Sloan Management Review,* 32(1), Fall, 77-82.

Honda Motor Co.'s experience demonstrates that two factors are prerequisite to overcoming cultural differences. First, management must clearly understand the goals to be attained in countries involved. Second, each country's role must be recognized and agreed upon. In promoting internationalization, Honda places the utmost importance on localization which means to adapt activities to the nations where it operates. The strategy stresses the localization of several elements including products, profits, production, and management. Honda's activities in North America are perhaps the best examples of the localization of production. In its plants in Ohio, the company attaches particular importance to three policies: maintaining cooperative relations between the management and the workforce, promoting harmony with the local community, and giving top priority to maintaining high quality in its products.

4.2.31

Vandermerwe, Sandra and Michael Chadwick (1989), "The Internationalization of Services," *Service Industries Journal,* 9(1), January, 79-93.

The authors propose a classification system to illustrate modes of service internationalization as a guide for managers taking their services into world markets. The system has two axes: the relative involvement of goods and the degree of consumer-producer interaction. The result of this two way classification system is a general 6-sector matrix, including: (1) low goods-lower interaction, (2) medium goods-lower interaction, (3) high goods-lower interaction, (4) low goods-higher interaction, (5) medium goods-higher interaction, and (6) high goods-higher interaction. This matrix is a useful conceptual tool as services tend to cluster within it.

4.2.32

Verhage, Bronislaw J., Lee D. Dahringer, and Edward W. Cundiff (1989), "Will a Global Marketing Strategy Work? An Energy Conservation Perspective," *Journal of the Academy of Marketing Science,* 17(2), Spring, 129-136.

A study was conducted of standardization of marketing strategy across national boundaries. The study analyzed consumers in the US, the Netherlands, France, and Norway about their energy conservation behavior and attitudes. The results indicate that: 1. consumers in the Netherlands are concerned mostly with personal comforts, 2. US consumers are concerned with convenience and time involvement in relatively equal amounts, 3. consumers in France are concerned with convenience and energy conservation equally, and 4. consumers in Norway are concerned mostly with time involvement, but also with convenience to a lesser extent. A single global marketing strategy cannot be justified in the case of energy conservation products. The implementation of a single international strategy in all countries and markets would not be likely to offer optimal sales performance.

4.2.33

Walters, Peter G. P. and Brian Toyne (1989), "Product Modification and Standardization in International Markets: Strategic Options and Facilitating Policies," *Columbia Journal of World Business,* 24(4), Winter, 37-44.

The development of international product programs characterized by international uniformity can be an important source of competitive advantage to companies undertaking value-chain activities overseas. This article evaluates international product modification and standardization strategies and policies that facilitate the maximization of international product uniformity. There are three ways to develop standard products: (1) product extension, which involves "projecting" the product presentation developed for a single market, (2) a premium prototype approach which involves the development of a product that meets the needs of the most demanding group of customers in overseas markets and the most stringent product-use conditions, and (3) a global common denominators policy, where the goal is to identify a global segment of demand in which consumer traits and conditions of use are relatively homogeneous.

4.2.34

Whitelock, Jeryl M.(1987), "Global Marketing and the Case for International Product Standardisation," *European Journal of Marketing,* 21(9), 32-44.

Levitt's view that a single product can be offered worldwide offers substantial benefits for international marketers, but a review of empirical findings in the literature suggests that this theory should be adopted with caution. A study of a group of 10 UK bed linen companies exporting to Europe was conducted. Data were from face-to-face interviews, telephone interviews, or written questionnaires. Most of the discussion concerned the firm's products, and an attempt was made to ascertain how far amendments and changes were needed to enable sales to European nations. Focus was on the tangible product. The seven companies that followed a program of some modification also were those with the highest export turnover. All modifications were discretionary, made as a result of consumer need. The decision to standardize was acknowledged as the reason for low export performance by two companies. The results support previous empirical studies on the practice of multinational corporations—that modification depends upon conditions of use.

4.2.35

Wills, James, Coskun A. Samli, and Laurence Jacobs (1991), "Developing Global Products and Marketing Strategies: A Construct and a Research Agenda," *Journal of the Academy of Marketing Science ,* 19(1), Winter, 1-10.

Multinational corporations must develop better international products and understand when to globalize or localize their marketing strategies. The authors develop a global product and marketing strategy decision model which incorporates the following dimensions: learning, involvement, diffusion-adoption, and culture context. The successful development of international marketing strategies depends on being global while acting local. The implementation of this strategy begins with an understanding of international markets at the macro level and consumer behaviors.

4.2.36

Yip, George S. (1989), "Global Strategy ... In a World of Nations?" *Sloan Management Review,* 31(1), Fall, 29-41.

Whether and how to globalize have become two of the most important strategy issues for managers around the world. A global strategy offers benefits, including cost reduction, improved quality, and increased competitive leverage; however, it also has drawbacks that are found in areas such as product standardization and uniform marketing. The most successful worldwide strategies find a balance between overglobalizing and underglobalizing that matches the level of strategy globalization to the globalization potential of the industry. To achieve the benefits of globalization, the managers of a worldwide business need to recognize when industry conditions provide the opportunity to use global strategy levers. These conditions can be grouped into four categories: (1) market drivers, (2) cost drivers, (3) government drivers, and (4) competitive drivers.

4.3 Strategic Alliances and Interaction Perspective

4.3.1

Campbell, N. C. G. (1985), "Buyer/Seller Relationships in Japan and Germany: An Interaction Approach," *European Journal of Marketing*, 19(3), 57-66.

The development and handling of relationships between suppliers and customers in Germany and Japan were studied using the interaction approach developed by the International Marketing and Purchasing Group. Focusing on the packaging industry, 25 interviews were conducted using a semi-structured questionnaire. Differences among four groups of variables were used to compare the countries. Differences seemed to outweigh similarities. Japan shows: (1) fewer takeovers between suppliers, (2) a more dynamic technical environment, (3) a more harmonious, trusting social system, (4) a more competitive business climate, and (5) more frequent and extensive personal contacts. German firms show: (1) more movement of staff between companies, (2) more willingness to change suppliers, and (3) more extensive use of legal agreements. Innovation is more important to the Japanese relationships, and cultural differences apparently account for the differences in buyer/seller relationships.

4.3.2

Contractor, Farok J.(1990), "Contractual and Cooperative Forms of International Business: Towards a Unified Theory of Modal Choice," *Management International Review*, 30(1), 31-54.

Interfirm cooperation and contracts comprise distinct strategy alternatives to the internalized expansion of the multinational enterprise via fully owned subsidiaries. The question arises of why a firm would agree to share its proprietary technical and administrative expertise. An overall framework for the international business modal choice, ranging from pure or quasi-arms-length contracts to joint ownership and full ownership of foreign operations is presented. The framework unifies the perspectives of internalization and transaction cost theories with the perspectives of the strategy literature. The optimum strategy is influenced by underlying variables in the environment for international business.

4.3.3

Devlin, Godfrey and Mark Bleackley (1988), "Strategic Alliances—Guidelines for Sucess" *Long Range Planning*, 21(5), October, 18-23.

In contrast to the old style of cooperative agreement, strategic alliances take place in the context of a company's long-term strategic plan and seek to improve or change a company's competitive position. Possibly the greatest stimulus to alliance formation has been the emergence of global competition. Other influences include: (1) the rapid pace of technological development, (2) the high costs of research and development, (3) the concentration of players in mature industries, and (4) governments. Senior management must be involved in the strategic alliance process, paying particular attention to the decision to form such an alliance, the choice of the alliance partner, and the alliance's planned management. An organizational structure with clear lines of accountability and responsibility must be established. Only high-quality staff should be recruited for the alliance.

4.3.4

Geringer, J. Michael (1991), "Strategic Determinants of Partner Selection Criteria in International Joint Ventures," *Journal of International Business Studies*, 22(1), 41-62.

Previous studies are vague regarding determinants of criteria for choosing complementary partners for international joint ventures. In this article, a distinction is made between task and partner-related dimensions of selection criteria. It is argued that the relative importance of task-related selection criteria is determined by the strategic context of the proposed joint ventures and the parent firm. In particular, it is determined by the critical success factors of the venture's competitive environment and the parent's static and dynamic position.

4.3.5

Gerlach, Michael (1987), "Business Alliances and the Strategy of the Japanese Firm," *California Management Review*, 30(1), 126-142.

US managers have begun to consider capital market relationships as a part of their overall corporate strategies, due to the transformation of global capital markets. These strategies are investigated from the viewpoint of Japan, where firms have forged special business alliances linking banks, shareholders, and trading partners into coherent groupings of mutual interest. The alliances have brought about close investor-management relationships that have shaped other areas of Japanese business. The Japanese firm is perceived as a social collective to be preserved and protected within the framework of the joint business alliance. Japanese industry has been characterized by rapid entry into new fields by companies that have the early and continuing support of affiliated firms.

4.3.6

Hallen, Lars, Nazeem Seyed Mohamed, and Jan Johanson (1989), "Relationships and Exchange in International Business," *Advances in International Marketing,* Vol.3, 7-23.

The purpose of this paper is to make international comparative analysis of customer-supplier relationships. An analysis model is developed that includes short-term and long-term aspects of customer-supplier interaction. For the long-term aspect, the adaptations by either or both parties are selected. The short-term aspect is represented by the current information exchange in terms of extensity, intensity, and information sharing within the dyad.

4.3.7

Hamel, Gary , Yves L. Doz, and C.K. Prahalad (1989), "Collaborate With Your Competitors—And Win," *Harvard Business Review,* 67(1), January-February, 133-139.

The issue of strategic alliances is analyzed. According to the authors, companies that benefit most from competitive collaboration adhere to a set of simple but powerful principles. (1) Collaboration is competition in a different form. Successful companies never forget that their partners may be out to disarm them. They understand how their partners' objectives compare with their own. (2) Harmony is not the most important measure of success. Occasional conflict may be the best evidence of mutually beneficial collaboration. Few alliances remain win-win undertakings forever. (3) Partners must defend against competitive compromise. What information gets traded is determined daily, often by junior engineers and operating managers. Successful companies inform employees at all levels about what skills and technologies are off-limits to the partner. (4)Learning from partners is paramount. Successful companies view each alliance as a window on their partner's broad capabilities. They use the alliance to build skills in areas outside the formal agreement and to diffuse acquired knowledge throughout their organizations.

4.3.8

Harrigan, Kathryn Rudie (1987), "Strategic Alliances: Their New Role In Global Competition," *Columbia Journal of World Business,* 22(2), Summer, 67-69.

Joint ventures and other forms of alliance are used with increasing frequency to restructure industries, create new products, keep abreast of rapidly-changing technologies, and ease problems of worldwide excess productive capacity. Since they will be such an important tool in global strategy, savvy managers are taking aggressive, but methodical steps to meet the new challenges of strategic alliances.

4.3.9

Harrigan, Kathryn Rudie (1988), "Strategic Alliances and Partner Asymmetries," *Management International Review*, 28(5), 53-72.

This research investigates the question of whether the attributes of sponsoring firms and their relationships to each other influences the efficacy of their strategic alliances. The influence of the sponsoring firm's asymmetries—in relative asset size, national origin, and venturing experience levels—on venture performance is tested by analyzing 895 strategic alliances competing in 23 industries for the period 1924-1985. The results indicate that ventures are more successful when partners are related (in products, markets, and/or technologies) to their ventures or horizontally related to them than when they are vertically related or unrelated to their ventures. Ventures also seem to last longer between partners of similar cultures, asset sizes, and venturing experience levels and when venture activities are related to both sponsors. Finally, sponsor traits and sponsor venture relationship traits do not appear to offer much explanatory power in models of venture survival, duration, and success.

4.3.10

Killing, J. Peter (1982), "How to Make a Global Joint-venture Work," *Harvard Business Review*, 60(3), May-June, 120-127.

Drawing from a research with 37 joint ventures involving mostly North American and Western European companies, this research explores the different ways executives can tailor their management approach to the specific needs of the enterprise. How fast should the joint venture grow? What constitutes good or bad management of it? The answers to these questions are critical to venture success.

4.3.11

Kobayashi, Noritake (1988), "Strategic Alliances with Japanese Firms," *Long Range Planning*, 21(2), April, 29-34.

Both the Japanese and Western automotive industries are facing the mature industry syndrome and must deal with five factors affecting the development of the automobile industry. Those factors are: (1) the expansion of affluence among automobile consumers all over the world, (2) the development of advanced technology, (3) a stronger emphasis on software adding value to hardware, (4) the advance of the information revolution, and (5) the increased demand for the internationalization of business activities. The major auto manufacturers find that they do not have the resources to meet these challenges alone. Joint ventures, such as the successful association of Ford and Mazda, as well as other methods of cooperation, are expected to become commonplace in the future. Unfortunately, many Westerners are suspicious of forming alliances with the Japanese, largely due to cultural and management differences.

4.3.12

Lei, David (1989), "Strategies for Global Competition," *Long Range Planning,* 22(1), February, 102-109.

Corporate strategy requires top management to consider certain critical strategic decisions that directly affect a company's long-term competitive state. These decisions include: (1) strategic alliances, (2) internal development and acquisition of new technologies and businesses, and (3) dynamic thinking through time. The use of strategic alliances may be called the "foreign policy" dimension of strategy, while finding a balance between internal development and acquisitions relates to a company's "domestic policy." The time element is one that US managers all too often neglect in their strategic thinking. Although joint ventures offer the recipient considerable short-term benefits, dangers also are involved.

4.3.13

Morris, Deigan and Michael Hergert (1987), "Trends in International Collaborative Agreements," *Columbia Journal of World Business,* 22(2), Summer, 15-21.

This article reports on the findings of an ongoing research program conducted at the INSTEAD business school in Fontainebleau, France into the use of international collaborative agreements. The findings show that collaboration between international partners has become an important aspect of international commerce. However, a growing number of companies have initiated joint projects, perhaps without fully realizing the many obstacles they are likely to confront. Collaborative agreements offer the potential to share risks and rewards beyond the capabilities of individual firms. It will only be the companies with skill and sensitivity toward resolving the managerial challenges who are likely to realize success from collaboration.

4.3.14

Nueno, Pedro and Jan Oosterveld (1988), "Managing Technology Alliances," *Long Range Planning,* 21(3), June, 11-17.

Formation of technology alliances has increased in Europe during the past four years. Among the most important frameworks are the European Strategic Programme for Research and Development in Information Technology and Basic Research in Industrial Technologies for Europe. In order to provide suggestions for improving the management of technological alliances, a study was conducted based on the in-depth analysis of 15 alliances between European companies. There are a number of driving forces behind the decision to create an alliance, but the most important difference among partnerships is whether they are intended to facilitate access to a technological capability or to seek access to a market. Some aspects of differentiation between various categories of alliance include objectives, decision level, time horizon, and risk.

4.3.15

Ohmae, Kenichi (1989), "The Global Logic of Strategic Alliances," *Harvard Business Review,* 67(2), March-April, 143-154.

In a world of rapid globalization, forging of an alliance is not a tool of convenience but a critical instrument for serving customers. Today, customer needs and preferences all over the world are converging. Technology is dispersing as well. No one company can keep the relevant technology in-house; nothing can stay propreitary. These two forces mean that companies face increasing fixed costs—wether for R&D, promoting a brand, creating a sales and distribution network, or developing a competitive management information system. All these fixed costs point toward forging alliances.

4.3.16

Turnbull, Peter W. (1987), "Interaction and International Marketing: an Investment Process," *International Marketing Review,* 4(4), Autumn, 7-19.

The interaction approach to studying international marketing activities of industrial firms is now an established research stream. Initiated by a team of European researchers, the interaction approach focuses on the process of managing interactions between supplier and customer units. In this article, the author elaborates on the features of the interaction approach and illustrates it using a company case study.

4.3.17

Turnbull, Peter W. (1985), "The Image and Reputation of British Suppliers in Western Europe," *European Journal of Marketing,* 19(6), 39-52.

The generalized reputation of a country affects the ability of companies in that country to attract export business. Research concerning the views of buyers in Europe about UK, German, and French suppliers shows that, in general, German and French suppliers have a good reputation with buyers, while UK suppliers are seen as less customer-oriented than their French and German counterparts and less competent technically. UK suppliers are also perceived as providing the worst delivery speed and reliability. Britain also ranks last in terms of the quality of business relationships with European buyers and is criticized for failing to translate documents and technical data into foreign languages. The research suggests several areas of concern for UK marketers, including customer service, the ability to provide technical solutions, and the quality of delivery services.

V. *International Marketing Management*

5.1 *Market Selection, Entry, Expansion, Segmentation, and Positioning*

5.1.1

Akaah, Ishmael P. and Attila Yaprak (1988), "Identifying Target Segments for Foreign Direct Investment Attraction: an Application of Conjoint Methodology," *International Marketing Review,* 5(3), Autumn, 28-37.

Conjoint methodology can be used by recipient countries to segment the donor market for foreign direct investment, thereby enhancing the effectiveness of their FDI attraction efforts. The study results indicate that FDI donors can be clustered into segment based on the FDI benefits they seek. The article concludes with normative and practical implications of the methodology for investment policy makers in recipient countries.

5.1.2

Amine, Lyn S., Edward Vitale and S. Tamer Cavusgil (1983), "Launching a Weaning Food in a Developing Country: the Moroccan Experience," *European Journal of Marketing,* 17(5), 44-54.

This ariticle deals with a weaning food in Morocco and examines the marketing procedures followed to launch the product. The project proved to be total failure. The authors' objective here is to identify the reasons for this failure and propose a revised marketing plan which might lead to success, leaving aside any political or administrative implications which are beyond the scope of this study. Research in this field shows that problems are commonly encountered in this type of venture in developing countries. Reasons may relate to governmental inefficiencies, weaknesses in the retailing infrastructure, marketing errors, or a combination of these and other factors specific to the individual country.

5.1.3

Calantone, Roger J. and C. Anthony di Benedetto (1988), "Defensive Marketing in Globally Competitive Industrial Markets," *Columbia Journal of World Business,* 23(3), Fall, 3-14.

The authors develop a practical, analytical model of competitive strategy for firms selling industrial products in international markets. Competitive launches, repositionings and retaliations are modeled using per-dollar maps. The model is applied to three illustrative real cases based on actual industrial marketing situations in global settings.

5.1.4

Carlsson, Ch. and S. O. Hansen (1982), "Innovation and Export Market Strategies in the Pharmaceutical Industry: A Taxonomical Approach," *Management International Review*, 22(3), 45-53.

5.1.5

Crawford, John C., Barbara C. Garland and G. Ganesh (1988), "Identifying the Global Pro-Trade Consumer," *International Marketing Review*, 5(4), Winter, 25-33.

This article examines the extent to which there is a global pro-trade consumer segment that cuts across levels of economic development. This study, involving two different methodological techniques, identifies and profiles the pro-trade consumer segments in four countries representing two developed/developing nations pairs, using demographic variables, intrapersonal variables and global marketplace variables. The results demonstrate that there is an intermarket pro-trade segment among consumers, which can be described by a common set of indicators with a fair degree of accuracy.

5.1.6

Daniels, John D. (1983), "Combining Strategic and International Business Approaches Through Growth Vector Analysis," *Management International Review*, 23(3), 4-15.

5.1.7

Day, Ellen, Richard J. Fox and Sandra M. Huszagh (1988), "Segmenting the global Market for Industrial Goods: Issues and Implications," *International Marketing Review*, 5(3), Autumn, 14-27.

Although the viability of global marketing is disputed, the best opportunities for pursuing basically the same strategy across national borders are in industrial marketing. However, because of the disparities across world markets, segmentation is essential to assessing opportunities for a standardized marketing approach. Segmentation based on economic indicators represents the first step in identifying potential markets. In this study, 96 countries were grouped into six segments. Implications for industrial marketers are presented, along with issues relating to using stages of economic development as a basis for segmentation.

5.1.8

Douglas, Susan P., and Dong Kee Rhee (1989), "Examining Generic Competitive Strategy Types in U.S. and European Markets," *Journal of International Business Studies*, 20(3), Fall, 437-463.

Identification of generic competitive strategy types has recently attracted considerable attention. However, most of this research has focused on competitive strategy of U.S. businesses in their domestic market. This study extends these findings to European market, based on a sample of industrial businesses drawn from the PIMS database. Similar dimensions underlying competitive strategy and similar generic types are found among businesses in the U.S. and in Europe. Some differences in the performance and business characteristics of certain strategy types were observed between U.S. and European Markets.

5.1.9

Edstrom, Anders and Peter Lorange (1984), "Matching Strategy and Human Resources in Multinational Corporations," *Journal of International Business Studies,* 15(2), Fall, 125-137.

Strategy is implemented by people. The characteristics of the major strategic levels and tasks in a multinational corporation are identified, along with their implications for strategic human resource management. Through observations within four Swedish MNCs, the process by which human resources have gained a place in strategic management is examined.

5.1.10

Eppink, D. Jan and Bas M. van Rhijn (1989), "International Strategies of Dutch Insurance Companies," *Long Range Planning,* 22(1), 41-47.

The internationalization of three large Dutch insurance companies is examined. The data were collected over the period from 1970 to 1985 by interviews and the study of company records and other publications. All three companies have sold foreign businesses, generally because the prospects in the market were not very good or because it was not possible to have enough say in running the company. While various modes of entry have been used, the three companies preferred to use acquisition for entry into foreign markets because it gave them full control of the foreign operations. Direct investments and joint ventures were chosen if no other options were available. All the companies treat their foreign operations as profit centers with a large degree of local autonomy in dealing with their local markets, and all were managed by local managers.

5.1.11

Erramilli, M. Krishna and C.P. Rao (1990), "Choice of Foreign Market Entry Modes by Service Firms: Role of Market Knowledge," *Management International Review,* 30(2), 135-150.

This article attempts to explain the variation of foreign market entry mode choice in the service sector. A convenience sample of 463 service firms that appeared to be engaged in international business activities was taken from Dun and Bradstreet's

Million Dollar Directory and from Consultants and Consulting Organizations Directory. A mail survey of these firms yielded 175 usable responses. The research indicates that some types of service firms can and often do export their products. The analysis also shows that service firms exhibit significantly greater aggressiveness in choosing entry modes when following their existing clients than when serving new customers. This is shown in their choice of higher involvement levels and in their preference to not team up with outsiders.

5.1.12

Goodnow, James D. (1985), "Developments in International Mode of Entry Analysis," *International Marketing Review,* 2(3), Autumn, 17-30.

Theories on international trade and investment as well as those relating the nature of the product to the length of the channel suggest that mode of entry decisions should result from the analysis of a wide variety of factors. This article shows how such theories might be related to practice through the development of decision support tools. Emphasis is given to a microcomputer software package developed to aid international mode of entry assessment.

5.1.13

Greer, Thomas V. (1986), "Beating Food Shortages: A Call for Co-operation," *International Marketing Review,* 3(1), Spring, 50-60.

Co-operation among multinational food corporations, public health agencies and charities to combat food shortages and inadequate nutrition is worthy of serious, objective consideration. Unfortunately, there is some suspicion, hostility, and lack of understanding among different parties. The private sector has valuable expertise and a customer/client orientation that is usually missing elsewhere. Several interventions and difficulties are discussed. It is concluded that significant amounts of responsible co-operation are vital and possible.

5.1.14

Griffin, Tom (1982), "Linking the Use of Modern Marketing Methods to Company Success," *Columbia Journal of World Business,* 17(3), Fall, 52-57.

The author surveys 49 Puerto Rican food manufacturers, measuring the use of "modern" marketing methods and the degree of company success. Significant correlation is shown between the two variables. The author recommends that these measurement instruments be applied to other industries and additional Hispanic centers.

5.1.15

Hamel, Gary and C.K. Prahalad (1989), "Strategic Intent," *Harvard Business Review,* 67(3), May-June, 63-76.

New perspectives on strategy are offered. Canon and other world-class competitors make strategy in a different way: on the basis of strategic intent. They begin with a goal that exceeds the company's present grasp and existing resources: "Beat Xerox," "Encircle Caterpillar." Then they rally the organization to close gap by setting challenges that focus employees' efforts in the near to medium term:"Build a personal copier to sell for $1,000." "Cut product development time by 75%." Year after year, they emphasize competive innovation: building a portfolio of competitive advantages; searching markets for "loose bricks" that rivals have left underdefended; changing the terms of competitive engagement to avoid playing by the leader's rules. The result is a global leadership position and an approach to competition that has reduced larger, stronger Western rivals to an endless game of catch-up ball.

5.1.16

Hanink, Dean M. (1985), "A Mean-Variance Model of MNF Location Strategy," *Journal of International Business Studies,* 16(1), Spring, 165-174.

A theoretical model of portfolio is presented to directly incorporate the effect of interdependence among national markets. Such a model can be useful in the analysis of an MNF's explicit location decisions. A numerical mean-variance portfolio model is developed and applied to the case of geographical expansion of the MNF. While international diversification may not be considered a necessary and sufficient cause for FDI, its effect on firm earnings should not be ignored in the MNF's location decisions.

5.1.17

Hawes, Jon M. and C.P. Rao (1983), "A Market Share Analysis of International Trade," *International Marketing Review,* 1(1), Autumn, 59-67.

A significant development during the 1970's was the empirical verification provided by the PIMS project of the positive relationship between a firm's market share and its profit ability. The authors propose that the PIMS findings may also apply for an aggregation of firms—namely, world traders. A market share analysis of the export trade performance of the U.S., the E.E.C., and Japan is presented, the implications of this research are discussed, and some directions for future research are provided.

5.1.18

Hitt, Michael A. and R. Duane Ireland (1987), "Building Competitive Strength in International Markets," *Long Range Planning,* 20(1), Feburary, 115-122.

Pressures for growth and the benefits of product diversification have led to the development of the large, multinational corporations. However, many of these firms have experienced problems in recent years. One major risk is the inability to manage the diversity resulting from diversification of the firm's operations. Internationalization opens new markets but also produces more competition at home. While the theory of managing diversification through developing an appropriate matching structure has been influential, this structure may not be the major conduit for implementation of diversification strategy. As firms become more diversified, they must ensure some degree of integration, while permitting more autonomy to divisions. The degree of commonality among a corporation's businesses has been linked to performance. Commonality is therefore a strategy for achieving integration.

5.1.19

Hoskins, C. and S. McFadyen (1991), "International Marketing Strategies for a Cultural Service," *International Marketing Review,* 8(2), 40-52.

The role of culture in international marketing strategies for television programming is examined. The focus is on how non-U.S. television program producers can exploit opportunities in the foreign marketplace by adopting a marketing approach that analyzes the needs of foreign buyers and audience in terms of the options available for segmenting the market. One approach is to identify a cross national segment where the producer possesses a competitive advantage. Another is to offer customized attributes desired by viewers in a major foreign market. An international coalition helps assure this. Paradoxically we find that this strategy may not always be inconsistent with standardization.

5.1.20

Jatusripitak, Somkid, Liam Fahey, and Philip Kotler (1985), "Strategic Global Marketing: Lessons from the Japanese," *Columbia Journal of World Business,* 20(1), Spring, 47-53.

As international market opportunities increased, Japan's global marketing strength became evident while American global market shares fell. Having secured its domestic markets, Japan expanded into developing and developed countries. It also pursued a strategy of producing products to sell in selected segments. Concurrent with this expansion was the development of a global marketing network which included the important stage of establishing production facilities around the world. The authors document these two strategies and provide a case example of how Japan's consumer electronics industry became dominant via global marketing. The lessons for U.S. companies are obvious.

5.1.21

Kale, Sudhir and D. Sudharshan (1987), "A Strategic Approach to International Segmentation," *International Marketing Review,* 4(2), Spring, 60-70.

This article proposes an approach to international segmentation which capitalizes on the inherent similarities across groups of consumers in different countries. By making the customers and not countries the basis of a firm's international marketing strategy, this approach not only facilitates increased consumer orientation, but also offers the potential to optimize the profits of a multinational firm at a global level.

5.1.22

Kelichi, Koseki (1990), "Marketing Strategies as Adopted by AJINOMOTO in Southeast Asia," *Journal of Advertising Research,* 30(2), April-May, 31-34.

Monosodium glutamate, or AJI-NO-MOTO—its patented name—was invented in 1908 by Kikunae Ikeda, a professor at Tokyo University. In order to create public awareness of this new and unknown product, advertising took the public crier approach. Soon, sales of AJI-NO-MOTO moved toward domestic and overseas countries and markets through a very strenuous effort. In Thailand, Malaysia, and Singapore, sole agents were set up to sell the original AJI-NO-MOTO package, mainly 100-gram cans and 3-ounce bottles. In the Philippines and Indonesia after World War II, it was easier to import the product in bulk from Japan. From 1965 to 1971, the market share of AJI-NO-MOTO brand retail products increased by more than 90%. The small packages are very economical and have become quite competitive with repackaged products. Radio advertising was most often used because of its enormous reach.

5.1.23

Kogut, Bruce (1985), "Designing Global Strategies: Comparative and Competitive Value-Added Chains (Part 1)," *Sloan Management Review,* 26(4), Summer, 15-28.

A value-added chain concept is used to analyze the competitive position of firms in a global industry and to examine the interaction between comparative and competitive advantage in international strategy. This suggests three modes of competition. One mode rests on the dispersion of the links in the chain of comparative advantage among countries, while another rests on differences in the chain of competition among firms. The third consists of the interplay between competitive and comparative advantage along a value-added chain. Sources of sustainable global advantage include: (1) increased economies of scale, (2) greater economies of scope, and (3) experience. Competing on the initial transfer of an advantage differs from competing on the basis of subsequent advantages gained by being global, and this advantage may not be sustainable.

5.1.24

Lewis, Geoffrey, John Clark, and Bill Moss (1988), "BHP Reorganizes for Global Competition," *Long Range Planning,* 21(3), June, 18-26.

The Broken Hill Proprietary Co. Ltd. (BHP), the dominant steelmaker in Australia, has undergone a large strategic change following its recognition of: (1) the collapse of world steel prices, (2) the Bass Strait oilfield's finite life, and (3) a slowdown in growth of the Australian economy. Moving from restricted Australian markets to international market competition was essential for BHP, and as a company of this size could not be managed centrally, a fundamental organizational change was required. The new management philosophy was built around: (1) sensitivity to the market, (2) the importance of human resources, (3) commitment to a "can do" philosophy, (4) innovation, (5) superiority of product/service, (6) technical excellence, and (7) adherence to honesty and fairness. The reorganization entailed moving from centralization to autonomous business units and developing a greater international focus.

5.1.25

Mascarenhas, Briance (1986), "International Strategies of Non-dominant Firms," *Journal of International Business Studies,* 17(1), Spring, 1-25.

This article documents the use of international strategies by some non-dominant firms to avoid direct competition with industry leaders. 25 cases of international strategies used by non-dominant firms in a variety of industries were cluster-analyzed to identify common strategies. Seven different strategies were identified together with their attendant firm characteristics, stage of industry internationalization, and underlying competitive logic.

5.1.26

Naylor, Thomas H. (1985), "The International Strategy Matrix," *Columbia Journal of World Business,* 20(2), Summer, 11-19.

Since 1968, a number of multinational corporations have adopted the international matrix to cope with the complexities of international management. The strategy matrix extends the scope of matrix management beyond short-term project management to long-term international strategic management. The experiences of four major corporations with the international strategy matrix show that it can be used to compete more effectively on a global scale.

5.1.27

Newman, Richard G. (1990), "The Second Wave Arrives: Japanese Strategy in the U.S. Auto Parts Market," *Business Horizons,* 33(4), July-August, 24-30.

The US automotive parts industry has come under increasing competitive pressures over the last five years because of a literal invasion of this market, especially by firms from Japan. The first sign of parts industry penetration surfaced with the arrival of the Japanese auto assemblers in the US in the area known as Auto Alley. Individual states invested millions of dollars to attract the transplants, but prosperity has not occurred as anticipated. Instead, the Japanese parts and component suppliers have arrived and have appeared in three forms: direct migration, purchase of an existing company, and joint ventures with US firms. Answers to the problem of Japanese transplants include stringent content laws that are clear and unambiguous and a federal limitation on joint ventures until a quid pro quo relationship can be established with Japanese firms.

5.1.28

Rugman, Alan M. (1987), "Strategies for National Competitiveness," *Long Range Planning,* 20(3), June, 92-97.

This article examines the Canadian experience with high technology and industrial policy, the role of US multinational corporations in Canada, and the emergence of Canadian multinationals investing in the US. Scott argues that the erosion of the US competitive position is a result of government emphasis on social justice at the cost of efficiency, and focus on soft managerial aspects of strategic policy rather than on hard issues of economics and productivity. Other theories emphasize micro-aspects as the vital elements in a firm's success and consider micromanagement failures as the more likely cause of productivity problems than macrolevel government policies. Canada has a group of globally successful multinational enterprises that lack firm-specific advantages in technology, but possess marketing and other advantages that more than compensate for lack of high technology.

5.1.29

Schuster, Camille P. and Charles D. Bodkin (1987), "Segmentation Practices of Exporting Companies," *Industrial Marketing Management,* 16(2), May, 95-102.

Marketing segmentation practices of industrial companies currently exporting their products are assessed. Data were gathered by telephone from 68 Virginia companies of various sizes. All of the respondents marketed products to international customers, and the range of industries was broad. Marketing activities between domestic and international customers were differentiated by 71% of the respondents. Selling activities among international customers were differentiated by 22% of those sampled. The marketing mix elements that were most often varied were price and distribution, both at 67%, followed by product specifications, product, and service, with responses at 60%.

5.1.30

Scott, Bruce R. (1984), "National Strategy for Stronger U.S. Competitiveness," *Harvard Business Review,* 62(2), March-April, 77-91.

The author takes issue with mainstream economists who argue that our economic problems are manageable within the current policy framework. Part of the problem is the theoretical structure with which they view the economy. The thoery of comparative advatage, for example, is based on a view of the world that is almost 200 years old. He argues that today's world requires that we turn the theory on its head as the Japanese have done. He suggests how the U.S. might take a similar approach to creating and implementing an economic strategy.

5.1.31

Seringhaus, F. H. Rolf and Charles S. Mayer (1988), "Different Approaches to Foreign Market Entry Between Users and Non-Users of Trade Missions," *European Journal of Marketing,* 22(10), 7-18.

Among the broad range of export support services provided by government and other institutions in many exporting nations, trade missions seem especially suited to a firm beginning foreign market involvement. They combine several important export marketing facets, such as establishment of direct contacts and a high profile in a target market, first-hand assessment of market opportunities, and exchange of experience with other participants. A 3-group quasi-experimental research design based on the experiences of Canadian industrial manufacturing firms is used in an effort to capture the differences in managerial behavior related to the use of trade missions in offshore market entry. Group 1 respondents are exporters who used a trade mission in their most recent market entry; Group 2 are exporters who did not use a trade mission, and Group 3 are firms not involved in offshore markets. Results indicate that the trade mission firms are more aware of or use more governmental programs.

5.1.32

Sims, J. Taylor (1986), "Japanese Market Entry Strategy at Work: Komatsu vs. Caterpillar," *International Marketing Review,* 3(3), Autumn, 21-32.

Elaborating on the positions of two key players in the global earthmoving and construction industry, this article discusses the Japanese market entry strategies. Alternative strategies for retaliation against Japanese competition are also examined.

5.1.33

Swamidass, Paul M. (1990), "A Comparison of the Plant Location Strategies of Foreign and Domestic Manufacturers in the U.S.," *Journal of International Business Studies,* 21(2), 301-317.

5.1.34

Walle, A. H. (1987), "Localised Marketing Strategies and the Bible of International Business," *European Journal of Marketing,* 21(1), 26-36.

The author draws an analogy between modern international management and the conflicting marketing strategies of the New Testament. Jesus Christ set up an organization initially consisting of 12 members. When he left, Peter, the new chief executive officer, favored multinational involvement strongly, but internal politics plus his limited sophistication blocked attempts at moving forcefully in that direction. The potential Gentile market was in danger of being saturated by a rival Eastern religion, Mithraism. A franchise was granted to Paul, who was responsible for introducing Christianity to the Gentiles. Paul simplified and generalized the product and marketing mix of the church and showed great skill in setting up subfranchises that were simultaneously independent and integrated into a greater network. Paul built autonomy services into every church.

5.1.35

Wolfe, Bonnie Heineman (1991), Finding the International Niche: A "How to" for American Small Business," *Business Horizons,* 34(2), March-April, 13-17.

It is argued that finding an international market niche for small businesses means targeting a few selected countries, and finding the right local distributors. The US government is a good source of information for a small business seeking a market niche. When targeting countries as potential markets, national wealth is an obvious consideration. The cost barriers to entering a foreign market include transportation, tariffs, and import regulations. Because regulations vary among countries and change over time, US business owners need to review the regulations frequently. US companies can directly market their products abroad through government and quasi-government agencies.

5.2 Foreign Direct Investment and Joint Ventures

5.2.1

Afriyie, Kofi (1988), "Factor Choice Characteristics and Industrial Impact of Joint Ventures: Lessons from a Developing Economy," *Columbia Journal of World Business,* 23(3), Fall, 51-61.

5.2.2

Arpan Jeffrey S. and David A. Ricks (1986), "Foreign Direct Investment in the U.S., 1974-1984," *Journal of International Business Studies,* 17(3), Fall, 149-163.

This study compares the pattern of foreign direct investment as of 1974, 1978 and 1984 and concludes that the pattern has remained more consistent than might have been expected. The number of foreign-owned firms has risen dramatically, but the foreign investments tend to be in the same states and industries and from the same countries as they were in 1974.

5.2.3

Beamish, Paul W. and John C. Banks (1987), "Equity Joint Ventures and the Theory of the Multinational Enterprise," *Journal of International Business Studies,* 18(2), Summer, 1-16.

The internalization approach is extended to the theory of the multinational enterprise to include an expanded role for equity joint ventures. Using the transaction cost paradigm of Williamson, this paper explains why joint ventures may sometimes be preferred over wholly owned subsidiaries.

5.2.4

Beamish, Paul W. (1987), "Joint Ventures in LDCs: Partner Selection and Performance," *Management International Review,* 27(1), 23-37.

A study was conducted to determine how the performance of joint business ventures in developing countries could be improved, focusing specifically on the contributions of each partner to the venture. The analysis was based on data from twelve core ventures between the US, the UK, or Canadian multinational enterprises (MNE) and local private firms. Eighteen questionnaires were administered to parent-company executives and general managers involved in the core ventures. It was found that MNE executives in high-performing ventures looked to their local partners for greater contributions than did MNE executives in low-performing ventures. The former executive relied on local partners for specific contributions in two general areas: local knowledge and local management. In contrast, MNE executives in low-performing ventures were less interested in local partners for specific contributions. Rather, they wanted a partner to satisfy existing or expected government requirements for local ownership or to avoid political intervention.

5.2.5

Beamish, Paul W. (1985), "The Characteristics of Joint Ventures in Developed and Developing Countries," *Columbia Journal of World Business,* 20(3), Fall, 13-19.

By analyzing recent empirical evidence, the author shows that certain characteristics of joint venture multinational enterprises differ between developed and developing countries, and that joint ventures in LDCs are characterized by a higher instability rate and greater managerial dissatisfaction.

5.2.6

Boddewyn, Jean J. (1983), "Foreign and Domestic Divestment and Investment Decisions: Like or Unlike?" *Journal of International Business Studies,* 14(3), Winter, 23-34.

The managerial literature on foreign investment and divestment is mush less developed than the economic literature on foreign direct investment theory. Nevertheless, surveyed with the purpose of better understanding foreign divestment decisions, the research to date reveals some noticeable differences between investment and divestment decisions- whether foreign or domestic—and even more substantial differences between foreign divestment and domestic divestment decisions.

5.2.7

Chao, Paul (1989), " Export and Reverse Investment: Strategic Implications For Newly Industrialized Countries," *Journal of International Business Studies,* 20(1),Spring, 75-91.

This study investigates consumer evaluations of product quality and purchase intent of two electronic products currently imported into the U.S. from a company in a newly industrialized country and one electronic product currently not manufactured by the same company.

5.2.8

Chaudhuri, Adhip (1988), "Multinational Corporations in Less-Developed Countries: What Is in Store?" *Columbia Journal of World Business,* 23(1), 57-64.

When Multinational Corporations get involved in production in LDCs, they create benefits for both parties. The actual share of the benefits which will accrue to each will be determined by their relative bargaining strengths and skills. The author argues that Multinational Corporations will find the governments of LDCs to be more pragmatic and less ideological than in the 1970s. However, success in reaching mutually beneficial agreements will require more flexibility on the part of the Multinational Corporations in accommodating the economic needs and aspirations of the LDCs.

5.2.9

Chernotsky, Harry I. (1987), "The American Connection: Motives for Japanese Foreign Direct Investment," *Columbia Journal of World Business,* 22(4), Winter, 47-54.

Japan's evolving overseas investment strategy is reviewed with particular emphasis on the organizational push and pull factors underlying the surge of foreign direct investment in the U.S. Japanese firms have sought to capitalize on existing opportunities and to protect themselves from emerging threats to their corporate interest. Perhaps more importantly, they have been drawn to the U.S. to insure market access in the face of mounting bilateral trade friction.

5.2.10

Choi, Jongmoo Jay (1989), "Diversification, Exchange Risk, and Corporate International Investment," *Journal of International Business Studies,* 20(1), Spring, 145-155.

5.2.11

Christelow, Dorothy B. (1987), "International Joint Ventures: How Important Are They?" *Columbia Journal of World Business,* 22(2), Summer, 7-13.

This paper estimates the importance of joint venture in international investment and in the national economies where joint ventures are sited. The estimates draw on Department of Commerce data on ownership patterns in foreign affiliates operating in the U.S. and U.S. affiliates operating abroad and numerous countries' estimates of the importance of foreign affiliates in their domestic economies.

5.2.12

Cieslik, Jerzy (1989), "Relationships and Contractual Arrangements in East-West Trade," *Advances in International Marketing,* Vol.3, 25-35.

The author identifies major characteristics of the Western firms entering into contractual arrangements with Polish partners and evaluate the existing contractual arrangements as to determine to what extent they contributed to the strengthening and stabilizing of interfirm linkages.

5.2.13

Connolly, Seamus G. (1984), "Joint Ventures with Third World Multinationals: A New Form of Entry to International Markets," *Columbia Journal of World Business,* 19(2), Summer, 18-22.

Third World firms have advantages such as lower labor and management costs, lower input costs, a more appropriate technology supplied without strings, and a greater familiarity with the business and working environment that is characteristic of Third World Nations. However, these companies lack capital, are often subject to exchange controls in their own country, and lack a flow of up-to-date and improved technologies in manufacturing. These are the complementary assets that firms from the U.S. and other industrialized countries can provide in a joint venture partnership as well as providing management and marketing skills and head office services that often are scarce resources for many Third World firms. There are certain situations in Third World countries where the combined advantages of the U.S. and Third

World firms make market entry or survival possible where otherwise neither could go it alone.

5.2.14

Contractor, Farok J. (1990), "Ownership Patterns of U.S. Joint Ventures Abroad and the Liberalization of Foreign Government Regulations in the 1980s: Evidence from the Benchmark Surveys," *Journal of International Business Studies,* 21(1), 55-73.

The 1980s saw a remarkably global liberalization of government attitudes to foreign ownership. Data from the US Department of Commerce's Benchmark Surveys show a small but unmistakable across-the-board reduction in the equity limits imposed on foreign investors in the early 1980s. The result was a small but also unmistakable reduction in the proportion and share of sales of 50-50 and minority affiliates in all but a few nations. There is still a huge variation in the proportion of 50-50 and minority affiliates out of all US affiliates in a nation. The variation ranges from below 5% in such nations as Ireland, Switzerland, and Argentina to above 75% in such nations as India and the Republic of Korea. Host government-imposed limits and performance requirements induce a greater use of minority and 50-50 affiliates.

5.2.15

Contractor, Farok J. and Peter Lorange (1988), "Competition vs. Cooperation: A Benefit/Cost Framework for Choosing Between Fully-Owned Investments and Cooperative Relationships," *Management International Review,* 28(5), 5-18.

In entering a new market or undertaking a new business, a firm must choose between a fully owned investment and the alternative of cooperating with another firm in a joint venture, licensing, or co-production agreement, a joint research or exploration consortia, or some other type of negotiated arrangement. This internalization versus cooperation choice can be examined in terms of a benefit-cost framework that can be used for both strategic and project cash flow analyses. A cooperative effort may have the effect of increasing the project's revenues and/or decreasing costs over what could have been earned by a fully owned subsidiary. On the other hand, certain drawbacks might decrease revenues and/or increase costs. Therefore, both direct and indirect incremental benefits and costs must be examined.

5.2.16

Davidson, William H. (1987), "Creating and Managing Joint Ventures in China," *California Managememt Review,* 29(4), 77-94.

Establishing a joint venture in China is a complicated and time-consuming task, with no guarantee of success or survival. In general, international joint ventures in other countries have high rates of failures. Despite the problems, joint ventures promise to be one of the most important forms of economic interaction between the US and

China. A study examined 47 US firms that operated joint ventures in China during 1984-1985. The firms' experiences in creating and managing Chinese joint ventures illustrate a number of common issues and themes. One of the most notable was the length of time and difficulty associated with establishing a joint venture. Recommendations for managing the negotiation process include: (1) Prepare an initial written agreement. (2) Use translators. (3) Know who the negotiators are. (4) Know who the authorities are.

5.2.17

Diamantopoulos, A. and B.B. Schlegelmilch (1987), "Comparing Marketing Operations of Autonomous Subsidiaries," *International Marketing Review,* 4(4), 53-64.

5.2.18

Franko, Lawrence G. (1989), "Use of Minority and 50-50 Joint Ventures by United States Multinationals During the 1970s: The Interaction of Host Country Policies and Corporate Strategies," *Journal of International Business Studies,* 20(1), Spring, 19-40.

This article examines geographical, sectoral and corporate trends in the use of minority and 50-50 joint ventures by U.S. multinational manufacturing and mining firms in less developed countries during the 1970s.

5.2.19

Geringer, J. Michael and Louis Hebert (1991), "Measuring Performance of International Joint Ventures," *Journal of International Business Studies,* 22(2), 249-263.

International joint ventures are increasing in frequency and strategic importance. However, efforts to identify variables associated with IJV performance have been constrained by disagreements regarding the comparability and reliability of alternative performance measures and methods. This study tests several hypotheses regarding the reliability and comparability of a range of objective and subjective measures of joint venture performance. The results show that objective measures were positively correlated with parent firm's reported satisfaction with IJV performance and with perceptions of the extent to which an IJV performed relative to its initial objectives. In addition, joint ventures perceived by their parents as performing more successfully were more likely to remain in operation than those that were evaluated as being less successful.

5.2.20

Gomes-Casseres, Benjamin (1990), "Firm Ownership Preferences and Host

Government Restrictions: An Integrated Approach,'' *Journal of International Business Studies,* 21(1), 1-22.

An integrated approach is proposed to explain how multinational enterprises (MNE) select ownership structures for subsidiaries. The approach integrates the MNEs preferable structures which minimize the transaction costs of doing business abroad and the ownership structures which are determined by negotiations with the host government. Statistical analysis is used to separate the effects of the two approaches within the integrated approach. The results support one of the more important hypotheses of the bargaining power approach which holds that attractive domestic markets increase the relative power of host governments. The analysis does not support other hypotheses of this approach, such as those predicting that firms in marketing and R&D intensive industries will have more bargaining power than others.

5.2.21

Gomes-Casseres, Benjamin (1989), ''Joint Ventures in the Face of Global Competition,'' *Sloan Management Review,* 30(3), Spring, 17-26.

5.2.22

Grosse, Robert(1988), ''The Economic Impact of Foreign Direct Investment: A Case Study of Venezuela,'' *Management International Review,* 28(4), 63-78.

The evaluation of the economic costs and benefits of foreign direct investment (FDI) on home and host countries remains a topic of active public policy debate. New empirical evidence is presented, and a simple methodology for conducting such evaluations in host countries is proposed. The economic impacts analyzed are grouped into three categories: (1) the employment effects of FDI on the host country, (2) the ways in which multinational enterprises affect national income, both its level and its distribution, and (3) the influence of FDI on the country's balance of payments. Specific evidence is presented from a survey of manufacturing firms in Venezuela. The results tend to support the argument that manufacturing FDI raises the host country income and improves the balance of payments relative to what would have occurred in the absence of FDI.

5.2.23

Harrigan, Kathryn Rudie (1984), ''Joint Ventures and Global Strategies,'' *Columbia Journal of World Business,* 19(2), Summer, 7-16.

A framework is proposed to predict whether firms will cooperate in forming joint ventures or other forms of interfirm cooperation. The framework also posits which forces destabilize cooperative ventures, and suggests conditions where strategic needs are best served by joint ventures.

5.2.24

Hennart, Jean-Francois (1986), "Internalization in Practice: Early Foreign Direct Investments in Malaysian Tin Mining," *Journal of International Business Studies,* 17(2), 131-143.

This paper looks at the historical record of early foreign direct investment in Malaysian tin mining and draws its implications for the theory of the MNE.

5.2.25

Hennart, Jean-Francois (1989), "Can the 'New Forms of Investment' Substitute for the 'Old Forms?' A Transaction Costs Perspective," *Journal of International Business Studies,* 20(2), Summer, 211-234.

Transaction costs theory is utilized to explain the features of the new contractual alternatives to foreign direct investment, to assess their efficiency, and to forecast their future development.

5.2.26

Kim, Wi Saeng and Esmeralda O. Lyn (1987), "foreign Direct Investment Theories, Entry Barriers, and Reverse Investments in U.S. Manufacturing Industries," *Journal of International Business Studies,* 18(2), Summer, 53-66.

This is an empirical study that investigates whether industrial organization-oriented FID theories explain the recent phenomenon of reverse foreign direct investment in the U.S. Based on the distribution of FDI in two-digit SIC manufacturing industries, the authors find that capital and advertising intensities act as entry barriers to foreign investments in the U.S. They also observe that foreign multinationals are attracted by the U.S. market size, and that they invest heavily in industries with intensive R&D combined with marketing efforts.

5.2.27

Kogut, Bruce (1988), "A Study of the Life Cycle of Joint Ventures," *Management International Review,* 28(5), 39-52.

The author examines the proposition that the motivations for the creation of a joint venture often are responsible for its termination. Data on instability rates suggest that the question is not whether but how quickly joint ventures terminate. Two explanations for the creation of joint ventures and their instability see joint ventures as a response to the competitive rivalry within an industry or between the partners. A third explanation emphasizes the transfer of organizational skills. In testing several hypotheses, the results discount any simple statement on the causes of joint venture instability. Then, the motivations for the creation and termination of a joint development agreement are examined in the context of the Honeywell Corp.—L. M. Ericsson joint venture. The conclusions of the case indicate that termination is not always the outcome of the competitive pulls on cooperation but often a reflection of the successful competition of the transfer of organizational knowledge.

5.2.28

Laurita, Tom and Michael McGloin (1988), "US-Soviet Joint Ventures: Current Status and Prospects," *Columbia Journal of World Business,* 23(2), 43-51.

This article describes the political, economic, and human problems emerging in the present efforts to negotiate and establish US-Soviet joint ventures. It attempts to evaluate the current status of these efforts from the points-of-view of US firms and of relevant Soviet organizations, and to anticipate possible means to overcoming barriers now being encountered based on the strategic commercial and economic interests of both sides. It further assesses the overall prospects for success, and points to related innovations that may arise in the realm of East-West commercial relations.

5.2.29

Lyles, Marjorie A. (1987), "Common Mistakes of Joint Venture Experienced Firms," *Columbia Journal of World Business,* 22(2), Summer, 79-85.

Four multinational firms with extensive experience in international joint ventures were surveyed to determine what mistakes they had made while joint venturing. They agree that mistakes often had little impact on the success or failure of the joint venture in meeting its objectives, but they do impact what the firms have learned from their joint venture experiences. This paper reports on the nature of these mistakes, the apparent causes of these mistakes, and the learning that results.

5.2.30

Madura, Jeff and Ann Marie Whyte (1990), "Diversification Benefits of Direct Foreign Investment," *Management International Review,* 30(1), 73-85.

5.2.31

Markide, Constantinos C. and Norman Berg (1988), "Manufacturing Offshore is Bad Business," *Harvard Business Review,* 66(5), 113-120.

Some U.S. companies have moved manufacturing operations overseas to take advantage of lower wage rates, defending the practice as the only way to stay competitive. But is it? Companies like Kodak and Black & Decker have been doing well while staying home. Also Japanese can manufacture in the U.S. and be successful. According to the authors, for many companies, offshore manufacturing is a poor option for gaining competitiveness. For one thing, it involves extra transportation, communication, and paperwork. These costs can offset any potential savings. Also, when direct labor is a small percentage of total costs, as it is for much of manufacturing, labor savings are less critical to the bottom line.

5.2.32

Mattsson, Lars-Gunnar (1989), "Development of Firms in Network: Positions and Investments," *Advances in International Marketing,* Vol.3, 121-139.

Two major questions are discussed: (1) Given that a firm is established in a market, how can its further development be described and understood as dependent on the positions it has established during the entry process? (2)Are the activities cumulative in the sense that positions are created that in themselves constituted driving forces for future development?

5.2.33

Meredith, Lindsay (1984), "Marketing Determinants of U.S. Direct Investment in Canadian Manufacturing Industries," *Columbia Journal of World Business,* 19(3), Fall, 72-78.

The study evaluates the applicability of "marketing related"variables to the explanation of U.S. multinational direct investment among Canadian manufacturing industries. The tentative conclusion is that a link does exist between U.S.-Canadian manufacturing industries. This implies taking a "global" view of the advertising budget.

5.2.34

O'Reilly Anthony J.F. (1988), "Establishing Successful Joint Ventures in Developing Nations: A CEO's Perspective," *Columbia Journal of World Business,* 23(1), 65-71.

A case study of H.J. Heinz Company's approach to doing business in developing countries, this article first discusses the strategy adopted by Heinz to ensure success. The author then focuses on Heinz' joint venture in Thailand, the People's Republic of China and Zimbabwe, and offers insights about Heinz's strategy "in action."

5.2.35

Paliwoda, Stanley J. and Marilyn L. Liebrenz (1984), "Expectations and Results of Contractual Joint Ventures by US and UK MNCs in Eastern Europe," *European Journal of Marketing,* 18(3), 51-66.

Using ten case studies the authors intend to illustrate technology transfer to Eastern Europe which takes the form of contractual joint ventures. Known in Eastern Europe as industrial co-operation, a term used also by the UNECE, they constitute large and usually industrial export-intensive projects which are financed over a number of years partly with an agreed buyback of the goods manufactured under the licence of the Western partner.

5.2.36

Reich, Robert B. and Eric D. Mankin (1986), ''Joint Ventures with Japan Give Away Our Future,'' *Harvard Business Review,* 64(2), 78-86.

To avert rising U.S. protectionist sentiment, Japanese companies are setting up plants in the United States, either as joint ventures or on their own; to obtain high-quality, low-cost products and components, U.S. companies are making joint venture agreements with Japanese companies. At the same time, U.S. companies are licensing their new inventions to the Japanese. However, the authors conclude the big competitive gains come from learning about manufacturing processes and the result of the new multinational joint ventures is the transfer of that learning from the United States to Japan.

5.2.37

Reynolds, John I. (1984), ''The 'Pinched Shoe' Effect of International Joint Ventures,'' *Columbia Journal of World Business,* 19(2), Summer, 23-29.

International joint ventures are tickets of admission to certain markets. International joint ventures also allow a multinational to spread scarce resources over a larger geographical area than otherwise would be possible. Joint venture operations, however, involve some inherent extra costs, including the loss of complete autonomy over costs, and the loss of complete autonomy over ''global'' decisions. It is an empirical question where international joint ventures ''fit'' in the strategies of multinationals. This study found that the ventures' ''fit'' usually becomes somewhat uncomfortable as time passes.

5.2.38

Rosten, Keith A. (1991), ''Soviet-U.S. Joint Ventures: Pioneers on a New Frontier,'' *California Management Review,* 33(2), Winter, 88-108.

Representatives of US-Soviet joint ventures were interviewed. The major incentive for the US partner is to utilize a distribution from the joint venture in freely convertible currency. However, a number of US companies participate in the joint venture for the increased opportunities. Negotiations in the Soviet are an arduous process. Fundamental rules that can enhance the possibility of success for other Western companies include selecting the appropriate partner, evaluating other cooperation arrangements, formulating a sound business strategy, structuring the agreement to meet the needs of the parties, and maintaining an active role in operations.

5.2.39

Sabi, Manijeh (1988), ''An Application of the Theory of Foreign Direct Investment to Multinational Banking in LDCs," *Journal of International Business Studies,* 19(3), Fall, 433-447.

5.2.40

Sharma, D. Deo (1989), "Technical Consultancy as a Network of Relationships," *Advances in International Marketing,* Vol.3, 57-74.

This article describes the working process and the network of relationships in a technical consultancy assignment through the analysis of a project awarded to a Swedish civil engineering firm which hired a number of independent technical consultancy firms to execute the various sections of the assignment.

5.2.41

Tesar, George (1987), "West European Direct Investment in the U.S.," *International Marketing Review,* 4(1), Spring, 52-60.

Research suggests that the small-and medium-sized Western European firms interested in direct investment in the United States are reluctant to co-operate with the state governments in formulating investment decisions. Research findings in the Upper Mid-west indicate that the primary motivation of these firms to invest in the Upper Mid-west is to shelter capital. The amount of importance the individual state governments place on reverse direct investment politicizes the entire process of solicitation of potential direct investors. As a result, the small-and medium-sized Western European firms tend to seek direct investment assistance from professional private sources.

5.2.42

Tyebjee, Tyzoon T. (1988), "A Typology of Joint Ventures: Japanese Strategies in the United States," *California Management Review,* 31(1), 75-86.

By investigating the trigger event in 21 Japanese joint ventures in the US, four categories of these ventures are identified: (1) adoption, i.e., the acquisition of an equity position in a young, high growth US firm by a Japanese company, (2) rebirth, which is the infusion of state-of-the-art technology by a Japanese company into an ailing subsidiary of a US firm, (3) procreation, i.e., the beginning of a new business entity by 2 independent parents, and (4) family ties, in which a joint venture evolves out of horizontal linkages between suppliers to a key account or vertical connections between suppliers and manufacturers. In-depth interviews with top managers in the 21 joint ventures reveal that these four types of joint ventures vary in terms of: (1) the relative size of the partners, (2) their relative power in the relationship, (3) the strategic contribution each partner makes, and (4) the territorial limitations placed on the joint venture's marketing activities.

5.2.43

Vasconcellos, Geraldo M. (1988), ''Factors Affecting Foreign Direct Investment in the Brazilian Manufacturing Sector: 1955-1980,'' *Management International Review,* 28(4), 53-62.

Factors that have affected the ability of the Brazilian economy to attract foreign direct investment (FDI) are investigated. Macroeconomic factors are empirically examined that influenced FDI in the Brazilian manufacturing sector in the period 1955-1980. The empirical analysis is restricted to US-based multinational corporations operating in Brazil during that period. The results indicate that local macroeconomic variables, although far from being the only factor, seemed to have been an important causal factor for the capital investment decisions of US-based firms. The findings suggest some implications for policies based on tax incentives. Several possibilities for future research include the inclusion of new local economic variables and the extension of the model to other countries.

5.2.44

Webster, D. Robert (1989), ''International Joint Ventures with Pacific Rim Partners,'' *Business Horizons,* March-April, 65-71.

The joint venture may be the only way of gaining market access to countries whose nontariff barriers and import restrictions make direct exporting difficult or impossible. The joint venture also presents the opportunity for the US partner to acquire technology and marketing expertise. The US closely monitors the export of all goods and services, particularly the transfer of technology to communist countries. Any proposal for this type of transfer should be examined for compliance with the applicable controls. There are several steps that both parties should follow to fully document the joint venture agreement, including the preparation of an information exchange-confidentiality agreement and the preparation of a letter of intent.

5.2.45

Weigand, Robert (1983), ''International Investments: Weighing the Incentives,'' *Harvard Business Review,* 61(4), July-August, 146-152.

5.3 Contractual Agreements, Licensing and Technology Transfer

5.3.1

Akaah, Ishmael P. and Edward A. Riordan (1988), ''Applicability of Marketing

Knowhow in the Third World,'' *International Marketing Review,* 5(1), Spring, 41-55.

Although considerable attention has been focused on marketing in the Third World, debate persists as to the extent to which marketing knowhow is applicable in Third World countries. In light of this , this paper investigates the incidence and regularity of performance of marketing-mix activities in Third World business contexts. The results support a relatively high level of incidence and regularity of performance of marketing-mix activities—thus implying their ''applicability.'' However, the results suggest that corporate factors influence the performance of marketing-mix activities.

5.3.2

Benvignati, Anita M. (1983), ''International Technology Transfer Patterns in a Traditional Industry,'' *Journal of International Business Studies,* 14(3), Winter, 63-75.

This research examines the factors influencing the speed of transfer of 40 textile machinery innovations between the United States and leading foreign competitors. Statistical analysis is based on detailed information identifying the first U.S. and foreign producers to introduce innovations, and indicating the timing of their introductions. Empirical relationships suggest that the speed of international transfer has been greater as time has passed and as commercial transactions between industrialized nations have increased. The speed has been slower when the innovating domestic firm was technologically nondominant and the imitating foreign firm was technologically dominant.

5.3.3

Boisot, Max (1983), ''The Shaping of Technological Strategy: European Chemical Firms in South East Asia,'' *Management International Review,* 23(3), 16-35.

5.3.4

Carstairs, Robert T. and Lawrence S. Welch (1982), ''Licensing and the Internationalization of Smaller Companies: Some Australian Evidence,'' *Management International Review,* 22(3), 33-44.

Australian firms were surveyed to determine the factors leading to the adoption and success of technological licensing. Most firms involved in licensing were small to medium in size, and had limited access to foreign export markets and limited abilities to engage in foreign investment. Those with the greatest amount of success in licensing had some previous experience in exporting which provided the skills and understanding to deal with international markets. Licensing success was also strongly dependent upon effective and long-term interactions between the licensor and licensee.

5.3.5

Cho, Kang Rae (1988), "Issues of Compensation in International Technology Licensing," *Management International Review,* 28(2), 70-79.

Because international technology markets are imperfect, technology prices generally are determined by negotiations between licensors and licensees. This often leads to charges of overcompensation for technologies purchased by licensees and their governments. Licensee government policies on technology compensation generally try to lower short-run balance of payment costs by regulating various agreement-specific factors. These attempts are of doubtful effectiveness. A more effective policy would be one that seeks both to ensure a reasonable bargaining range between the licensor and licensee and to strengthen the licensee's bargaining leverage by influencing environment specific factors. This can be done by eliminating any chances of excessive profits in the licensee's market. An alternative method would be to lower the costs of developing the same or a similar technology domestically or of obtaining the technology from an alternative source.

5.3.6

Contractor, Farok J. (1983), "Technology Licensing Practice in U.S. Companies: Corporate and Public Policy Implications," *Columbia Journal of World Business,* 18(3), Fall, 80-88.

Licensing practice in a sample of 241 companies is analyzed for factors as the importance of patents and trademarks in the context of changes in government scrutiny of technology transfers. Regression equations statistically model the level of licensing activity in a firm, based on size, internationalization, patent incidence and other factors.

5.3.7

Daniels, John D. and Fernando Robles (1982), "The Choice of Technology and Export Commitment: the Peruvian Textile Industry," *Journal of International Business Studies,* 13(1), Spring/Summer, 67-87.

This study examines the relationship between the adoption of capital-intensive technologies and export commitment of Peruvian textile firms. The results suggested a positive relationship. One possible reason is that exporters must be more concerned with product quality perception and delivery reliability which may be higher through the use of labor-saving innovations. Another is that lower production costs may be more important in external markets which are more competitive. The study elaborates on the complex factors affecting technology choice, emphasizing that there are country, industry, product, and innovation specific variables which affect the use of so-called appropriate technology.

5.3.8

Dawson, Leslie M. (1987), "Transferring Industrial Technology to Less Developed Countries," *Industrial Marketing Management,* 16(4), November, 265-271.

Motivations for private industry to transfer technological knowledge to less developed countries (LDC) include: (1) stimulating new growth markets, (2) access to strategic materials, (3) investment protection, (4) moral imperative, and (5) world power shifts. Some of the more important technology targets for LDCs include the agriculture, infrastructure, and export stimulation sectors. New technologies, research by-products, and abandoned technologies are often examples of technologies that can be transferred by a firm without leading to competition with its primary business. The main mechanisms for direct transfer of technological innovations are direct investment, licensing and joint ventures, and free donations.

5.3.9

Hauptman, Gunter (1987), "Intellectual Property Rights," *International Marketing Review,* 4(1), Spring, 61-64.

Intellectual property infringement has become a serious problem in international trade. This article addresses the issue, using the IBM PC as an example. Problems arising within the U.S., those arising from imports to the U.S., and those occurring outside the U.S. are analyzed and ways to combat violations are suggested.

5.3.10

Ho, Suk-ching and Ho-fuk Lau (1988), "Development of Supermarket Technology: the Incomplete Transfer Phenomenon," *International Marketing Review,* 5(1), Spring, 20-30.

Irrespective of the potential benefits associated with international transfer of retail technology, the question over the appropriateness of marketing technology of Western origin in different socio-cultural settings is yet to be answered. Using the supermarket technology in Hong Kong as an example, this paper shows that the transference of the retail technology from one market to another is highly dependent on the socio-cultural environment. It concludes that in effecting an international transfer, a retailer may have to be satisfied with an incomplete transfer, proceed in a gradual, evolutionary process and maintain an adaptive interaction with the environment.

5.3.11

Ho,Suk-Ching and Yat-Ming Sin (1987), "International Transfer of Retail Technology: The Successful Case of Convenience Stores in Hong Kong," *International Journal of Retailing,* 2(3), 36-48.

The causes of rapid development of convenience stores in Hong Kong are explored. An underlying assumption is that a new retailing idea must be benefitial to consumers, so it is important to examine consumers' reactions to this technology. To do so, a survey of customer reactions was performed in Hong Kong at three 7-Eleven stores. Some 205 usable responses were obtained. It was found that convenience store characteristics are well matched to the consumers' characteristics and needs. This assisted the rapid development of convenience store technology in Hong Kong. A second analytical assumption is that the process of development of a retail technology is accelerated by the existence of complementary technology, such as supermarkets, and the aggressive actions of individual firms.

5.3.12

Kogut, Bruce (1986), "On Designing Contracts to Guarantee Enforceability: Theory and Evidence from East-West Trade," *Journal of International Business Studies,* 17(1), Spring, 47-61.

Literature on East-West trade and the choice of contracts can be integrated into recent work on the theory of the multinational corporation and contract enforceability. By using the properties of foreign direct investment as a benchmark, the article explains why one type of contract ends to prevail over another. The explanation rests on the premise that because of the prohibition on FDI, contracts are used which most closely replicate the benefits of intra-firm trade, while providing managerial and risk-shifting services to the eastern partner.

5.3.13

Kotabe, Masaaki and Janet Y. Murray (1990), "Linking Product and Process Innovations and Modes of International Sourcing in Global Competition: A Case of Foreign Multinational Firms," *Journal of International Business Studies,* 21(3), 383-408.

A taxonomy of sourcing strategies is developed to systematically identify a variety of sourcing patterns. Based on a few variables identified in the taxonomy, the performance implications of various sourcing strategies and innovative activities that accompany them are explored using a sample of subsidiaries of European and Japanese multinational firms operating in the U.S. It appears that product and process innovations are intertwined such that continual improvements in manufacturing processes lead to product innovations. The taxonomy shows that, when either one of the innovative activities is low while the other is high, the degree of internal sourcing of major components appears generally low.

5.3.14

Lo, Thamis Wing-chun, Oliver Hon-ming Yau and Yi-jing Li (1986), "International

Transfer of Service Technology: An Exploratory Study of the Case of Supermarkets in China," *Management International Review,* 26(2), 71-76.

The transfer of a new service technology from one country into another is not an easy task. Several requirements necessary for the transfer of technology are: (1) The new technology should serve the local consumers more satisfactorily than traditional means; (2) The consumers should perceive and realize the new service technology is better. The development of supermarkets in the Peoples' Republic of China illustrates some of the problems in the transfer of such an advanced technology in a centrally planned, developing country. The advantages of such transfers to China's present modernization success are discussed as is the role of foreign firms in the development of supermarkets and other service industries.

5.3.15

Madu, Christian N. (1989), "Transferring Technology to Developing Countries— Critical Factors for Success," *Long Range Planning,* 22(4), August, 115-124.

A decision framework is presented for technology transfer from developed countries to less developed countries (LDC). This framework considers technology to be an important strategic variable in national development planning. LDCs and MNCs may lessen the risks linked with the transfer of inappropriate technology by considering technology transfer in a formal planning process. The decision framework includes: (1) identifying the active participants, (2) studying the scope and limitations of traditional or existing technology, and (3) determining the strengths and weaknesses of LDCs in terms of production. Successful technology transfer will help to improve both the social and the economic condition of LDCs. The benefits of technology transfer include: (1) long-term economic growth as a result of technology progression, and (2) an increase in direct foreign investment.

5.3.16

Mansfield, Edwin (1989), "Technological Creativity: Japan and the United States," *Business Horizons,* 32(2), March-April, 48-53.

A two-year study by the National Science Foundation on technological development is presented. Data were obtained from a sample of 60 Japanese and US firms in the chemical, machinery, electrical equipment, and instruments industries. Three major conclusions emerged from the study. First, regarding the differences between the countries in innovation cost and time, while the Japanese have substantial advantage in the machinery industries, they do not have an advantage in others, such as the chemical industry. Second, a large part of the US problem seems traceable to its inability to match Japan as a quick and effective user of external technology. Third, the results support the contention that applied research and development in Japan have yielded a higher return in Japan than in the US. There is no evidence that the rate of return from basic research has been high in Japan.

5.3.17

Millman, A. F. (1983), "Technology Transfer in the International Markets," *European Journal of Marketing,* 17(1), 26-47.

Issues in technology transfer in the world market are discussed. The author finds that transfer of technology within and among multinational companies is well established. The reasons include: first, they seek to control the diffusion and exploitation of their technology as part of a global strategy; second, if they are to benefit from a sharing arrangement, they look for partners of similar standing. Until such time as alternative channels for technology are developed to the same level of efficiency, there is little doubt that multinationals will dominate technological activity in the private sector.

5.3.18

Sarathy, Ravi (1985), "High-Technology Exports from Newly Industrializing Countries: The Brazilian Commuter Aircraft Industry," *California Management Review,* 27(2), 60-84.

5.3.19

Welch, Lawrence S. (1989), "Diffusion of Franchise System Use in International Operations," *International Marketing Review,* 6(5), 7-19.

The spread of "second generation" franchise system use from a predominantly U.S. base is studied. The focus is on Australia as one of the major recipient countries. Australia has moved rapidly through a process of adoption and imitation of U.S. companies' franchise systems in the 1970s and 1980s. Having applied the franchise system in domestic operations, a number of Australian companies have now begun to develop an international thrust, including an interest in the U.S. market.

5.3.20

Welch, Lawrence S. (1985), "The International Marketing of Technology: an Interaction Perspective," *International Marketing Review,* 2(1), Spring, 41-53.

The author analyzes the nature and demands of technology licensing as an international marketing strategy from the perspective of small to medium-sized firms and as a connection between unrelated organizations.

5.4 Export Marketing and Countertrade

5.4.1

Aggarwal, Raj (1989), "International Business Through Barter and Countertrade," *Long Range Planning,* 22(3), June, 75-81.

Countertrade can be classified into four major categories: (1) barter, (2) clearing arrangements, (3) switch trading, and (4) compensation agreements. The four categories differ in complexity with regard to time period and the degree to which money is involved. Reasons for countertrade include protectionism, limited access to hard currency, and the potential to develop new markets. The effects of market imperfections can be classified along two general dimensions: (1) quota-type effects that limit quantities, and (2) tax-type effects that raise costs. Corporate strategy for using countertrade should be guided by the nature of countertrade and the business skills needed to use it successfully. Firms also must examine the potential problems involved with countertrade, which include the lack of flexibility and the limited range of products available for countertrade.

5.4.2

Amine, Lyn S., S. Tamer Cavusgil, and Robert I. Weinstein (1986), "Japanese Sogo Shosha and the U.S. Export Trading Companies," *Journal of the Academy of Marketing Science,* 14(3), Fall, 21-32.

The sogo shosha are studied for the light they can shed on US export trading companies (ETC). Sogo shosha offer their suppliers three primary services: (1) specialization in providing intermediary services, (2) risk-reduction through extensive information channels, and (3) significant financial assistance. Three new areas are emerging as the sogo shosha shift from reactive to proactive trading: more third-country trade, increased participation in product areas requiring sophisticated distribution, and greater participation in high-risk overseas "mega" projects. The emerging ETCs in the US are those formed by consortia of smaller suppliers, service-oriented firms, multinational corporations, and quasi-public organizations or public entities. Some of the largest ETCs are competing directly with the sogo shosha in world markets.

5.4.3

Amine, Lyn S. and S. Tamer Cavusgil (1986), "Export Marketing Strategies in the British Clothing Industry," *European Journal of Marketing,* 20(7), 21-33.

Specific company export marketing policies and company traits were related systematically to export performance in a sample of firms selected from the UK clothing industry. These firms represented a wide range of company size and degree of export involvement. A combination of mail and personal interviews was employed to collect data, and 48 usable returns were obtained. Data analysis was conducted through use of cross-tabulation and Pearson correlation analyses. The main characteristics of company exporting were: (1) company attitude and commitment to exporting, (2) the process of market selection, and (3) marketing mix decisions. Correlates of export performance were examined. Export performance seemed to improve with more experience. Conditions for export success were highly industry-specific. Concentration on key markets was found to be mostly irrelevant in the clothing export business.

5.4.4

Axinn, Catherine N. (1988), "Export Performance: Do Managerial Perceptions Make a Difference?" *International Marketing Review,* 5(2), Summer, 61-71.

This article reports on a study of the relationship between the perceptions managers have on exporting and the export performance of their firms. Although the study also examines relationships between exporting and other manager-related and firm-related variables, a key finding links perception of export-based growth opportunities with firm export performance. Although a variety of measures have been used to evaluate export performance, in this study export performance is measured by the percentage of sales which a firm obtains by exporting.

5.4.5

Ayal, Igal and Seev Hirsch (1982), "Marketing Factors in Small Country Manufactured Exports: Are Market Share and Market Growth Rate Really Important," *Journal of International Business Studies,* 13(2), Fall, 73-80

5.4.6

Barrett, Nigel J. and Ian F. Wilkinson (1985), "Export Stimulation: A Segmentation Study of the Exporting Problems of Australian Manufacturing Firms," *European Journal of Marketing,* 19(2), 53-72.

Manufactured exports are critical to the future economic performance of Australia. The authors attempt to identify different types of manufacturing organizations in Australia in terms of their actual and perceived exporting problems, and to suggest the types of assistance that might be needed. The data analyzed are taken from a 1969 study of 340 Australian manufacturing firms. The firms are grouped into 5 clusters using a K-means method of nonhierarchical cluster analysis. The conclusions include: (1) Firms that report primarily environmentally related problems, such as price competition, need financially based incentives with minimal direct involvement by change agents. (2) Firms that emphasize problems concerning the process of exporting require assistance through more direct involvement by change agents. (3) Firms experiencing both types of problems need a combination of financial incentives and direct involvement. As firms achieve export success, the process problems diminish while the environmental problems assume greater significance.

5.4.7

Bates, Constance (1986), "Are Companies Ready for Countertrade," *International Marketing Review,* 3(2), Summer, 28-36.

This paper presents the results of a study designed to gather empirical data about countertrade activity by U.S. firms. The focus of the study was to determine the number of firms engaging in countertrade, their general characteristics, their motivations for countertrading, and their expected future level of involvement in countertrade.

5.4.8

Bilkey, Warren J. (1985), "Development of Export Marketing Guidelines," *International Marketing Review*, 2(1), Spring, 31-40.

Optimal export marketing practices are identified for a given business condition. The author also estimates the extent to which firms use sub-optimal export marketing practices and possible means for developing guidelines that would enable managements to identify which export marketing practices would be optimal for their particular firm at a given point in time.

5.4.9

Cavusgil, S. Tamer and Jacob Naor (1987), "Firm and Management Characteristics as Discriminators of Export Marketing Activity," *Journal of Business Research*, 15(3), June, 221-235.

Characteristics associated with the export marketing activity of manufacturing firms were examined. A literature review revealed four sets of firm-related constructs that influence export activity: unique firm advantages, decision-maker characteristics, resource commitment to exporting, and perceived attractiveness of exporting. Data were taken from a survey of 310 manufacturing firms. Results indicate that the characteristics useful in discriminating between exporting and nonexporting firms include the scope of the firm's U.S. market, perceived risks of exporting, company size, management expertise, and the existence of national middlemen network for the firm. It was concluded that the four constructs vary in their ability to discriminate between exporters and nonexporters.

5.4.10

Cavusgil, S. Tamer and Ed Sikora (1988), "How Multinationals Can Counter Gray Market Imports," *Columbia Journal of World Business*, 23(4), Winter, 75-85.

Gray or parallel import marketing has always concerned multinational companies and their dealer networks. This article proposes a range of both reactive and proactive strategies that companies can adopt to counter gray market channels. Each strategy is illustrated by actual management responses. The principal thesis is that long-term and assured resolution of gray market problems can result from deliberate management planning and action. Such a response is made imperative in light of the May 1988 US Supreme Court decision upholding the legality of gray market imports.

5.4.11

Cho, Kang Rae (1987), "Using Countertrade as a Competitive Management Tool," *Management International Review,* 27(1), 50-57.

The basic types of countertrade are counterpurchase, compensation, offset, barter, and switch. Countertrade can (1) offer a means of creating an export opportunity, (2) provide a method of securing reliable sources of raw materials and intermediate products over the long term, and (3) help a company solve financial problems associated with trade debt or blocked funds. However, countertrade also has potential pitfalls, including: (1) a limited list of countertrading goods offered for payments, (2) the higher level of uncertainty associated with countertrading goods to be received, (3) a danger of nurturing competition against goods the company is to receive and/or the goods it or its major client produces, and (4) complexity. A countertrade decision-making process consists of evaluating the countertrading country, identifying countertrading goods, examining the effects on the company, and developing a negotiation strategy. Companies need a corporatewide concerted approach to use countertrade properly as a competitive management tool.

5.4.12

Cohen, Stephen S. and John Zysman (1986), "Countertrade, Offsets, Barter, and Buybacks," *California Management Review,* 28(2), 41-56.

With the development of monetary trading systems, various forms of barter came to be viewed as marginal transactions. However, incidence of international trade accomplished through barter, countertrade, buybacks, and offsets has increased in recent years, perhaps accounting for as much as 30% of world trade. These trade forms have reemerged due to increased government intervention into economic development. Barter forms also have been spurred by the increased availability of development funds during the 1970s, arms trade, and the need to manage surplus capacity. Use of trade by developing states as an instrument of national economic policy has served to restrict the degree to which the flow of commodities is determined by market factors.

5.4.13

Cooper, Robert G. and Elko J. Kleinschmidt (1985), "The Impact of Export Strategy on Export Sales Performance," *Journal of International Business Studies,"* 16(1), Spring, 37-55.

This article reports the results of an extensive empirical study of the export strategies of a large sample of high technology electronics firms, and the performance results of adopting alternate export strategies. Six strategy scenarios were identified. The results show that the types of foreign markets selected, segmentation strategies and product strategies all have a pronounced impact on export sales and export growth.

5.4.14

Czinkota, Michael R. and Michael L. Ursic (1983), "Impact of Export Growth
   Expectations on Smaller Firms," *International Marketing Review*, 1(2) Winter,
   26-33.

The findings of a survey of export attitudes and behavior of small-and-medium-sized
U.S. manufacturing firms are presented. Companies are differentiated according to
their growth expectations and the behaviors of firms that have export growth
expectations are compared to the behavior of firms that do not anticipate export
growth. The authors suggest that the export growth expectations of a firm shape its
behavior in terms of contact activities and its perceptions of export problems.

5.4.15

Czinkota, Michael R. and Wesley J. Johnston (1983), "Exporting: Does Sales
   Volume Make a Difference?" *Journal of International Business Studies*, 14(1),
   Spring/Summer, 147-153.

This study investigates the effect that the size of a firm has on export activities,
perceived problems in exporting, and attitudes toward exporting. The results indicate
that broad generalizations concerning the size of firms and exporting appear to be
inappropriate.

5.4.16

Czinkota, Michael R. and Michael Ursic (1991), "Classification of Exporting Firms
   According to Sales and Growth into a Share Matrix," *Journal of Business
   Research*, 22(3), May, 243-253.

An export growth-share matrix that divides firms into four categories based on
export percentage and anticipated growth is developed. Implications are developed
for each category of firms to help governments encourage exporting and to improve
managerial decisions. While firms that export a small percentage of sales should be
reached by promoting awareness of selling abroad, firms that export a large
percentage of sales need more concrete help. Low-growth firms have more product
experience and less international orientation. This indicates that the nature of help
given to these firms should be more strategy-oriented than product oriented.

5.4.17

Darling, John R. (1985), "Keys for Success in Exporting to the US Market,"
   European Journal of Marketing, 19(2), 17-30.

The authors identify 10 keys to success in exporting to the US market: (1) Analyze
market opportunity, (2) Evaluate product potential, (3) Establish a market entry
mode, (4) Make a firm commitment, (5) Allocate the necessary resources, (6)
Identify technical issues, (7) Develop a strategic marketing plan, (8) Organize an

operational team, (9) Implement the marketing strategy, and (10) Assess and control operations. These 10 points should be viewed as interrelated issues that must be carefully reviewed and analyzed by the executive anticipating a successful entry and penetration of the US market.

5.4.18

Delacroix, Jacques (1984), "Export Strategies for Small American Firms,"*California Management Review,* 26(3), 138-153.

It is widely believed that the US export market is basically the preserve of large corporations, despite the fact that the majority of US firms are classified as small businesses. Two reasons are given as to why size should affect export capability: (1) Large production units enable economies of scale, which promote lower prices; (2) Large firm size may be a prerequisite of effective international marketing. The experience of US agricultural exports indicates that smallness does not automatically preclude export success. The argument that low product differentiation explains the export performance of US firms is undercut by import examples, such as Brie cheese from France. The global convergence of lifestyles generates demands faster than they can be satisfied by domestic producers, thus providing an opening to exporters.

5.4.19

Dichtl, E. M. Leibold, M. H. G. Koglmayr, and S. Muller(1984), "The Export-Decision of Small and Medium-Sized Firms: A Review," *Management International Review,* 24(2), 49-60.

The economic difficulties of the past few years have led to an intensification of the discussion regarding the possible contribution of the export business to overcome this structural crisis. Especially in the area of small- and medium-sized business it is assumed that considerable underutilized export reserves exist. A critical analysis is made of major works that touch upon the fundamental decision of small and medium-sized firms to commence with an export activity for the first time. The present level of research in this direction is disappointing, and the first steps toward improving the situation involve operationalization of the constructs used.

5.4.20

Duhan, Dale F. and Mary Jane Sheffet (1988), "Gray Markets and the Legal Status of Parallel Importation," *Journal of Marketing,* 52(3), July, 75-83.

The authors describe how and why gray marketing occurs in the context of legal and illegal marketing activities. The regulatory and judicial decisions relating to gray marketing activities are reviewed and the implications of an upcoming Supreme Court ruling on gray marketing are discussed.

5.4.21

Ernst, Maurice (1990), "U.S. Exports in the 1990s," *Business Horizons,* 33(1), January-Feburary, 44-49.

The economic environment will be favorable to US exporters well into the 1990s. Over the past 25 years, US exports have grown faster than the economy as a whole. Since 1985, the real dollar exchange rate has fallen more than 30%, and export market share has begun to increase. The general trends of real exchange rates indicate that: (1) the basic forces that have put downward pressure on the dollar have not disappeared, (2) the growing economic integration of the European Community (EC) increasingly puts all of Western Europe under the tight monetary discipline of its most powerful member, Germany, and (3) there is a good chance that international cooperation in economic policy will be closer than in the past. Several of the most important US markets are likely to be both fast growing and more open to imports. These include Canada, Western Europe, Japan, and the Republic of Korea.

5.4.22

Green, Robert T. and Trina L. Larsen (1986), "Sudden Wealth/Sudden Poverty: Implications for Export Opportunities," *Columbia Journal of World Business,* 21(4), Winter, 3-12.

Export marketers face rapidly changing conditions in the international markets. These changes may have a significant effect on the opportunities that exist for their products in those markets. A study was undertaken to examine the experiences of three nations that recently have suffered severe economic shocks that resulted in a contraction in imports—Mexico, Nigeria, and Brazil. The changes that took place in the demand for different categories of imports are analyzed, and the similarities and differences in the responses of the three nations are examined. In all three countries, the three categories of sophisticated capital goods, electric and nonelectric machinery, and transport equipment all displayed wide swings in response to economic conditions. Basic commodities appear to gain import share during hard times, but Mexico displayed this trend more than the other two countries.

5.4.23

Green, Robert T. and Ajay K. Kohli (1991),Export Market Identification: The Role of Economic Size and Socioeconomic Development," *Management International Review,* 31(1), 37-50.

The relationship between a nation's imports of manufacturing goods and its economic size and level of socioeconomic developments are investigated. The findings suggest that the quantity exported to a nation is a function of its economic size, with elite-oriented consumer products representing a partial exception. On the other hand, socioeconomic development exhibits a more complex relationship with export volume. While exports of basic consumer products and sophisticated industrial products are related to a nation's level of socioeconomic development, exports of basic industrial goods and sophisticated consumer products are not. These findings dictate the cautious use of economic size and socioeconomic development as indicators of export market potential.

5.4.24

Kedia, Ben L. and Jagdeep Chhokar (1986), "Factors Inhibiting Export Performance of Firms: An Empirical Investigation," *Management International Review,* 26(4),33-43.

Various studies have focused on the perceived inhibitors to exporting. An attempt is made to identify those factors that are both important and difficult to counter. 96 Louisiana firms form the sample. Cited as the most important inhibitors of export activity are: (1) knowing how to market overseas, (2) obtaining information on overseas prospects and markets, (3) knowing foreign business practices, (4) knowing export procedures, (5) pricing for foreign markets, (6) competing with foreign and US firms overseas, and (7) dealing with a strong US dollar. There are differences between which of these factors are cited by exporting and nonexporting firms. Thus, different educational and export-promotion programs are needed to address the needs of firms at different stages of the export process.

5.4.25

Kaynak, Erdener and Vinay Kothari (1984), "Export Behaviour of Small and Medium-Sized Manufacturers: Some Policy Guidelines for International Market-ers," *Management International Review,* 24(2) 61-69.

This cross-national study compares the degree of export orientation in a number of manufacturing industries and points out differences which might exist in such orientations among exporting and non-exporting manufacturing firms. The study also explores the strategic approaches to be used by North American manufacturers to be successful in their major foreign markets.

5.4.26

Ganitsky, Joseph (1989), "Strategies for Innate and Adoptive Exporters: Lessons from Israel's Case," *International Marketing Review,* 6(5), 50-65.

This article compares corporations established expressly to serve foreign markets (innate exporters) with those that first served domestic markets and later broadened their scope to foreign markets (adoptive exporters). It examines their respective reasons for export involvement, managerial attitudes and practices, risk profiles, strategic postures in four competitive scenarios, and key distinctive success factors.

5.4.27

Hennart, Jean-Francois (1990), "Some Empirical Dimensions of Countertrade," *Journal of International Business Studies,* 21(2), 243-270.

Countertrade is used to describe six types of transactions: barter, clearing arrangements, switch trading, buy-back, counterpurchase, and offset. Implications of recent theories of countertrade are compared with data obtained from Countertrade Outlook, a comprehensive database of countertrade transactions. The findings indicate that the relationship between a country's credit rating and its propensity to countertrade is not as strong as commonly held. On the other hand, the data support the rival hypothesis that some forms of countertrade, such as buy-back and counterpurchase, are substitutes to foreign direct investment. The most important finding is that each countertrade type seems to have its own separate motivations.

5.4.28

Holden, Alfred C. (1989), "US Official Export-Finance Support: Can American Exporters Expect a Competitive EXIMBANK to Emerge?" *Columbia Journal of World Business,* 24(3), Fall, 33-46.

5.4.29

Howard, Donald G. and James M. Maskulka (1988), "Will American Export Trading Companies Replace Traditional Export Management Companies?" *International Marketing Review,* 5(4), Winter, 41-50.

This paper examines the American Trading Company as authorized under the Export Trading Company Act of 1982. It reviews the three critical elements necessary for AETCs to become a significant force in world markets—capital, product/production skills, and international marketing skills. Specifically, this article investigates an important potential source of international marketing skills, the Export Management Company, to determine their interest in participating in an AETC.

5.4.30

Huszagh, Sandra M. (1986), "International Barter and Countertrade," *International Marketing Review,* 3(2), Summer, 7-19.

Barter and countertrade will be significant trade tools throughout the 1980s. Presently confronted by saturated established markets and debt-burdened new markets, firms of all sizes in all industry sectors must evaluate these trading approaches. This paper describes the forms of barter and countertrade, products typically traded, markets served, and objectives advanced by each form. The intent is to explore opportunities and problems accompanying each form, so that managers can assess the utilities of these transactions to their firms' international marketing strategies.

5.4.31

Huszagh, Sandra M. and Hiram C. Barksdale (1986), "International Barter and Countertrade: An Exploratory Study," *Journal of the Academy of Marketing Science,* 14(1), Spring, 21-28.

Executives from a sample of eighteen firms were surveyed about their barter/countertrade arrangements, the products and markets involved, and the advantages and disadvantages of these arrangements. Barter/countertrade arrangements generally involved commodities or low-technology products. Firm product/market diversity was associated with more complex countertrade agreements and the establishment of special organizational structures to deal with alternative trade forms. Firms that provided a single product line were subject to fluctuating demand and tended to prefer barter over countertrade arrangements, while firms having diverse product lines tended to prefer countertrade transactions. Barter/countertrade agreements were advantageous for entering new markets and could be used to reduce foreign currency exchange risk.

5.4.32

Huszagh, Sandra M. and Fredrick W. Huszagh (1987), "Understanding Agricultural Export," *International Marketing Review,* 4(1), Spring, 16-30.

This article's basic theorem is that effective export programs must be simultaneously founded on grass-roots political support, economic comparative advantage, and domestic vertical development. The mechanics for establishing broad-based political support are addressed first, followed by criteria for targeting to international markets with the most favorable demand and government incentives. The evolutionary aspects of comparative advantage are discussed in the context of long-term economic and political support from producers, processors and related technology suppliers involved in targeted export strategies.

5.4.33

Johansson, Johny K. and Ikujiro Nonaka (1983), "Japanese Export Marketing: Structures, Strategies, Counterstrategies," *International Marketing Review,* 1(2), Winter, 12-25.

Against the success of Japanese exporting companies during the last decade, this paper presents a comprehensive review of the factors behind their performance. Based on a combination of secondary and primary data, the structures within which the exporting companies operate are spelled out and integrated. The integration is shown to lead naturally to a particular strategic posture dominated by a long-run perspective and a high quality/price ratio in products meticulously adapted for very specific market segments. Potentially valuable counterstrategies drawing upon the Japanese experiences and military analogies are developed.

5.4.34

Katsikeas, Constantine S. and Nigel F. Piercy (1991), "The Relationship Between Exporters from a Developing Country and Importers Based in a Developed Country: Conflict Considerations," *European Journal of Marketing,* 25(1), 6-25.

Conflict issues in exporter-importer trading relationship are investigated through field work in Greece and the UK. Data on 28 export-import dyads were matched to examine perceptual differences among the dyad members. The results show that the export-import relationship was governed by some conflict between the involved parties. However, in the overwhelming majority of conflict areas, its magnitude was associated with low levels. In most of the subvariables, most of the matched pairs investigated were marked by perceptual differences between the dyad members, with respect to the degree of conflict in the relationship. In the majority of the conflict areas investigated, the identified differences in the reported perceptions of the dyad members had no systematic character.

5.4.35

Kaynak, Erdener and Metin N. Gurol (1987), "Export Marketing Management in Less-Developed Countries: A Case Study of Turkey in Light of the Japanese Experience," *Management International Review,* 27(3), 54-66.

Less developed countries rely on export marketing to obtain much needed foreign currencies that are required for their socioeconomic and technological development. The dependence of most LDCs upon agricultural products, semiprocessed products, and raw materials has proved to be disadvantageous. In order to meet development objectives, LDCs must give high priority to the marketing of manufactured products abroad. Turkey is an LDC struggling to shift the majority of its exports from raw materials and agricultural commodities to industrial goods. Turkey must accomplish this objective by 1995, when it becomes a member of the European Economic Community, or free competition within the EEC will push the country back into an agrarian economy. An expert marketing model for Turkey is proposed that is based on the international product life cycle and the experience curves.

5.4.36

Kim, W. Chan (1986), "Global Diffusion of the General Trading Company Concept," *Sloan Management Review,* 27(4), Summer, 35-43.

In recent years, General Trading Companies (GTC) have spread to other countries besides Japan. GTCs provide a transaction-cost approach which helps facilitate trading activities. They also provide a centralized intermediary approach which increases the efficiency of distribution of goods by acting as a marketing intermediary. This is particularly helpful in developing countries whose distribution channels are highly fragmented. Finally, GTCs act as information-gathering services which create economies of scale for small firms. There are five institutional environmental factors that contribute to the formation of GTCs: (1) an underdeveloped infrastructure, (2) an industrial base dominated by small- and medium-sized firms, (3) standardized products, (4) highly fragmented distribution channels, and (5) strong government support for GTC-like organizations.

5.4.37

Korth, Christopher M. (1991), "Managerial Barriers to U.S. Exports," *Business Horizons,* 34(2), March-April, 18-26.

The failure of US exports is mainly attributed to managerial barriers within the companies. The managerial barriers can be broken down into several categories, including (1) limited ambition, which may reflect satisfaction with opportunities in the US domestic market, (2) unrecognized opportunities, which may be due to inadequate knowledge of international markets, (3) a culpable lack of necessary resources, including exporting skills, managerial time, necessary financing, and productive capacity, and (4) unrealistic fears of such elements as operational difficulties, environmental differences, and risks. Reducing these managerial barriers should be an important goal for both corporate managers and governmental agencies.

5.4.38

Lecraw, Donald J. (1989), "The Management of Countertrade: Factors Influencing Success," *Journal of International Business Studies,* 20(1),Spring, 41-59.

5.4.39

Lee, Chong S. and Yoo S Yang (1990), "Impact of Export Market Expansion Strategy on Export Performance," *International Marketing Review,* 7(4), 41-51.

An operationalization scheme is presented in which export market expansion strategy is measured as a multidimensional construct. In addition, the effect of the choice of an export market expansion strategy on the export performance of firms is examined. Multiple measures of export performance were compared across the three strategic groups of export market expansion developed through the three-stage classification scheme. The primary data were collected in 1985 through field interviews with 55 top managers of small and medium-sized high technology manufacturing firms. It was found that exporting firms with a market diversification strategy perform significantly better in terms of export level and export sales growth, compared to other groups with a market concentration or a concentric diversification strategy. No statistically significant difference was found among the thee groups in terms of perceived export sales growth and the three export profitability measures.

5.4.40

Lim, Jeen-Su, Thomas W. Sharkey, and Ken I. Kim (1991), "An Empirical Test of an Export Adoption Model," *Management International Review,* 31(1), 51-62.

A four-construct hierarchical export adoption model was developed. The four constructs included awareness, interest, intention, and adoption. The model's validity was tested by application of LISREL. The results of the LISREL analysis provided strong support for the model's ability to explain the export behavior of the firm. The incremental fit index and chi-square difference test confirmed a significant improvement in goodness of fit for the hypothesized model. The direct causal paths from awareness to interest, from interest to intention, and from intention to adoption were found to be significant.

5.4.41

Lutz, James M. and Robert T. Green (1983), "The Product Life Cycle and the Export Position of the United States," *Journal of International Business Studies,* 14(3), Winter, 77-93.

This study analyzed trade in 4-digit level manufacturing categories over time for four nations, including the United States, to ascertain the relevance of the product life cycle theory to such trade. The level of technological input was controlled. The results indicate that the theory has at least some explanatory relevance for three of the four countries, including the United States.

5.4.42

Madsen, Tage Koed (1989), "Successful Export Marketing Management: Some Empirical Evidence," *International Marketing Review,* 6(4), 41-57.

The main results of a survey of 134 export activities in manufacturing firms in Denmark are presented. The author analyzes the association between export performance on the one hand and export marketing policy, firm characteristics and market characteristics on the other hand. Bivariate and multivariate analyses are performed with the purpose of identifying critical export marketing success factors.

5.4.43

Malekzadeh, Ali R. and Samuel Rabino (1986), "Manufacturers' Export Strategies," *International Marketing Review,* 3(4), Winter, 27-33.

In this empirical study, export strategies of 131 California exporting manufacturers were examined. A factor analysis of 50 variables yielded five factors which were analyzed subsequently through multiple discriminant analysis. Two of the five factors, strategic planning and export strategies, were found to be meaningful in discriminating between small and large exporters.

5.4.44

Mesdag, Martin van (1987), "Winging it in Foreign Markets," *Harvard Business Review,* 65(1), January-February, 71-74.

Kellogg's cornflakes, Heineken beer, and Hero products sell like mad all over the world. The shot-in-the-dark marketing strategy—a seemingly sloppy, irresponsible, and decidely risky way to approach global markets—helps explain their success. This strategy doesn't take products into foreign markets with studied, country-by-country targeting. Nor does it resemble "global marketing." Instead, it's opportunistic. Companies merely take existing products from their home markets and give them a hard try in suitable foreign markets. This approach doesn't give marketers the license to be careless, and they can still alter their products lightly to meet foreign needs.

5.4.45

Michaels, Pavlos (1989), "General Export Trading Companies: A Tri-Country Study of Japan, Korea, and the United States," *Singapore Marketing Review,* Vol.4, 45-54.

When the export trading companies(ETCs) of Japan, Korea, and the United States are compared, the Japanese Sogo-shosha are found to be the most successful, followed by the Korean general trading companies (GTCs). The U.S. ETCs have not been successful. In fact U.S. business reponse to the ETC Act of 1982 has been poor and the act's impact has been slight. The differences in ETCs are deeply rooted in the specific cultural, societal, and business structures and values of the three countries. The article concludes that , while the operational ability of the Sogo-shosha is to be envied, it is doubtful that it could or should be copied indiscriminately. The U.S. experience is different. The GTC concept is country-specific and can only be adopted successfully as an extension of cultural norms, business practices, and historical experience for a country.

5.4.46

Mirus, Rolf and Bernard Yeung (1986), "Economic Incentives for Countertrade," *Journal of International Business Studies,* 17(3), Fall, 27-39.

Countertrade using standard economic theory is examined. The authors show that in many circumstances countertrade is a rational response to transaction costs, information asymmetry, moral hazard-agency problems, and other market imperfections. It also investigates countertrade into international business theories.

5.4.47

Neale, C. W. and David Shipley (1990), "Empirical Insights into British

Countertrade with Eastern Bloc Countries," *International Marketing Review,* 7(1), 15-31.

5.4.48

Nicholls, J.A.F., Marlene Lyn-Cook, and Sydney Roslow (1989), "Strategies for Export Marketing of Non-Traditional Products," *International Marketing Review,* 6(4), 58-72.

5.4.49

Palia, Aspy P. (1990), "Worldwide Network of Countertrade Services," *Industrial Marketing Management,* 19(1), Feburary, 69-76.

Faced with an increasing number of countertrade demands, marketing managers are required to accept a wide range of commodities in payment for the goods that they sell. Lacking the expertise to market these countertraded commodities, marketing managers seek the assistance of countertrade service organizations which provide a variety of services and specialize by product category and by geographic region served. Based on 1988 data, attention is given to the services offered, products handled, regions covered, and clients served by these companies. It is shown that the countertrade service industry has rapidly attained worldwide proportions. Ninety-three organizations providing countertrade services make up this industry.

5.4.50

Palia, Aspy P. and Charles F. Keown (1991), "Combating Parallel Importing: Views of US Exporters to the Asia-Pacific Region," *International Marketing Review,* 8(1), 47-56.

The extent of parallel importing encountered by US exporters using exclusive or sole agents in the Asia-Pacific region is investigated using data obtained via a mail survey of US exporters to Asia. About 29% of the exporters reported that their exclusive-sole agents were experiencing problems with parallel imports. Almost 41% of the respondents reported experiencing parallel distribution problems in the past. The strategy perceived to be most effective in minimizing parallel distribution was to refuse orders from nonappointed agents. Strategies considered as somewhat effective included price reductions, special promotional allowances, recognition of warranties only on products sold by the appointed agent, and specially labeled products.

5.4.51

Palmer, John D. (1985), "Consumer Service Industry Exports: New Attitudes and Concepts Needed for a Neglected Sector," *Columbia Journal of World Business,* 20(1), Spring, 69-74.

The fast food restaurant represents an industry that is neglected in international trade. This can be generalized to include most consumer services. However, American fast food chains have successfully expanded into international markets and the export of consumer services probably has higher growth potential than merchandise trade services. This sector of trade can no longer be ignored, for the implications from these trends will have an impact on the strategy of the firm and the trade policy of the U.S. in the future.

5.4.52

Piercy, Nigel (1983), "Export Marketing Management in Medium-Sized British Firms," *European Journal of Marketing,* 17(1), 48-65.

This study focuses on the export market strategy decision and the base for export competition in medium-sized firms, while taking the internationalization of the firm and its export objectives as important situational influence. The hypothesis on which this approach is founded is that decisions on export strategy and competition shape the operational policies which are possible. The issues that have been studied in the paper include: (1) internationalization and export objectives, (2) export market strategy, (3) export marketing information, (4) export competition, (5) export price discrimination and export pricing methods, and (6) export invoice currency strategy.

5.4.53

Rabino, Samuel and Kirit Shah (1987), "Countertrade and Penetration of LDC's Markets," *Columbia Journal of World Business,* 22(4), Winter, 31-37.

Countertrade can be utilized to complement export entry strategies, especially when dealing with less developed markets. A framework that models the interaction between an American high-technology vendor and a developing country leading to a countertrade agreement and technology transfer is presented.

5.4.54

Rao, C. P., M. Krishna Erramilli, and Gopala K. Ganesh (1990), "Impact of Domestic Recession on Export Marketing Behaviour," *International Marketing Review,* 7(2), 54-65.

Through conducting a mail survey of 185 US exporting firms, the authors intended to investigate how a firm's export marketing activities are affected by a recession. The findings suggest that recessions can have a significant impact on firms' export marketing activities. Some firms appear to intensify their exports in response to adversity in the domestic market due to a recession. These firms tend to employ marketing tactics, such as competitive pricing, that can stimulate export sales quickly without the need for long-term resource commitment. There is some tentative evidence that exporters increase their exports to areas of the world less affected by the recession. The results indicate that public and private export promotion programs are considered ineffective.

5.4.55

Reisman, Arnold, Duu-Cheng Fuh, and Gang Li (1988), "Achieving an Advantage with Countertrade," *Industrial Marketing Management,* 17(1), February, 55-63.

This study provides a taxonomy for classifying countertrade. The advantages to the trading partners depend on the respective levels of economic development in their home countries. Many transactions involve product bundling. The more commodities bundled together the wider are the quantity ranges within which a trade will be profitable to both sides, assuming that comparative advantage is enjoyed by the trading partners in their respective product lines. The principles for setting a corporate countertrade policy are similar to those for setting a price structure. Although the issues are generic, some specific examples are demonstrated to illustrate countertrade with the Peoples' Republic of China.

5.4.56

Reisman, Arnold, Raj Aggarwal, and Duu-Cheng Fuh (1989), "Seeking Out Profitable Countertrade Opportunities," *Industrial Marketing Management,* 18(1), February, 65-71.

A proactive approach for use by large and small enterprises to locate countertrade opportunities is presented. It is based on an analysis of the demand and supply of countertraded goods and on defining the likelihood of profitable countertrade and the concepts of market synergy. Suitable countertrade opportunities are most likely in the presence of the following: (1) excess capacity due to fluctuating demand conditions, (2) low marginal cost ratios, and (3) the ability to clearly segment customers at a sufficiently low cost. Countertrade also makes good sense if marketing synergy can be established between the goods acquired by way of the countertrade and the firm's existing lines. Countertrade is particularly effective in opening up new vistas at the input and output sides of a manufacturing process.

5.4.57

Samiee, Saeed (1990), "Strategic Considerations of the EC 1992 Plan for Small Exporters," *Business Horizons,* 33(2), March-April, 48-52.

The plan of the European Community (EC) to eliminate remaining internal barriers to trade is apt to influence the ability of small exporters to remain competitive in the EC. Personal interviews were conducted with division heads and officials of the Organization for Economic Cooperation & Development, General Agreement on Tariffs and Trade, and the European Conference of the Ministries of Transport. All officials interviewed felt that smaller firms with highly differentiated products will be able to effectively compete in the post-1992 EC. Small firms tend to use pricing policies that are indiscriminant with regard to host-country market conditions. Three forces will maintain status quo within the EC for the intermediate future: (1) Proposed changes will be implemented over a period of years; (2) Purchasing agents are not likely to change their behavior immediately; (3) There is a heterogeneous nature of management philosophy, backgrounds, and orientation in EC countries.

5.4.58

Schlegelmilch, Bodo B. (1986), "Controlling Country-Specific and Industry-Specific Influences on Export Behaviour" *European Journal of Marketing*, 20(2), 54-71.

An analysis of the determinants of differing export behavior of firms was attempted by controlling for country-specific and for industry-specific behavior. In 1982, a 4-part questionnaire containing 194 independent variables was sent to 1,500 managing directors of UK and German firms. The 310 replies showed a bias toward exporters as measured by the exporters to nonexporters ratio. A set of summary statistics was performed to obtain an indication of the distributional characteristics of the employed variables. The scope for data reduction was checked by a factor analysis. The main part of the research consisted of a stepwise discriminant analysis. Findings verified the hypothesis that country and industry differences influence the structure of the characteristics that distinguish between nonexporters and exporters.

5.4.59

Schroeder, Dean M. and Alan G. Robinson (1991), "America's Most Successful Export to Japan: Continuous Improvement Programs," *Sloan Management Review,* 32(3), Spring, 67-81.

Continuous improvement programs (CIP) were developed in the US long before they were introduced into Japan. CIPs unleash and utilize employee experience and creativity to improve both products and performance. Despite the long history and the benefits of such systems, few US companies have invested efforts to adopt them. Direct Japanese investment in the US, coupled with the desire to imitate successful Japanese competitors, has resulted in the widespread introduction of CIPs into US companies. Requirements for successful CIP management include: (1) improvements at first cause dislocation require time to be proven worthwhile; (2)operating practices that restrict the flow of ideas must be eliminated; and (3) employees must be continuously trained and developed.

5.4.60

Seifert, Bruce and John Ford (1989), " Are Exporting Firms Modifying Their Product, Pricing and Promotion Policies?" *International Marketing Review,* 6(6), 53-71.

Firms in the electrical machine tool builders, food processing equipment, and fluid power industries were surveyed concerning their export marketing policies, Except in promotion, most of these industrial firms follow a standardized marketing approach. Their export budgets are smaller than their domestic budgets. Also the firms indicated that they were only lukewarm about their overall export performance; those most satisfied with their export performance tend to be larger, more experienced in exporting, or spend equal or greater amounts on export promotion than on comparable domestic product line promotion.

5.4.61

Seringhaus, F. H. Rolf (1989), "Trade Missions in Exporting: State of the Art," *Management International Review,* 29(2), 5-16.

5.4.62

Sharkey, Thomas W., Jeen-Su Lim, and Ken I. Kim (1989), "Export Development and Perceived Export Barriers: An Empirical Analysis of Small Firms," *Management International Review,* 29(2), 33-40.

Decision makers' perceptions about export obstacles for firms at various stages of development are examined using data collected from small businesses via a mail survey. A total of 438 usable responses were received from US businesses. A factor analysis of questionnaire items provided five barrier factors that were consistent with prior research: governmental policy, procedural and technical complexity, contextual differences, perceived strategic limitations, and local competition. Analysis of variance is used for each of the five barrier factors across three stages of development: nonexporters, marginal exporters, and active exporters. Marginal exporters are found to perceive more barriers than active exporters in two out of five barrier classes, yet no difference is found between the barrier perceptions of marginal exporters and nonexporters.

5.4.63

Sullivan, Daniel and Alan Bauerschmidt(1988), "Common Factors Underlying Incentive to Export: Studies in the European Forest Products Industry Journal," *European Journal of Marketing,* 22(10), 41-55.

The consensus in the literature was used as a framework for integrating existing knowledge about attention-evoking factors relating to high export initiation in an attempt to determine whether there is a structure of relationships. The data used were gathered from managers in the European forest products industry, and they were generated through a questionnaire that asked the managers to indicate the importance of 30 potential incentives to export. A 5-point Likert scale was used that ranged from "not at all important" to "extremely important." Results support the contention of literature that incentives to export make up a multidimensional structure. In particular, two notions—the life-cycle concept and strategic versus tactical -provide insights instrumental to clarifying the complexity.

5.4.64

Sullivan, Daniel and Alan Bauerschmidt (1989), "Common Factors Underlying Barriers to Export: A Comparative Study in the European and U.S. Paper Industry," *Management International Review,* 29(2), 17-32.

A study was conducted to examine the characteristics of barriers to export. The data were collected during two research projects. One project obtained questionnaire responses from 117 US firms with active involvement in export, and the other obtained responses from 62 European firms. Analysis of the attitudes of managers in the US forest products industry showed a cluster of barriers to export that were linked to the international commitment of the firm, governmental trade policies, and market conditions. Factor analysis of the data collected from the European firms revealed both similarities and differences between European and US respondents. The European managers regarded export barriers as a challenge arising from firm-specific conditions, while the US respondents interpreted the barriers to export as the consequences of country-specific conditions.

5.4.65

Turnbull, Peter W. and G. F. Welham (1985), "The Characteristics of European Export Marketing Staff," *European Journal of Marketing,* 19(2), 31-41.

The authors propose that individual characteristics such as educational level and competence, together with attitudinal sets, are significant factors affecting the ease with which relationships can be initiated, developed, and maintained in export marketing. Attention is focused on the characteristics and quality of the individuals who are key to successful interaction. Three primary characteristics of individual marketers from Germany (64 marketers), France (95), Italy (60), Sweden (80), and the UK (108) are examined: (1) experience of relevant product technology and foreign country markets, (2) training and educational achievements, and (3) communication skills and foreign language ability. The evidence suggests that (1) the German marketers lead the rest by a large percentage in terms of experience in living and working abroad, (2) the UK marketers lead in terms of technical education qualifications, and (3) most marketers are not technically fluent in languages other than English.

5.4.66

Vernon-Wortzel Heidi, Lawrence H. Wortzel, and Shengliang Deng (1988), "Do Neophyte Exporters Understand Importers?" *Columbia Journal of World Business,* 23(4), Winter, 49-56.

This study identifies and analyzes the supply selection criteria and information sources US importers use. It then compares these criteria with perceptions of suppliers from the People's Republic of China and analyzes the differences between US importers' choices and PRC exporters' perceptions of importers' choices. While exporters' perceptions may be idiosyncratic to exporters from the PRC, they strongly reflect the PRC buyers' environment and organization culture. Thus, these results support the more general proposition that neophyte exporters' perceptions reflect their home country's business environment and culture.

5.4.67

Weigand, Robert E. (1989), "The Gray Market Comes to Japan," *Columbia Journal of World Business,* 24(3), Fall, 18-24.

The grey market may provide the greatest single hope that US consumer goods will win their way into Japan's markets. Unauthorized goods now reach Japan's consumers through parallel imports, reimports, mail order, and personal imports. Authorized channels counteract the mavericks by ignoring the matter, warning customers that they may be buying counterfeit products, pointing out product differences, narrowing the price differential, limiting the validity of a warranty to the country targeted for a product's sale and buying up unauthorized goods that leak into grey market channels. The lower value of the dollar and the Japanese government's apparent efforts to encourage imports suggest export opportunities for US business. Reasons for this include: (1) many Japanese now believe foreign products are about as good as domestic goods; (2) Japanese consumers are showing signs of Western rationality; and (3) many Japanese are unsure about trade liberalization.

5.4.68

Weigand, Robert E. (1991), "Parallel Import Channels—Options for Preserving Territorial Integrity," *Columbia Journal of World Business,* 26(1), Spring, 53-60.

Parallel importation or parallel marketing channels are often called gray marketing and are closely related to the practice of reimportation. The rise of gray market is due to three main factors, including exchange rate differences, the power of the discriminating monopolist, and opportunistic behavior by members of administered marketing channels. Reducing the price differentials between the authorized and gray market product is a powerful tool for reducing the attractiveness of the parallel import. Perhaps the most powerful reactive strategy available to the manufacturer is to terminate the opportunistic middleman.

5.4.69

Williamson, Nicholas C. (1984), "Export Management Companies: the Implications for Developing the American Export Trading Company," *International Marketing Review,* 1(4), Autumn/Winter, 24-39.

5.4.70

Williamson, Peter (1991), "Successful Strategies for Export," *Long Range Planning,* 24(1), February, 57-63.

Export strategies adopted by British, Japanese, and West German companies in entering the U.S. market are compared and analyzed. Japan has been the most successful exporter in aspects of market share, product differentiation, and brand awareness. The success can be attributed to Japanese long-term commitment to stable prices and heavy investment in marketing and distribution. British exporters may learn from the Japanese in their emphasis on push marketing. British and West German exporters have not capitalized on the importance of local distributors. West German exports have achieved relatively stable market shares by emphasizing their technological advantage and price sensitive segment. British exports' low market share, volatile price, and low brand loyalty may be due to their inadequate short-term strategy.

5.4.71

Wills, James, Laurence Jacobs, and Aspy Palia (1986), "Countertrade: the Asia-Pacific Dimension," *International Marketing Review,* 3(2), Summer, 20-27.

The Asia-Pacific region, one of the world's fastest growing markets is experiencing wide and growing use of countertrade. This paper explores some of the factors leading to increased use of countertrade deals in the Asia-Pacific market. Recent examples of countertrade transactions in the region are reviewed and the implications for management are explored.

5.4.72

Yaprak, Attila (1985), " A Empirical Study of the Differences Between Small Exporting and Non-Exporting U.S. Firms," *International Marketing Review,* 2(2), Summer, 72-83.

The research focus of this article is on exploring selected demographic, functional and behavioral characteristics of small-to-medium-sized exporting vs. non-exporting firms. While evaluating the findings from an empirical survey, the study comments on their congruence or incongruence with relevant previous research, and provides managerial and normative implications.

5.4.73

Yavas, Ugur, Secil Tuncalp, and S. Tamer Cavusgil (1987), "Assessments of Selected Foreign Suppliers by Saudi Importers: Implications for Exporters," *Journal of Business Research,* 15(3), 237-246.

A study was conducted to examine how importers in Saudi Arabia assess suppliers from four leading exporting countries: the US, Japan, the UK, and Taiwan. Personal interviews were conducted with 54 major importers in the Eastern Province of Saudi Arabia. Results indicated that Saudi importers evaluated Japanese suppliers in the most favorable way. Japanese companies ranked first on such dimensions as ease of placing order, advertising support, attractive styles and appearance, and provision of satisfactory repair and maintenance services. In addition, Japanese products were received well by both Saudis and expatriates. Suppliers from the US ranked 2nd behind the Japanese. The main disadvantages of US products were their high prices and the high transportation costs. However, US products were rated as having a high-quality image. The poorest overall image was attributed to Taiwanese suppliers.

5.5 Product, Branding, and Sourcing Strategies

5.5.1

Arnold, Ulli (1989), ''Global Sourcing—An Indispensable Element in Worldwide Competition,'' *Management International Review,* 29(4), 14-28.

Global sourcing involves globalization in two respects—the internationalization of purchasing activities and the adoption of a strategic orientation for all resource management. The goal of global sourcing is to utilize purchasing potential on the worldwide level. Global sourcing can be a critical factor in a variety of competitive strategies, such as: (1) supporting a global strategy by realizing economies of scale through materials inputs, (2) supporting a multinational strategy by developing potentials for differentiation and by having an active influence on quality standards, and (3) supporting a regionally limited strategy concerning the general improvement of input-output relations or preparing export activities by building up a strategic bridgehead in target markets. The efficiency of global sourcing primarily depends on whether the concept is introduced as a binding cognitive orientation.

5.5.2

Bello, Daniel C. and Lee D. Dahringer (1985), ''The Influence of Country and Product on Retailer Operating Practices: A Across National Comparison,'' *International Marketing Review,* 2(2), Summer, 42-52.

This study examines the extent to which retailer's country of origin and product assortment influence retailer operating practices. Although conventional wisdom suggests practices are likely to vary by country, universal aspects of the retailing task may lead to similarities in retailing practices for a given product, regardless of national setting. To empirically investigate whether country or product is the dominant influence in determining retailer behavior, the authors examine data on retailer activities in India and Africa.

5.5.3

Chan, Allan K. K. (1990), "Localization in International Branding: A Preliminary Investigation on Chinese Names of Foreign Brands in Hong Kong," *International Journal of Advertising,* 9(1), 81-91.

The process of brand localization is investigated. 261 localized Chinese brand names of foreign brands in Hong Kong were studied. These localized brand names were found to be of reasonable length, easily pronounceable, and containing either positive or neutral connotations by themselves. Viewing these localized brands in terms of translation from their original counterparts, most of them were found to be similar in length to their originals, reading similarly in Cantonese to the original names' pronunciation, and containing dissimilar connotations to those of the original names. Contextualization in international branding has been practiced as exhibited in the creation of Chinese brand names in terms of physical, vocalized, and connotative appearance.

5.5.4

Cho, Kang Rae (1990), "The Role of Product-Specific Factors in Intra-Firm Trade of U.S. Manufacturing Multinational Corporations," *Journal of International Business Studies,* 21(2), 319-330.

This study examines the role of major product-specific factors in the product patterns of intrafirm trade of US manufacturing multinational corporations. Intrafirm trade is defined as the international exchange of goods and services among affiliated firms. Using pooled time series, cross-sectional regression analysis of nineteen products, it is found that the technology intensity of a product has a strong positive effect on the propensity of the product to intrafirm trade. In contrast, the economies-of-scale level seems to have a constraining effect on the propensity. The vertical integration intensity and the international production intensity are found to have no significant bearings on the propensity. This study results in no new evidence regarding the nature of the relationship between a product's intrafirm trade dispensity and its international production intensity.

5.5.5

Czinkota, Michael and Masaaki Kotabe (1990), "Product Development the Japanese Way," *Journal of Business Strategy,* 11(6), November-December, 31-36.

During the post-World War II period, Japanese companies relied heavily on licensed US and European technology for product development. Continued major investment in research and development earmarked for product innovation heralded the technological maturation within Japan's firms, where the quality and productivity levels began to match or even surpass those of the original licensor. Because of its incrementalist product development approach, Japanese firms have been able to increase the speed of new product introductions, meet the competitive demands of a rapidly changing marketplace, and capture market share. Japanese firms are willing to take the progress achieved through incrementalism and develop a new market approach around it. They also prefer down-to-earth methods of information gathering for market research.

5.5.6

Eroglu, Sevgin A. and Karen A. Machleit (1989), "Effects of Individual and Product-specific Variables on Utilizing Country of Origin as a Product Quality Cue," *International Marketing Review,* 6(6), 27-41.

This research advances the country of origin research stream by addressing some of the theoretical and methodological issues given as limitations in past studies. A conceptual model based on the cue paradigm was developed to investigate the relative impact of country of origin as a quality indicator in a causal framework. Results indicate that the country of origin cue is indeed a significant indicator of product quality; however, its relative effect varies by product category as well as by certain individual and product variables.

5.5.7

Ghoshal, Sumantra (1988), "Creation, Adoption, and Diffusion of Innovations by Subsidiaries of Multinational Corporations," *Journal of International Business Studies,* 19(3), Fall, 365-388.

This article presents findings of a multiphased and multi-method study on the organizational attributes that facilitate creation, adoption, and diffusion of innovations by subsidiaries of multinational companies.

5.5.8

Gillespie, Kate and Dana Alden (1989), "Consumer Product Export Opportunities to Liberalizing LDCs: A Life-Cycle Approach," *Journal of International Business Studies,* 20(1), Spring, 93-112.

5.5.9

Globerman, Steven (1988), "Addressing International Product Piracy," *Journal of International Business Studies,* 19(3), Fall, 497-504.

The economic consequences of international product counterfeiting are reviewed. It cautions that while such piracy has net costs, widespread retaliation through trade protectionism could also prove costly. It recommends a policy approach that facilitates "private" protection of property rights.

5.5.10

Hill, John S. and William L. James (1991), "Product and Promotion Transfers in Consumer Goods Multinationals," *International Marketing Review,* 8(2), 6-17.

This article sheds light on MNC product transfers to subsidiaries—whether from the U.S. or from third party markets—and on promotion transfers. Research findings indicate that consumer goods subsidiaries have product mixes with heavy U.S. orientations, but that this orientation diminishes over time. Promotion synergies are also shown to decrease with time. Overall, this research confirms the Levitt thesis that U.S. products can in many cases be globalized, and that MNCs perceive inter-market similarities to be more important than differences in their formulating of international product strategies.

5.5.11

Johansson, Johny K. (1989), "Determinants and Effects of the Use of "Made In" Labels," *International Marketing Review,* 6(1), Spring, 47-58.

Selected empirical findings on the effects of a product's "made-in" label are integrated with theoretical developments in consumer information processing and the economics of consumer search. The result is an internally consistent theory of how country-of-origin effects vary across situations, individuals and products. The new perspective explains why country stereotyping influences decisions more among well-informed buyers and dismisses the idea that country-of-origin cues are necessarily misleading or bad. It also generates predictions of when country-of-origin effects are greater and when they are smaller.

5.5.12

Kotabe, Masaaki and Glenn S. Omura (1989), "Sourcing Strategies of European and Japanese Multinationals: A Comparison," *Journal of International Business Studies,* 20(1), Spring, 113-129.

Based on a typology of sourcing strategies, this study identifies various sourcing patterns adopted by European and Japanese multinational manufacturing firms in serving the U.S. market. The study has found that the product's market performance is not at all related to its life-cycle stage in world trade or to production location, but is positively related to the internal components sourcing and negatively related to the product adaptation. The findings strongly support Levitt's call for a global product.

5.5.13

Kotabe, Masaaki (1990), "Corporate Product Policy and Innovative Behavior of European and Japanese Multinationals: An Empirical Investigation," *Journal of Marketing,* 54(2), April, 19-33.

The author empirically examines the product policies of European and Japanese multinational firms in relation to product and process innovations. He also investigates linkages between corporate product policy and manufacturing strategy and their implications for product and process innovations in an era of global competition. These foreign multinational firms, in particular the Japanese firms, increasingly stress the simultaneous strategic importance of product and process innovations. Findings indicate that Levitt's argument for the development of a globally acceptable product has gained momentum among European and Japanese multinational firms that lead in product and process innovations. In a marketing context, it has become important for them to expand commonalities across national boundaries rather than focusing on customer differences based on nationalities.

5.5.14

Mullor-Sebastian, Alicia (1983), "The Product Life Cycle Theory: Empirical Evidence," *Journal of International Business Studies,* 14(3), Winter, 95-105.

This paper presents three empirical tests of the product life cycle theory based on U.S. trade data and on a relatively new data series providing information about a larger number of products and at a lower level of aggregation than the data used previously. The results of the tests strongly support the hypothesis that industrial product groups behave in the manner predicted by the product life cycle theory on world markets. In the case of individual products, however, the results provide less support for the theory. The policy implication is that development strategies should rely on industrial sectors rather than on individual commodities.

5.5.15

Narasimhan, Ram and Joseph R. Carter (1990), "Organisation, Communication and Co-Ordination of International Sourcing," *International Marketing Review,* 7(2), 6-20.

The materials management structure of an organization affects materials acquisition and distribution activities of a company's international operations. There are three major classifications of organizational structure for materials management: centralized, decentralized, and matrix. Each of these forms can be further segmented by product, geography, or both. The particular organizational structure that will work best is contingent on the firm, product characteristics, the sourcing environment, and other characteristics. The matrix organizational structure is more likely to flourish under three conditions: (1) leverage is needed to deal with a few powerful suppliers, (2) higher volumes of strategically important items are sourced internationally, and (3) the purchased items are nonsophisticated.

5.5.16

Onkvisit, Sak and John J. Shaw (1983), "An Examination of the International

Product Life Cycle and Its Application within Marketing," *Columbia Journal of World Business,* 18(3), Fall, 73-79.

The international product life cycle is a relatively unknown and often overlooked concept. The authors argue that it can be a valuable tool for multinational companies to use for marketing new products abroad.

5.5.17

Onkvisit, Sak and John J. Shaw (1989), "The International Dimension of Branding: Strategic Considerations and Decisions," *International Marketing Review,* 6(3), 22-34.

The strategic, legal, and research implications of trademark decisions in an international context are examined. The focus of the investigation is on the strengths and limitations of each branding strategy. The legal dimension of international branding, a topic usually ignored in the marketing literature, is also covered.

5.5.18

Pitcher, A. E. (1985), "The Role of Branding in International Advertising," *International Journal of Advertising,* 4(3), 241-246.

As international markets become more homogeneous, prospects for world branding are increasing. A brand, which represents the set of beliefs consumers hold about a product's benefits and risks, influences whether the product will be considered for purchase. For a brand to succeed internationally, it must be characterized by a commonality of favorable consumer beliefs and expectations across countries and cultures. Implementation of an effective world branding strategy will depend on: (1) wide product availability, possibly through common distribution channels, (2) the ability to compete with local brands, (3) wide existence of supportive consumer usage segments, (4) the ability to apply common advertising strategy across markets, (5) possession of a distinctive advertising property, such as a logo or slogan, that is applicable for worldwide marketing, and (6) development of a sophisticated organizational structure capable of supporting world brand execution.

5.5.19

Poh, Lai Yuen (1987), "Product Life Cycle and Export Competitiveness of the UK Electronics Industry (1970-1979), " *European Journal of Marketing,* 21(7), 28-37.

Advanced industrial countries generally are regarded as possessing a comparative advantage and being export competitive in "new" and "growth" products. This hypothesis was tested by plotting a logistical growth curve using data from the electronics industry. The analysis assumed a 3-stage product life cycle—new, growth, and maturity. Findings that supported the hypothesis included: (1) The electronics industry in the UK is highly export competitive. (2) Industrial sectors in the growth state were the best performers. (3) A link exists between export competitiveness and the growth stage.

5.5.20

Ronkainen, Ilkka A. (1983), "Product-Development Processes in the Multinational Firm," *International Marketing Review,* 1(2), Winter, 57-65.

This research focuses on the product-development process and ways to make it multinational in scope. Data collected by interview from four industrial companies are used to discuss the means and objectives of multinational program management.

5.5.21

Rosen, Barry Nathan, Jean J. Boddewyn and Ernst A. Louis (1989), "U.S. Brands Abroad: An Empirical Study of Global Branding," *International Marketing Review,* 6(1), Spring, 7-19.

Based on a survey of U.S. brand managers of consumer products, this study found that while some 66% of the responding brands are used abroad and most are internationally standardized, approximately 80% of sales still come from the U.S. market. Overseas, U.S. brands generate most of their sales in culturally similar markets, specifically Canada and the United Kingdom.

5.5.22

Still, Richard R. and John S. Hill (1985), "Multinational Product Planning: A Meta-Market Analysis," *International Marketing Review,* 2(1), Spring, 54-58.

The concept of meta-markets has been around a long time, with numerous references to the European market, the South American market and so on. This article examines MNC consumer product transfers into four OECD-recognized meta-markets. It is demonstrated that in some cases regional cultures affect MNC product adaptation strategies.

5.5.23

Takada, Hirokazu and Dipak Jain (1991), "Cross-National Analysis of Diffusion of Consumer Durable Goods in Pacific Rim Countries," *Journal of Marketing,* 55(2), April, 48-54.

The Bass new product growth model is used for cross-national analysis of diffusion processes of durable goods in four major Pacific Rim countries including the US, Japan, the Republic of Korea, and Taiwan. The estimated coefficients are used to test the hypotheses on country-specific effects and on lead- and lag-time effects on the diffusion rates of consumer durable goods in these countries. The result shows that the model fits the data on diffusion of consumer goods remarkably well in all of the countries and it predicts the time to peak and peak sales accurately. The empirical results show that the rate of adoption in countries characterized by high context culture is higher than that in countries with low context culture.

5.5.24

Thorelli, Hans B., Jeen-Su Lim and Jongsuk Ye (1989), "Relative Importance of Country of Origin, Warranty, and Retail Store Image on Product Evaluations," *International Marketing Review,* 6(1), Spring, 35-46.

This research investigates the relative importance of country of origin, product warranty, and retail store image on consumers' product quality perception, overall attitude toward the product, and purchase intentions. A 2x2x2 full factorial design with two levels of country of origin, warranty and retail store image is utilized. ANOVA results show that country of origin and warranty cues have significant impacts on the three dependent measures. The interaction effects of all three independent variables are significant for the quality perception and overall attitude towards the product but are not significant for the purchase intentions. In addition excellent warranty terms combined with store reputation has a greater impact on the dependent variables than the country-of-origin cue.

5.5.25

Yavas, Ugur and Guven Alpay (1986), "Does an Exporting Nation Enjoy the Same Cross-National Commercial Image?" *International Journal of Advertising,* 5(2), 109-119.

Prevailing consumer attitudes toward made-in US, Japan, Germany, Italy, UK, and Taiwan labels in Bahrain and Saudi Arabia were examined. A structured questionnaire was administered to 59 Bahraini students attending the Gulf Polytechnic Institute and 94 Saudi students attending the University of Petroleum and Minerals. Japan attained the highest rating on 10 of 14 attributes in both samples. Made-in US label ratings closely followed those of the Japanese labels. Both groups had unfavorable reactions to made-in Taiwan labels. When a test statistic was applied to the data, it was found that the two groups agreed in their assessments. This finding supported the conjecture that cultural proximity leads to similar perceptions of made-in labels and suggested that multinational marketers in the Gulf countries can employ standardized campaigns fruitfully.

5.6 *Pricing Strategies*

5.6.1

Al-Eryani, Mohammad F., Pervaiz Alam, and Syed H. Akhter (1990), "Transfer Pricing Determinants of U.S. Multinationals," *Journal of International Business Studies,* 21(3), 409-425.

The influence of environmental and firm-specific variables on the selection of international transfer pricing strategies is examined using data obtained from 164 multinational enterprises by means of a questionnaire. The responses were analyzed by performing factor analysis and constructing a Probit model. The findings show that the legal and size variables are significantly associated with the use of market-based transfer pricing strategies. These results suggest that legal considerations, such as compliance with tax and custom regulations, are influential in the use of market-based transfer pricing. Economic restrictions, such as exchange controls and price controls, political-social conditions, and the extent of economic development in host countries are unimportant or secondary determinants of a market-based transfer pricing strategy. The results indicate that US multinationals closely abide by the US tax regulations.

5.6.2

Cavusgil, S. Tamer (1988), "Unraveling the Mystique of Export Pricing," *Business Horizons,* 31(3), May-June, 54-63.

Export pricing for U.S. firms is a complex issue and simple decision rules often are inadequate due to the large number of variables affecting international pricing decisions. In order to provide a better understanding of export pricing issues and identify propositions for further testing, a study was conducted using personal interviews with executives at 24 Midwestern companies. From the study the author identifies six variables which influence export pricing: (1) the nature of the product or industry, (2) the location of the production facility, (3) the system of distribution, (4) the location and environment of foreign market, (5) US government regulations, and (6) the attitude of the firm's management. Approaches to pricing used by firms include the rigid cost-plus, flexible cost-plus, or dynamic incremental strategies. The article also describes a multi-step decision framework for export pricing.

5.6.3

Choi, Jongmoo Jay (1986), "A Model of Firm Valuation With Exchange Exposure," *Journal of International Business Studies,* 17(2), 153-160.

The issue of how the firm's exposure to exchange rate uncertainty influences its valuation is analyzed. The author identifies the variables affecting the firm's economic and accounting exchange exposure as well as the cost of capital in a formal unified model.

5.6.4

Demirag, Istemi S. (1988), "Assessing Foreign Subsidiary Performance: the Currency Choice of U.K. MNCs," *Journal of International Business Studies,* 19(2), Summer, 257-275.

The author studies the extent of foreign currency and/or parent company currency financial measures used by 105 U.K-based MNCs in the process of evaluating foreign subsidiary operations and their managers' performance.

5.6.5

Drumm, Hans Juergen (1983), "Transfer Pricing in the International Firm," *Management International Review,* 23(4), 32-43.

The high number of unsolved theoretical problems of transfer pricing in the international firm seems to be reduced only by the standardization approaches of the Organization for Economic Cooperation & Development (OECD) model of double taxation agreements. The recent restrictive prescriptions to transfer pricing given by the OECD model and the German Minister of Finance and the theoretical solutions for transfer pricing in national firms have provided the basis for examination of transfer pricing. The purposes of optimal allocation and a fair distribution of profits have failed in the international firm if they follow the theoretically based rules for transfer pricing; this is due to the profit relocating effects of some transfer price types and the restrictive, paradigmatic rules of the OECD model. In international firms, allocation decisions must be made without regard for transfer prices.

5.6.6

Johansson, Johny K. and Gary Erickson (1985), "Price-Quality Relationship and Trade Barriers," *International Marketing Review,* 2(3), Autumn, 52-63.

This article presents some rather complicated empirical work employing econometric modelling to demonstrate the validity of a quite simple proposition: the use of a product's price as an indicator of quality is only justified when the market is free of trade barriers and other imperfections. It demonstrates that individuals are well aware of this fact, making use of price as a quality indicator only where trade barriers have not distorted prices. Thus, it is not possible to make very strong generalizations about the existence of a universal price quality relationship.

5.6.7

Mathur, Ike and David Loy (1984), "The Use of Foreign Currency Futures to Reduce Exchange Rate Risk," *International Marketing Review,* 1(3), Spring/ Summer, 58-65.

5.6.8

Srinivasan, Venkat and Yong H. Kim (1986), "Payments Netting in International Cash Management: a Network Optimization Approach," *Journal of International Business Studies,* 17(2), Summer, 1-20.

5.6.9

Thach, Sharon V. and Catherine N. Axinn (1991), "Pricing and Financing Practices of Industrial Exporting Firms," *International Marketing Review,* 8(1), 32-46.

Relationship between commitment to exporting and level of export achievement is examined through a mail survey of senior executives at machine tool manufacturing companies in Ontario and Michigan. The results seem to support the existence of a relationship between commitment and success. However, the relationship between specific marketing practices and success is not supported by the data. Successful exporters did not differ from less successful exporters with respect to any pricing or financing practice. Commitment was found to have some influence on relationships between country of origin and financing practices, and financing practices and success. Exporters from Canada were shown to use pricing strategy more competitively and seemed to use government incentives and credit supports more than US exporters.

5.7 Channels of Distribution and Logistics

5.7.1

Alawi, Hussein M.A. (1986), "Saudi Arabia: Making Sense of Self-Service," *International Marketing Review,* 3(1), Spring, 21-38.

Self-service food stores are a new emerging form of retail technology in Saudi Arabia. By focusing on relevant institutional, planning and operational dimensions, this study describes and analyzes the process by which this form of food retailing was adopted. Data were collected from 96 stores located in three metropolitan areas of the Kingdom, and the results suggest that the sudden proliferation of these stores during the past decade was characterized by the lack of rational planning, short-term decision making orientation, and limited concern for promotional activities.

5.7.2

Alexander, Nicholas (1990), "Retailers and International Markets: Motives for Expansion," *International Marketing Review,* 7(4), 75-85.

International operations and specific attitudes to the European internal market planned for 1992 are examined. Twenty-six large UK retailers with retail interests outside the UK were surveyed. The chief executives of the companies were mailed questionnaires, with 80 usable responses obtained. The results show that the UK multinational retailer places a greater emphasis on opportunities in new markets than on the lack of opportunities in home markets. The findings emphasize positive rather than negative motivations for international expansion. UK retailers in the 1980s were eager to seek new opportunities where they occurred, not because other markets were closing to them.

5.7.3

Anderson, Cristina P. and Patriya S. Tansuhaj (1990), "Exploring Third World Export Distribution Strategies," *Advances in International Marketing,* Vol.4, 141-158.

Export distribution strategies used by companies in less developed countries are examined by taking a close look at the Philippines' furniture industry. The stage of export development is identified and the importance of the distribution function in their export efforts is explored. Although distribution is considered important among firms, there is an obvious lack of channel planning and strategy. Current support by the Philippines' Government is evaluated through a comparison of governmental support provided by a successful newly developed country, Taiwan. Both government support and improved distribution strategy are needed in order for a firm in a less developed country to successfully compete in the international marketplace.

5.7.4

Anderson, Erin and Anne T. Coughlan (1987), "International Market Entry and Expansion via Independent or Integrated Channels of Distribution," *Journal of Marketing,* 51(1), January, 71-82.

The authors explore the issue of downstream vertical integration through an emprical investigation of distribution channel choice in foreign markets by U.S. semiconductor companies. Using original interview data, they develop scales to measure key variables. With these measures they build a logistic regression model of what factors affect the form of the distribution channel chosen in various foreign markets. The results indicate that integration is associated with the degree of transaction specificity of assets in the distribution function and whether or not the product being introduced is highly differentiated. There is evidence that the product will be sold through whatever channel is already in place, if any. Further, American firms seem more likely to integrate the distribution channel in highly developed industrialized countries than in Japan and Southeast Asia.

5.7.5

Buckley, Peter J., C.L. Pass, Kate Prescott (1990), "Foreign Market Servicing by Multinationals: An Integrated Treatment," *International Marketing Review,* 7(4), 25-40.

Four propositions are presented concerning the integration of different approaches to the foreign market servicing strategies of multinational firms. First, the whole channel must be considered in making market servicing decisions. Second, when a part of the channel is externalized, activities that are downstream will not be internalized. Third, once part of a channel is located abroad, downstream activities will tend to be located abroad. Fourth, the control and monitoring of information is vital to the success of international channel management. Agents' functions, promotion, and transport traverse the integrated model and feed directly into the strategic decisions facing firms at the different levels of the channel. The categorization of foreign market servicing strategies into exporting, licensing, and foreign investment ignores the crucial role of channel management.

5.7.6

Burt, Steven (1989), "Trends and Management Issues in European Retailing," *International Journal of Retailing*, 4(4), 92-97.

Changes in the European consumer market have played a role in shaping the retail industry by their implications for consumer activity. Retailers are particularly vulnerable to consumer change as the final stages in the distribution channel. The retail response to this turbulent environment has increasingly involved elements of the strategic planning process, as the benefits of managing, rather than reacting, are appreciated. In their search for growth, retailers have pursued strategies involving diversification, product development, internationalization, and market penetration. The size and complexity of major European retailers raise fundamental issues for the management of these corporations. Investment in people and in developing their skills is necessary if new management systems are to be developed.

5.7.7

Carman, James M. (1990), "A Cross-National Comparison of Relations in Automobile Channels of Distribution," *Advances in International Marketing*, Vol.4, 1-32.

A comparative study of automobile channels of distribution was conducted in California and Norway in order to assess the impact of country culture, corporate culture, market environment, the distribution system, and interorganizational relations on opportunism, conflict and satisfaction. While there are many similarities, U.S. dealers appear to get their conflict out in the open and are more satisfied with their channel relationships. Norwegian dealers are less litigious but end up with frustrations and lower satisfaction.

5.7.8

Cavusgil, S. Tamer and Ugur Yavas (1987), "Supplier Selection in International Markets: A Study of Saudi Importers," *Industrial Marketing and Purchasing*, 2(2), 19-28.

Major importing distributors in Saudi Arabia were interviewed to investigate the relative importance of choice criteria that these importers adopted when making international supplier selection decisions. The importers were asked to rate the importance of 18 supplier selection criteria. Factor analysis reveals six underlying dimensions. These dimensions are core supplier benefits, preference by local customers, expatriate appeal, support services, price, and commercial risk. These six account for 68% of the variation in responses. It is shown that the major concern in the minds of the Saudi importers was the local market appeal of the imported products. Findings confirm the importance attached by Saudi importers to core supplier benefits, such as warranties, timely delivery, favorable transportation terms, and after-sales service.

5.7.9

Cavusgil, S. Tamer (1990), ''The Importance of Distributor Training at Caterpillar,'' *Industrial Marketing Management,* 19(1), February, 1-9.

Independent dealers play an especially critical role in international channels where the manufacturer-dealer partnership becomes essential. Using Caterpillar as a case study the importance of dealer training by the manufacturer was examined. In a comprehensive discussion of training issues, the following reasons were given for providing dealer support: better morale and control, increased sales, increased ability to stay ahead of the competition, and enhanced competitiveness in a changing marketplace. In addition, insights from the experience of Caterpillar in implementing its Sales Team Development System were presented. Caterpillar's customer offering extended beyond the equipment to include value-added benefits through quality service. The company broke out of the web of competition by strengthening its distribution networks and differentiating its product to include such customer services as parts availability and maintenance.

5.7.10

Czinkota, Michael R. (1985), ''Distribution of Consumer Products in Japan,'' *International Marketing Review,* 2(3), Autumn, 39-51.

This article examines the structure of the Japanese distribution channels for consumer products. It highlights the unique characteristics of the distribution process on both the wholesale and retail levels and shows how historical factors have contributed to these developments. Based on this information, recommendations are made to the importer of consumer products into Japan in order to aid in successful market penetration.

5.7.11

Czinkota, Michael R. (1985), ''Distribution in Japan: Problems and Changes,'' *Columbia Journal of World Business,* 20(3), Fall, 65-71.

The Japanese distribution system is frequently characterized as the major non-tariff barrier to imports. This article provides an overview of the existing distribution system in Japan and analyzes its effect on imports. Subsequently, the changes taking place in the system are highlighted and suggestions are made on how importers can take advantage of these changes in order to successfully penetrate the Japanese market.

5.7.12

Frazier, Gary L. and Sudhir H. Kale (1989), "Manufacturer—Distributor Relationships: A Sellers' versus Buyers' Market Perspective," *International Marketing Review,* 6(6), 7-26.

A conceptual framework is designed to explain how the initiation, implementation, and review of manufacturer-distributor relationships are likely to vary, based on whether such relationships take place in buyers' markets in developed countries or in sellers' markets in developing countries. Several cultural and structural dimensions of markets in developing countries also play an important role in the conceptual framework.

5.7.13

Habib, Ghazi M. and John J. Burnett (1989), "An Assessment of Channel Behavior in an Alternative Structural Arrangement: the International Joint Venture," *International Marketing Review,* 6(3), 7-21.

This article tests a number of channel behavior hypotheses in a unique structural arrangement—the joint venture. The results indicate that goal disparity is a significant predictor of conflict and that perceived conflict is related to member satisfaction, manifest conflict, and desire for change.

5.7.14

Marr, Morman E. (1984), "The Impact of Customer Service in International Markets," *International Marketing Review,* 1(4), Autumn/Winter, 17-23.

In the world of physical distribution the identification of customer needs and the measurement of their relative importance has in the past been ignored. This paper investigates this theme and concludes it is of paramount importance for would-be suppliers to obtain the view-points of their prospective customers.

5.7.15

Marr, Norman E. (1987), "Understanding Customer Service for Increased Competitiveness," *International Marketing Review,* 4(3), Summer, 45-53.

Many companies in the UK have been forced to export to survive. A large number of such companies have failed due to their lack of understanding about the customer service requirements of overseas customers. Understanding the relative influence of each of the components of customer service, a manufacturer will be able to develop a service package which will maximize customer satisfaction, thus giving as near as possible optimum use of limited resources. The procedures detailed in this article will enable marketers to benefit from understanding the needs of individual market segments.

5.7.16

Ramaseshan, B. and Leyland F. Pitt (1990), "Major Industrial Distribution Issues Facing Managers in Australia," *Industrial Marketing Management,* 19(3), August, 225-234.

A study of the industrial marketing managers of Australian organizations in the electronics, chemical, and mining equipment industries was conducted in order to determine the most critical distribution issues facing these managers over the next 3-5 years. The top ten issues were identified as: (1) inventory management and control, (2) an understanding by everyone in the organization of distribution's importance to customer service, (3) the effective use of computers in distribution to attain competitive advantage, (4) the recruitment and development of distribution personnel, (5) the handling, transportation, and storage of hazardous materials, (6) the minimization of distribution costs, (7) improved distribution planning, (8) the selection of distribution channels, (9) increased understanding of the role of distribution by top management, and (10) the integration of distribution with other marketing mix variables.

5.7.17

Ross, Randolph E. (1983), "Understanding the Japanese Distribution System: An Explanatory Framework," *European Journal of Marketing,* 17(1), 5-13.

The nature of the Japanese distribution system has been noted as a major problem area for the foreign producer seeking to penetrate the Japanese market. This study is an attempt to identify the nature of the problems faced by the foreign suppliers in selecting the appropriate local representatives, in gaining access to the relevant market segments, and in managing to compete successfully once entry to the market has been gained. The results reported in this article arise from structured interviews with the senior executives of 30 major firms now operating in Japan as well as with the commercial staffs in the Canadian and American embassies.

5.7.18

Rosson, Philip J. and David Ford (1982), "Manufacturer-Overseas Distributor Relations and Export Performance," *Journal of International Business Studies,* 13(2), Fall, 57-72.

The export arrangement which makes use of overseas distributors is examined in this article. Although this method is important for many manufacturers operating in foreign markets there are reservations about the performance levels that are achieved under such arrangements. It is suggested that there is an important link between the performance level achieved and the very nature of the relationship that exists between the manufacturer and overseas distributor. The authors also assert that the nature of the manufacturer-overseas distributor relationship is associated with certain characteristics of the participating companies; namely, their stake in the relationship, their experience, and their uncertainty surrounding the relationship.

5.7.19

Seifert, Bruce and John Ford (1989), "Export Distribution Channels," *Columbia Journal of World Business*, 24(2), 15-22.

In order to determine which distribution channels firms were using, a survey was sent to exporting firms in the electrical, machine tool builders, food equipment, and fluid power industries. The respondents were asked to choose among nineteen different distribution channels. An analysis of variance was run to determine whether there were any product line, firm, or industry characteristics that were linked to the overall satisfaction rating for the distribution system. The distribution channels most often used were sales representatives and export distributors. The respondents appeared satisfied with their overall distribution system but indicated some relative dissatisfaction with trading companies. The one firm variable that was positively linked to overall satisfaction with the export distribution system was the length of time the firm had been exporting. The results imply that firms that export industrial goods use distribution channel members identical to those used at home.

5.7.20

Seto, Hiroaki (1985), "A Comparative Study of Manufacturers' Sales Subsidiaries and Manufacturers' Sales Finance Subsidiaries in the UK, USA, Canada and Japan," *European Journal of Marketing*, 19(3), 41-47.

Manufacturers in the UK, US, and Canada were surveyed using a mailed questionnaire to study the roles and purposes of manufacturers' sales subsidiaries (MSS) and manufacturers' sales finance subsidiaries (MSFS) in different countries. The results were compared with quantitative data from Japanese manufacturers. From the marketing perspective, common purposes and roles of MSS are observed, but from the financial perspective, only Japanese manufacturers seek to produce sufficient cash flow to generate a high growth rate. Recent Japanese MSFS seek to release working capital quickly by financing money capital. British MSFS differ in management from those in Japan and the US.

5.7.21

Shipley, David D. (1984), "Selection and Motivation of Distribution Intermediaries," *Industrial Marketing Management*, 13(4), October, 249-256.

This article reviews factors requiring the application of effective selection and motivation criteria when using independent distributors. Data were drawn from a sample of 105 US and 108 UK manufacturing companies. Substantial similarity was found between companies in the two countries. The most widely selected criteria were: (1) market knowledge, (2) market coverage, and (3) salesforce management. All of these criteria bore directly on their ability to improve manufacturers' sales performance. Earlier findings suggested that intermediaries are motivated by manufacturers who provide them with attractive remuneration, physical support, and effective 2-way communication. Many of the respondents to the current survey offer these kinds of inducements and thus should be able to enjoy their intermediaries' commitment.

5.7.22

Stock, James R. and Douglas M. Lambert (1983), "Physical Distribution Management In International Marketing," *International Marketing Review*, 1(1), Autumn, 28-41.

The international physical distribution environment and channel of distribution strategies are analyzed. Management of the export shipment and physical distribution activities is also discussed.

5.8 Promotion and Advertising Strategies

5.8.1

Belk, Russell W. and Richard W. Pollay (1985), "Materialism and Status Appeals in Japanese and U.S. Print Advertising," *International Marketing Review*, 2(4), Winter, 38-47.

Content analyses of U.S. and Japanese magazine advertisements featuring products and services in a home setting reveal several significant differences over time and support hypotheses based on comparative cultural values and economic conditions. As expected, recent Japanese advertising has increasingly emphasized status to a much greater degree than recent U.S. advertising, and recent U.S. advertising has continued to emphasize personal efficacy to a much greater degree than does Japanese advertising. Both cultures are found to use materialistic themes in their advertisement.

5.8.2

Boddewyn, Jean J. and Monica Leardi (1989), "Sales Promotions: Practice, Regulation and Self-Regulation Around the World," *International Journal of Advertising*, 8(4), 363-374.

Many sales promotion techniques are controlled via industry codes, government regulations, and media acceptance rules. In 1987, the International Advertising Association conducted an international survey of these controls. Thirty-six countries answered, and half of them were developed nations. The use of premiums, gifts and competitions has been debated in light of their impact upon trade competition, consumer protection, and the general public interest. Unconditional gifts are least regulated because they are usually considered as a legitimate way of encouraging people to try a new product. Major arguments for and against premiums include: stimulation of competition, consumers benefiting directly, and diverting the interest of the consumer away from the main item. Major findings of the survey included: (1) All 36 countries forbid the false or misleading presentations of sales promotions. (2) The US and the UK are the most favorable to sales promotions. (3) Most developed countries strictly regulate sales promotions in order to prevent abuses. (4) Price reductions are by far the most popular sales promotions.

5.8.3

Clemens, John (1987), "Television Advertising in Europe: The Emerging Opportunities," *Columbia Journal of World Business,* 22(3), Fall, 35-41.

This study analyzes the current market for television advertising in Europe and predicts how it will change and grow over the next decade. The research also examines the implications for international marketers, and suggests how they can effectively organize to take advantage of the coming explosion in television advertising availability.

5.8.4

Foxman, Ellen R., Patriya S. Tansuhaj and John K. Wong (1988), "Evaluating Cross-National Sales Promotion Strategy: An Audit Approach," *International Marketing Review,* 5(4), Winter, 7-15.

Sales promotion is an important element of marketing communication strategy which accounts for more promotional expenditures than advertising in some countries. However, sales promotion has been generally ignored by researchers. This article briefly reviews the criteria used in the U.S. to evaluate sales promotions and these criteria are found inadequate to guide the formulation of sales promotion internationally. Environmental sensitivity factors are identified which are over-looked in domestic sales promotions and an audit approach to planning and evaluating cross-national sales promotion strategy is presented.

5.8.5

Head, David (1988), "Advertising Slogans and the 'Made-In' Concept," *International Journal of Advertising,* 7(3), 237-252.

An important part of modern international advertising is the use of verbal allusion to a product's country of origin as a selling point. The "made-in" concept has been established as one of the clearly identifiable strategies employed by many companies. However, opinion is divided regarding the importance of designation of origin as a selling point. With reference to slogans used in European ads, this article identifies the main strategies used in deployment of the made-in concept. They include an appeal to the national pride of the reader and the reputation enjoyed by certain countries for certain products. It is suggested that advertising slogans using made-in factors and similar nation-oriented selling points have an undeniable part to play in the marketing process.

5.8.6

Hill, John S. and Unal O.Boya (1987), "Consumer Goods Promotions in Developing Countries: An Empirical Study," *International Journal of Advertising,* 6(3), 249-264.

When multinational corporations (MNC) take consumer goods to less developed countries (LDC), they face advertising problems which include undeveloped economic infrastructures, adverse public attitudes, and poor production facilities. A study of 61 MNCs' advertising practices in LDCs found extensive use of print media. This may be due to the following factors: (1) Print is the most available medium; (2) The companies perceive their primary target markets to be the better educated segments; (3) Literacy rates for LDCs are growing. The study also found that television is used more than radio, possibly due to the high impact TV has on consumers and the increasing ownership of TVs.

5.8.7

Hong, Jae W., Aydin Muderrisoglu, and George M. Zinkhan (1987), "Cultural Differences and Advertising Expression: A Comparative Content Analysis of Japanese and U.S. Magazine Advertising," *Journal of Advertising,* 16(1), 55-62.

US and Japanese print advertisements are analyzed to examine how advertising expression and content differ in the two nations. The degree of emotional appeals, informativeness, and comparativeness of advertising are the dimensions explored. As theorized, Japanese ads are evaluated as more emotional and less comparative than American ads. In contrast to presumptive notions, Japanese ads are found to contain at least as many information cues as American ads. It is also observed that the Japanese ads tended to be longer.

5.8.8

Kale, Sudhir H. (1991), "Culture-specific Marketing Communications: An Analytical Approach," *International Marketing Review,* 8(2), 18-30.

Cultural factors have tremendous impact on cross-national communication, and it is in the area of cross-cultural communications that most blunders in international marketing occur. Using Hofstede's four discussions of culture, this article provides a generalizable framework to assess the effectiveness of cross cultural communication. The application of the proposed framework has been demonstrated in the context of promoting international tourism.

5.8.9

Kane, Michael J. and David A. Ricks (1988), "Is Transnational Data Flow Regulation a Problem?" *Journal of International Business Studies,* 19(3), Fall, 477-482.

5.8.10

Kaynak, Erdener and Ugur Yucelt (1987), "A Cross-National/ Cross-Cultural Study of Radio Listening Preferences: American and Canadian Consumers Contrasted," *International Journal of Advertising,* 6(4), 331-338.

5.8.11

Kedia, Ben L. and Jagdeep S. Chhokar (1986), "An Empirical Investigation of Export Promotion Programs," *Columbia Journal of World Business,* 21(4), Winter, 13-20.

This study evaluates 17 export promotion programs with respect to their familiarity, use, and benefits on the part of 49 exporters and 47 non-exporters. The results indicate that the low levels of awareness on the part of both exporters and non-exporters have caused the export promotion efforts to be ineffective. Among the small minority of firms who were aware of the programs, the participation rate was rather high. A large number of firms surveyed indicated a willingness to utilize the programs and expected to derive considerable benefits from such utilization. These results suggest that a greater exposure of the export promotional efforts should occupy a high priority.

5.8.12

Luqmani, Mushtaq, Ugur Yavas and Zahir Quraeshi (1989), "Advertising in Saudi Arabia: Content and Regulation," *International Marketing Review,* 6(1), Spring, 59-72.

5.8.13

Meredith, Lindsay (1988), "US Foreign Trade and Marketing in Canadian Manufacturing Industries," *International Journal of Advertising,* 7(4), 343-355.

This study explores the linkage between US-based advertising spillover into Canada and the differing degrees of market penetration achieved by US exports among Canadian manufacturing industries. The effect of US exports to Canada on Canadian local media usage was also evaluated. The results of an ordinary least squares regression indicated that US spillover advertising is negatively related to US export penetration of Canadian markets. Canadian local media usage appeared to be positively related to US export penetration of Canadian manufacturing industries. Implications for government policymakers include: 1. Spillover advertising may not be considered as a threat that allows imports to gain access to host country market shares at the expense of local producers. 2. The presence of US exports may contribute to the health of Canada's local media infrastructure.

5.8.14

Moncrief, William C. and Robert M. Landry (1985), "Print Advertising Strategies of International Firms—A Content Analysis," *International Journal of Advertising,* 4(4), 341-354.

Content analysis was used to examine the amount, format, and type of advertising by non-US firms in the US. A census was conducted of 7,954 advertisements by non-US firms found in Newsweek magazine from 1965 to 1982. The results indicate that automobiles and liquor were the most commonly advertised categories, but camera and home entertainment product ads grew as technology improved. Japan and Scotland were represented most often. Comparative ads were less common than is usual in the US, accounting for only 4.8% of the total. Sex appeal was used at the highest percentage during the 1960s; the pattern of its use was inconsistent. While ads were spread throughout the magazine, they were concentrated on the back inside cover and were usually a full-page or a double-page spread. Men were featured twice as often as women, but men were the target audience for most of the products.

5.8.15

Rau, Pradeep A. (1987), "Awareness Advertising and International Market Segmentation: An Analysis," *International Journal of Advertising,* 6(4), 313-321.

Awareness advertising and its implications for global market segmentation are analyzed. Awareness advertising is the practice of multinational firms buying paid advertising space in a market where the product is neither permitted to be commercially imported for sale nor locally manufactured. The main goals of awareness advertising are: to sensitize the target segments to brand names and/or product characteristics, to inform the target customer where the product can be purchased, and to reassure customers for the product that competent service agents are available locally in the event of repair or service problems. The single greatest benefit to the expenditure of advertising money lies in that initial users of such advertising can ensure a global presence for their product. This can be utilized later to counter companies which are slow to recognize that global segments do exist for many products.

5.8.16

Rosen, Barry Nathan, Jean J. Boddewyn, and Ernst A. Louis (1988), "Participation by US Agencies in International Brand Advertising: An Empirical Study," *Journal of Advertising,* 17(4), 14-22.

Many advertising agency executives observe that corporations are moving toward placement of their worldwide advertising through a single agency—a "mega-agency." To examine the extent to which US firms use the same agency to advertise abroad and in the home market, two-page questionnaires were mailed to brand managers in 1986-1987, soliciting data on foreign marketing activities and advertising agency selection policy. The total response was 85 of the original 651 brands. It was found that among the brands sold abroad only one-third are handled by the same agency at home and abroad. This proportion does not differ substantially with advertising budgets, by product class, or between standardized and nonstandardized brands. No single-agency group or mega-agency takes care of more than eight percent of the sample brands. No agency handles a majority of its US brands abroad.

5.8.17

Stewart, Sally and Nigel Campbell (1988), "Advertising in China and Hong Kong: A Preliminary Attempt at Some Comparisons of Style," *International Journal of Advertising,* 7(2), 149-154.

This study evaluates the style of advertisements in Beijing, China, that appeared during a selected week in October 1985. Using categories suggested by Kotler, the findings were compared with an analysis of 62 campaigns run in Hong Kong. A total of 91 advertisements shown on China Central Television were videotaped and grouped according to what Kotler called "execution styles." Results show that using the product in a normal setting was by far the most popular type of advertising used by Chinese advertisers, while those in Hong Kong employed mood or image to a much greater extent. It appeared that Hong Kong organizations referred the "slice-of-life" approach popular in China, while ads produced by foreign companies were more likely to use a mood or image style of TV commercial. In China, advertising was free to make claims about the health-giving properties of wine and other drinks, whereas in Hong Kong, the advertising of medicinal products on TV was very strictly controlled.

5.8.18

Tansey, Richard, Michael R. Hyman, George M. Zinkhan (1990), "Cultural Themes in Brazilian and U.S. Auto Ads: A Cross-Cultural Comparison," *Journal of Advertising,* 19(2), 30-39.

Automobile advertisements that appeared in the business magazines of Brazil and the US during the 1970s were examined to determine if Brazilian and US advertisers employ different themes in print advertisements. The research revealed that: (1) urban themes were used more frequently in Brazilian ads than in US ads, (2) leisure themes were used more frequently in US ads than in Brazilian ads, (3) work themes appeared as frequently in Brazilian ads as in US ads, and (4) work themes appeared more frequently in US ads as the 1970s progressed. The results suggest that values differ between the business subculture of Brazil and that of the US.

5.8.19

Waterson, M. J. (1988), "European Advertising Statistics," *International Journal of Advertising*, 7(1), 77-93.

5.8.20

Weinberger, Marc G. and Harlan E. Spotts (1989), "A Situational View of Information Content in TV Advertising in the U.S. and U.K." *Journal of Marketing*, 53(1), January, 89-93.

A study of the information content of U.S. and U.K. advertising was developed in the context of the Foote, Cone and Belding planning Matrix. The study illustrates that the amount of information content in ads is related closely to the decision-making situation defined by dimensions of the FCB matrix. Specifically, significant main effects are found but no interactions for degree of involvement or type of involvement. Overall, ads for high involvement and rational products have the most information, with generally higher levels in the U.S. than in the U.K.

5.8.21

Whitelock, Jeryl and Djamila Chung (1989), "Cross-Cultural Advertising: An Empirical Study," *International Journal of Advertising*, 8(3), 291-310.

The authors examine standardized advertisements within the European framework by measuring the cross-cultural standardization of ads appearing in printed media during the period July 1985 to June 1986. A proposed algorithm for evaluating the degree of standardization of ads is used to compare ads in Marie-Claire (France) with those in Woman's Journal (UK). The ads for six products out of 52 showed no point of comparison, and two others could not be compared because of their peculiarities. While 43 ads bore direct comparisons, only 7 ads out of 52 were exactly the same in both magazines. Only nine ads were considered to be cases of total standardization. The results of the test suggest that fully standardized advertising is the exception rather than the rule, and that partially standardized advertising is the most commonly found format.

5.9 Standardization Issues

5.9.1

Friedmann, Roberto (1986), "Psychological Meaning of Products: A Simplification of the Standardization vs. Adaptation Debate," *Columbia Journal of World Business*, 21(2), Summer, 97-104.

The psychological meaning that consumers derive from and ascribe onto products is shown to be useful in simplifying the debate as to whether or not one ought to standardize or adapt international marketing strategies. With theoretical support from a variety of disciplines, the psychological meaning of product is argued to provide decision makers with a diagnostic tool from which strategic marketing choices can be derived.

5.9.2

Hill, John S. and Richard R. Still (1984), ''Adapting Products to LDC Tastes,'' *Harvard Business Review,* 62(2), March-April, 92-101.

Findings of a survey of 61 subsidiaries of consumer goods manufacturers with operations in 22 LDCs are reported. The findings show that most consumer products that MNCs sell in developing countries originate in the companies' home markets. The temptation for many MNCs is to standardize their products across all markets. The authors find, however, that a ''more appropriate'' marketing strategy is to tailor consumer products to local customs and market conditions.

5.9.3

Mueller, Barbara (1991), ''Multinational Advertising: Factors Influencing the Standardized vs. Specialized Approach,'' *International Marketing Review,* 8(1), 7-18.

Print and television advertisements for US products appearing in the US, West Germany, and Japan are analyzed to explore the factors determining the adoption of standardized versus specialized approaches. The results suggest that messages transferred between Western markets, such as the US and West Germany, are more likely to be standardized than those transferred between Western and Eastern markets, such as the US and Japan. Product type is not found to play an influential role in the degree of standardization employed. However, standardization is found to be significantly more common in television than in print advertising.

5.9.4

Mueller, Barbara (1991), ''An Analysis of Information Content in Standardized vs. Specialized Multinational Advertisements,'' *Journal of International Business Studies,* 22(1), 23-39.

Print and television advertisements for US products appearing in the US, Germany, and Japan are evaluated to explore differences in the informational content of standardized versus specialized approaches to multinational advertising. The result shows that highly standardized messages contain significantly fewer consumer information cues than highly specialized messages. This characterization is true regardless of product category. The more standardized the message being transferred, the lower the level of consumer information contained within the commercial message. The quantity of information in a message is not independent of its quality or usefulness to the consumer.

5.9.5

Onkvisit, Sak and John J. Shaw (1987), "Standardized International Advertising: A Review and Critical Evaluation of the Theoretical and Empirical Evidence," *Columbia Journal of World Business,* 22(3), Fall, 43-55.

Standardized international advertising is a highly controversial practice which has attracted a great deal of attention over the last two decades. This paper provides a comprehensive review of related theoretical and research issues. The evaluation includes the examination of empirical evidence based on management and consumer responses. The validity of the three schools of thought (i.e., standardization, localization, and compromise) is critically examined. The paper also proposes a schematic framework which offers a pragmatic solution to the marketing question of whether and when standardization should be employed.

5.9.6

Peebles, Dean M. (1989), "Don't Write Off Global Advertising: A Commentary," *International Marketing Review,* 6(1), 73-78.

Some thoughts on the standardization of advertising in global markets are offered. They support a globalized perspective in international advertising.

5.9.7

Ryans, John K., Jr. and David G. Ratz (1987), "Advertising Standardization: A Re-Examination," *International Journal of Advertising,* 6(2), 145-158.

This study intends to measure the extent to which multinational corporations use standardized advertising. In addition, several relationships that have been postulated or supported in previous research were tested. The guiding variables were target markets and product positioning, while the strategy variables were campaign objectives, campaign themes, and media objectives. The survey instrument was designed to measure actual practice with respect to the standardization of advertising. The final sample included 34 usable responses. In contrast to the results of previous studies, the results revealed relatively high levels of standardization by the firms in the sample across all the relevant variables. An interesting finding was the high standardization of creative execution. Cultural similarity was found to be related to the extent of standardization.

5.9.8

Walters, Peter G.P. (1986), "International Marketing Policy: a Discussion of the

Standardization Construct and Its Relevance for Corporate Policy," *Journal of International Business Studies,* 17(2), Summer, 55-67.

An overview and evaluation of the standardization debate are presented. Central issues of interest include a discussion of the standardization construct and an evaluation of the evidence regarding corporate implementation of standardization strategies.

5.9.9

Wolfe, Alan (1991), "The Single European Market: National or Euro-Brands?" *International Journal of Advertising,* 10(1), 49-58.

Full implementation of a single European market is likely to be delayed long after 1992 because of remaining fiscal, legal, and operational problems, not the least of which will be the lack of harmonization of consumers. However, prospects appear promising for some traditional local brands and for new Euro-brands aimed at satisfying needs of the majority across Europe. A number of key factors affect the choice between local and Euro-brands, including customer needs, production and distribution costs, and legal constraints. The greatest changes will lie in management structure. The full benefits of a Euro-brand can be gained only if a single manager has ultimate responsibility for its profits horizontally.

5.10 Planning, Control, and Coordination

5.10.1

Baliga, B.R. and Alfred M. Jaeger (1984), "Multinational Corporations: Control Systems and Delegation Issues," *Journal of International Business Studies,* 15(2), Fall, 25-40.

This paper has two major objectives: first, to identify control and delegation issues confronting multinational corporation managers; second, to develop a conceptual model to assist multinational corporation managers in selecting appropriate control systems and determining the extent of delegation to be provided to subsidiary managers.

5.10.2

Bartlett, Christopher A. and Sumantra Ghoshal (1987), "Managing Across Borders: New Strategic Requirements (Part 1)," *Sloan Management Review,* 28(4), Summer, 7-17.

The demands of managing in an international operating environment have changed in recent years. There is a new need for the integration and coordination of activities. In addition, conditions have increased the value of more nationally responsive differentiated approaches. Finally, the ability to transfer knowledge and expertise from one part of the organization to others worldwide has become more important in building durable competitive advantage. Managers of multinational companies (MNC) are faced with the task of optimizing efficiency, responsiveness, and learning simultaneously. This suggests new strategic and organizational challenges. Discussions with 250 managers in nine of the world's largest MNCs revealed that limited organizational capability represents the most critical constraint in responding to new strategic demands.

5.10.3

Black, J. Stewart (1988), "Work Role Transitions: a Study of American Expatriate Managers in Japan," *Journal of International Business Studies,* 19(2), Summer, 277-294.

The author explores relationships between several variables and work role transition in the case of an overseas assignment to Japan. Role ambiguity and role discretion were found to influence work adjustment, while predeparture knowledge, association with local nationals, and family's adjustment were found to correlate with general adjustment of American expatriate managers in Japan.

5.10.4

Carapellotti, Lawrence R. and Saeed Samiee (1984), "The Use of Portfolio Models for Production Rationalization in Multinational Firms," *International Marketing Review,* 1(3),Spring/Summer, 5-13.

The use of portfolio models is analyzed to facilitate the production rationalization process in multinational firms. The degree to which portfolio planning is adopted will ultimately be determined by the perception of potential benefits within the individual firms. Adopting an ongoing production rationalization policy will enable decision makers to regularly and systematically raise questions about their firms' global outlook.

5.10.5

Davidson, William H. (1984), "Administrative Orientation and International Performance," *Journal of International Business Studies,* 15(2), Fall, 11-23.

This article examines how aspects of the firm's administrative orientation influence the choice of management modes, and how the choice of management modes impacts international performance.

5.10.6

Doz, Yves and C.K. Prahalad (1984), "Pattern of Strategic Control Within

Multinational Corporations," *Journal of International Business Studies,* 15(2), Fall, 55-72.

The management of the relationships between headquarters and subsidiaries within multinational companies is analyzed. The author discusses how various MNCs have approached the issue of headquarters control over subsidiary activities and what management systems and procedures are used, in which configurations, to exercise such control as is required. Findings suggest that selected tools must be used to manage data, to manage managers, and to manage conflicts; and that the successful companies blend an array of tools into a consistent management process. Companies with too narrow or too wide a repertory of tools and companies that fail to blend tools consistently face difficulties in trading off needs for responsiveness and needs for coordination.

5.10.7

Dymsza, William A. (1984), "Global Strategic Planning: a Model and Recent Developments," *Journal of International Business Studies,* 15(2), Fall, 169-183.

A comprehensive, dynamic model of strategic planning is developed for multinational corporations. The model depicts many aspects in MNC strategic planning systems, while recognizing that many variations exist among companies. Within the context of the model and experience of companies, certain approaches to competitive assessment, focusing on strategic issues, portfolio planning, and threat/opportunity analysis, are emphasized.

5.10.8

Egelhoff, William G. (1984), "Patterns of Control in U.S., UK, and European Multinational Corporations," *Journal of International Business Studies,* 15(2), Fall, 73-83.

This paper examines the type and level of control exercised by the parent headquarters of 50 U.S., UK, and European multinational corporations over their foreign subsidiaries. Patterns of control in the three national groups differ in significant ways, and these differences seem to have important implications for other characteristics of a company's organization design and managerial style.

5.10.9

Gates, Stephen R. and William G. Egelhoff (1986), "Centralization in Headquarters-Subsidiary Relationships," *Journal of International Business Studies,* 17(2), Summer, 71-92.

This study attempts to add clarity to the issue of standardization by re-testing many of the existing hypotheses with data from a study of centralization in 50 large U.S., U.K. and European MNCs. It examines how the degree of centralization inherent in the headquarters-foreign subsidiary relationship varies in response to a variety of company-wide and subsidiary level conditions.

5.10.10

Geringer, J. Michael and Colette A. Frayne (1990), ''Human Resource Management and International Joint Venture Control: A Parent Company Perspective,'' *Management International Review,* 30(3), 103-120.

Geringer and Hebert distinguished three dimensions that constitute the foundation of effective international joint venture (IJV) control systems: the focus of control, the degree of control sought by the parents, and the mechanisms used by the parents to exercise control. Recruitment and staffing of IJV employees may represent a crucial strategic control mechanism for an IJV parent; these mechanisms need not be limited to the start-up stage of the venture. It is critical that training be specific to the trainees' customs and the actual problems that are being faced. Performance appraisals are another strategy that parent firms can employ; appraisals should serve to identify strengths and weaknesses so that training and development programs can be suited to employee needs.

5.10.11

Geringer, J. Michael and Louis Hebert (1989), ''Control and Performance of International Joint Ventures,'' *Journal of International Business Studies,* 20(2), Summer, 235-254.

The authors review prior studies addressing the conceptualization and operationalization of control within IJVs, as well as the IJV control-performance relationship.

5.10.12

Ghertman, Michel (1988), ''Foreign Subsidiary and Parents' Roles During Strategic Investment and Divestment Decisions,'' *Journal of International Business Studies,* 19(1), Spring, 47-68.

Based on three in-depth analyses of different types of restructuring decisions, the author of the article finds that the foreign subsidiaries seem to carry most of the decision making effort for their own plant closures, while for strategic portfolio readjustment during which they change owners, they are not consulted.

5.10.13

Harvey, Michael G. (1989), ''Repatriation of Corporate Executives: An Empirical Study,'' *Journal of International Business Studies,* 20(1), Spring, 131-144.

5.10.14

Keegan, Warren J. (1983), ''Strategic Marketing Planning: The Japanese Approach,'' *International Marketing Review,* 1(1), Autumn, 5-15.

One of the most significant developments in marketing during the past decade has been the growing importance of Strategic Marketing Planning. This article focuses on the Japanese approach to strategic market planning and its role in the competitive performance. The implications of Japanese practice for Western marketers are also examined.

5.10.15

Kreder, Martina and Maria Zeller (1988), ''Control in German and U.S. Companies,'' *Management International Review,* 28(3), 58-66.

Managerial control is an ongoing process of adjustment to changing conditions that include setting goals, giving orders, setting up procedures, and monitoring results. A manager can control directly through personal intervention or indirectly by implementing plans, programs, and organizational rules. Control can be classified by a behavioral model, which is decentralized, direct, participative, and socioemotional, or a systems model, which is centralized, indirect, and task-oriented. To add to the empirical data on methods and concepts of control, control at the top management level was compared in large German and US companies. Findings show that management structures and processes in German companies tend to be more behavior-oriented, whereas in American companies, control is more systems-oriented.

5.10.16

Majaro, Simon (1983), ''Training Across National Boundaries,'' *International Marketing Review,* 1(1), Autumn, 16-27.

This article explores the role of training in small, medium and large organizations, then goes onto examine the plethora of complications that arise when a company with a large number of products in a large number of countries addresses the problem of marketing training.

5.10.17

Martinez, Zaida L. and David A. Ricks (1989), ''Multinational Parent Companies' Influence over Human Resource Decisions of Affiliates: U.S. Firms in Mexico,'' *Journal of International Business Studies,* 20(3), Fall, 465-487.

This research provides empirical evidence of the relationship between the degree of influence U.S. parent companies have over the human resource decisions of their Mexican affiliates and the affiliates' resource dependencies on the parent company and importance to the parent company. Both wholly-owned and joint venture affiliates are examined. The research shows that resource dependence was the factor most closely related to parent influence over affiliate human resource decisions.

5.10.18

McDonald, Malcolm (1983), "International Marketing Planning: The Gap between Theory and Practice," *International Marketing Review,* 1(1), Autumn, 42-58.

This study is based on a thesis which identifies and evaluates the marketing planning practices of British industrial goods companies operating internationally and examines the validity of the widespread belief that formalized marketing planning facilitates success.

5.10.19

McDonald, Malcolm H.B. (1982), "International Marketing Planning," *European Journal of Marketing,* 16(2), 3-32.

A conceptual approach to marketing planning is introduced. This approach is comparatively simple to identify and define as a logical sequence and a series of activities leading to the setting of marketing objectives and the formulation of plans for achieving them. The approach comprises the following steps: (1) gathering information on both the external environment and the company internally, (2) identifying major strengths, weakness, opportunities and threats, (3) formulating basic assumptions, (4) deciding on the marketing objectives of the business based on the information gathered, (5) laying down strategies for achieving the objectives, (6) formulating programs for implementing the strategies to include timing, responsibilities and costs, and (7) measuring progress towards achievement of the objectives.

5.10.20

Negandhi, Anant R. (1983), "Cross-Cultural Management Research: Trend and Future Directions," *Journal of International Business Studies,* 14(2), Fall, 17-28.

Historical perspectives on cross-cultural studies are illustrated. The emerging field of cross-cultural studies on organizational functioning is largely a result of partial integration between the cross-cultural comparative management field and organization theory areas. Although some cross-cultural organization studies were conducted prior to the 1950s, the large-scale projects on industrialization of developing countries at four major universities during the 1950s provided a major impetus to the comparative management area. Scholars from various social disciplines—psychology, sociology, social and cultural anthropology, economics, and political sciences—contributed toward these efforts. The differing backgrounds of these scholars are reflected in their conceptualizations and methodologies as well as in their specific findings. The conceptual and methodological approaches used by the comparative management theorists can be divided roughly into the following groups: the economic development orientation; the environmental approach; and the behavioral approach.

5.10.21

Reid, Stan (1983), ''Firm Internationalization, Transaction Costs and Strategic Choice,'' *International Marketing Review,* 1(2), Winter, 44-56.

The formal administrative arrangements that firms use for conducting foreign trade are peculiarly fitted to achieve specific export performances. The author shows how changes in these arrangements represent primarily organizational strategies for handling export transaction costs more efficiently.

5.10.22

Smeltz, Wayne J. and Belmont F. Haydel (1984), ''Fragmentation Between Home Office and Overseas Management,'' *International Marketing Review,* 1(4), Autumn/Winter, 60-68.

This research sought to test the existence of fragmentation between home office and overseas management and its potential impact on the planning and control of social responsiveness programs.

5.10.23

Tung, Rosalie L. (1984), ''Human Resource Planning in Japanese Multinationals: a Model for U.S. Firms?'' *Journal of International Business Studies,* 15(2), Fall, 139-149.

The efficient operation of a multinational corporation is contingent upon the availability of numerous resources—technology, capital, know-how, and people. In this paper, the argument is made that human power is a key ingredient to the successful operation of a multinational, without which all the other aforementioned resources could not be effectively and efficiently utilized or transferred from corporate headquarters to devote more attention to human resource planning, which is viewed as part of the overall planning and control process in a firm.

5.10.24

Verhage, Bronislaw J. and Eric Waarts (1988), ''Marketing Planning for Improved Performance: a Comparative Analysis,'' *International Marketing Review,* 5(2), Summer, 20-30.

Although many researchers suggest that strategic marketing planning is likely to improve a company's competitive position, little evidence is available to support this hypothesis. The few empirical studies conducted in this area have dealt with businesses in the United States and Britain. Therefore, it is difficult to generalize about the extent to which the implementation of the marketing concept, along with related planning and research techniques, actually impact the performance of companies.

5.10.25

Walters, Peter G. (1985), "A Study of Planning for Export Operations," *International Marketing Review,* 2(3), Autumn, 74-81.

Export planning activity is analyzed. Using a definition of planning as a one-cycle process, attention is focused on the propensity of a sample of forest products exporters to undertake certain planning activities and on differences between planners and non-planners. It was found that exporting was generally unplanned in the survey firms, and that the propensity to plan increased with size and the relative significance of export sales.

5.11 Negotiation Strategies

5.11.1

Campbell, Nigel C.G., John L. Graham, Alain Jolibert, and Hans Gunther Meissner (1988), "Marketing Negotiations in France, Germany, the United Kingdom, and the United States," *Journal of Marketing,* 52(2), April, 49-62.

The determinants of marketing negotiations in four cultures are investigated in a laboratory simulation. 138 businesses from the U.S., 48 from France, 44 from West Germany, and 44 from the UK participated in two-person, buyer-seller negotiation simulations. The American process of negotiations is found to be different from that of Europeans in several respects.

5.11.2

Ghauri, Pervez N. (1988), "Negotiating with Firms in Developing Countries: Two Case Studies," *Industrial Marketing Management,* 17(1), Feburary, 49-53.

The author provides an analysis of the negotiations between Swedish firms, as sellers, and firms in India and Nigeria as buyers. The two cases with developing nations as buyers are compared with a case where both the buyer and seller came from Sweden. The respective government and environmental variations emerge as factors on the process of negotiation itself. Western firms should particularly consider the following points: (1) time, (2) identification of the contents of the agreement, (3) understanding the other party's position, and (4) building up relative power. By gathering data on the other party, considering each side's position, and developing different alternatives, the negotiators can build up their power, as the party having more data automatically acquires more power.

5.11.3

Ghauri, Pervez N. (1986), "Guidelines for International Business Negotiations," *International Marketing Review,* 3(3), Autumn, 72-82.

Treating negotiations as a technique which can be learned and adapted to international business, this article takes a problem solving approach and endeavors to provide some guidelines for successful negotiating. It addresses the different stages of the negotiation process and provides a strategic planning model for negotiations.

5.11.4

Graham, John L. (1986), "Across the Negotiating Table from the Japanese," *International Marketing Review,* 3(3), Autumn, 58-71.

The process of negotiation in Japan differs from that in America. Americans must adapt their approach to establishing a rapport, information exchange, persuasion, and concession making if they are to be successful in dealing with Japanese clients and partners.

5.11.5

Graham, John L. and Roy A. Herberger, Jr. (1983), "Negotiators Abroad—Don't Shoot From the Hip," *Harvard Business Review,* 61(4), July-August, 160-168.

Influenced by their frontier past, many American business people come to the negotiating table with a do-or-die attitude that often defeats their purpose. They tend to "shoot first; ask questions later." But with the growing role of the United States in international trade, this naive attitude may cause them, instead of their adversaries, to bite the dust. By recognizing their own shortcomings and by learning more about other cultures and negotiating styles, Americans can improve their image and enhance their chances for sucess.

5.11.6

Graham, John L. (1983), "Brazilian, Japanese, and American Business Negotiations," *Journal of International Business Studies,* 14(1), Spring/Summer, 47-61.

This paper investigates in a laboratory experiment the determinants of the outcomes of business negotiations in three cultures. The outcomes of negotiations between Japanese businessmen result primarily from a situational constraint—the role of the negotiator (buyer or seller). Representational bargaining strategies, a measure of the process of the interaction, is the most important variable in American negotiations. In negotiations between Brazilian business people, deceptive bargaining strategies— also a process measure -is the key variable affecting outcomes.

5.11.7

Hawrysh, Brian Mark and Lynne Judith Zaichkowsky (1990), "Cultural Approaches to Negotiations: Understanding the Japanese," *International Marketing Review,* 7(2), 28-42.

This article reviews literature on negotiations between Japanese and Americans using an anthropological perspective. The negotiation articles concerning the Japanese can be organized around Graham and Sano's four-phase linear model of the negotiation process. Cultural differences between the Japanese and Americans are found with respect to the first and second stages of decision making, namely personal relationships, status, styles of decision making, and bidding. Cultural differences are not confirmed in the third and fourth stages of the negotiation process, namely persuasive tactics, concessions, and outcomes. Several authors have analyzed different Japan-US approaches to personal relationships, status distinctions, harmony, face, time, cognitive processes, and group action.

5.11.8

Heiba, Farouk (1984), "International Business Negotiations: A Strategic Planning Model," *International Marketing Review,* 1(4), Autumn/Winter, 5-16.

The accelerating interdependency among global societies and the growing role of U.S. and Western countries in international trade strongly necessitate learning, experience, and training in the task of negotiations. This paper suggests that true understanding of environmental determinants, styles, and tactics of international business negotiations is a must, if one is to achieve desirable outcomes. The old attitude of bargaining overseas and the John Wayne approach will not work anymore. "Go native" and "adaptability" will be the key words for successful international business negotiations in the future.

5.11.9

Rangaswamy, Arvind, Jehoshua Eliashberg, Raymond R. Burke, and Jerry Wind (1989), "Developing Marketing Expert Systems: An Application to International Negotiations," *Journal of Marketing,* 53(4), October, 24-39.

The development of NEGOTEX (negotiations expert) is discussed. This system offers guidelines to those preparing for international marketing negotiations. The knowledge base of NEGOTEX consists of definitions of objects and variables pertinent to the international negotiation domain as well as the relationships between these objects and variables. The inference engine manipulates the elements of the knowledge base, along with information supplied by the user, in a way that solves a specific problem. A prototype was developed by inputting the knowledge elements into the shell according to its conventions and syntax. The next stage in the development of the expert system was to validate the prototype system and the representational forms used to implement it.

5.11.10

Tung, Rosalie L. (1982), "U.S.-China Trade Negotiations: Practices, Procedures and Outcomes," *Journal of International Business Studies,* 13(2), Fall, 25-37.

This study sought to examine and identify (1) the mechanics of U.S.-China trade negotiations; (2)how a company prepares for such negotiations; (3) the factors that contribute to the success or failure of such negotiations; and (4) the outcomes of such negotiations. Data pertaining to these characteristics were collected from 138 U.S. firms engaged in China trade.

5.11.11

Weiss, Stephen E. (1987), "Creating the GM-Toyota Joint Venture: A Case in Complex Negotiation," *Columbia Journal of World Business*, 22(2), Summer, 23-37.

The creation of a joint venture hinges on successful negotiation by the prospective partners. In international business, this process is often complex. This article describes the GM-Toyota negotiations in detail and suggests steps that facilitate agreement.

5.12 Other Issues in International Marketing Management

5.12.1

Cavusgil, S. Tamer and Ugur Yavas (1984), "Transfer of Management Know-How to Developing Countries: An Empirical Investigation," *Journal of Business Research*, 12(1) , March, 35-50.

Management expertise transferred to developing countries through graduate university programs in advanced nations is analyzed. Research was conducted using about 70 managers from Turkey who acquired an M.B.A. in the United States. Three issues are highlighted: local applicability of certain skills, firm and individual factors linked to local applications of management expertise, and primary considerations in transfer impediments common to indigenous organizations. Frequently, technology is transferred to developing countries through licensing or multinationals' foreign direct investment. Foreign direct investment has been hampered by inappropriate transfers and problems related to foreign dominance.

5.12.2

Haegg, Claes (1983), "Sources of International Business Ethics," *Management International Review*, 23(4), 73-78.

Two sources can be employed when rules of international business ethics are constructed; theoretical analysis based on generally accepted postulates, and the body of guidelines which has been advanced by international organizations. This review discusses both sources of international business ethics and describes some situations that exemplify the kind of problems which international business ethics are intended to be able to solve. It appears that a deductive model can, at least in some cases, give more precise results than the guidelines of the Organization for

Economic Cooperation & Development (OECD), probably because the OECD guidelines are the result of a compromise and what they have gained in acceptance they have lost in precision. The publication of several codes of conduct by different international organizations may also lead to further confusion with respect to international business ethics. Thus, now appears to be the appropriate time for the development of a theoretical source of international business ethics.

5.12.3

Harvey, Michael G. and Ilkka A. Ronkainen (1985), "International Counterfeiters: Marketing Success Without the Cost and the Risk," *Columbia Journal of World Business,* 20(3), Fall, 37-45.

Counterfeit merchandise of all types has flooded the U.S. market and markets abroad, duping the brand-conscious consumer and costing firms millions of dollars. This article examines common counterfeiting methods, the impact of counterfeiting on U.S. based multinational corporations, and the efforts now underway to curb the manufacture and marketing of counterfeit goods.

5.12.4

Maisonrouge, Jacques G. (1983), "The Education of a Modern International Manager," *Journal of International Business Studies,* 14(1), Spring/Summer, 141-146.

This article is based upon a speech delivered by Jacques G. Maisonrouge, Senior Vice President, IBM Corporation at the Annual Meeting of the Academy of International Business, Washington, DC, when he became the first recipient of the International Business Leader of the Year award and was elected an Honorary Member of the Fellows of the Academy of International Business.

5.12.5

Mayo, Michael A., Lawrence J. Marks, and John K. Ryans Jr. (1991), "Perceptions of Ethical Problems in International Marketing," *International Marketing Review,* 8(3), 61-75.

U.S. international marketing practitioners identified the most difficult ethical problems they have encountered in foreign trade. These ethical problems were rated as occurring infrequently and having a moderate impact on a firm's overseas competitiveness. Conversely, the respondents saw ethical problems as likely to tarnish the firm's domestic image and to generate much concern for top management. This suggests such problems may have a stronger negative impact upon a firm's domestic public image but may not be a major factor inhibiting its international trade. The strategic alternatives to, and management implications of, avoiding markets which may pose ethical problems are discussed.

5.12.6

Papadopoulos, Socrates (1987), "Strategic Marketing Techniques in International Tourism," *International Marketing Review,* 4(2), Spring, 71-84.

The application of econometrics in the development of international tourism marketing strategies is discussed. In particular the author examines how empirical results can be related to a market choice matrix in identifying the most attractive countries for allocating marketing resources and limited promotional funds.

5.12.7

Shaikh, Muzaffar A. and Behram J. Hansotia (1985), "Industrial Market Structure Analysis in a Major Multinational Corporation," *International Marketing Review,* 2(1), Spring, 18-30.

VI. Decision Tools for International Marketing

6.1 International Marketing Research

6.1.1

Bartram, Peter (1990-1991), "The Challenge for Research Internationally in the Decade of the 1990s," *Journal of Advertising Research,* 30(6), December-January, RC3-RC6.

The size of the non-US market for marketing research is larger than it was and the US may no longer be the focus for development and innovation if such trends continue. Instead of being seen primarily as a means of helping managements exploit new opportunities effectively, the justification for marketing research will be based more on its ability to articulate new social values and expectations and to be a precise and objective means whereby consumers, voters, and active citizens can make their wishes known. In countries where research is still in its infancy, the basic issue is one of education and adoption. In countries where the industry's methods are established, the main issue tends to be one of application.

6.1.2

Berney, Karen (1989), "Market Research: Gizmos, Gadgets and Gimmicks," *International Management,* 44(7), July/August, 40-43.

With the advent of open economic borders after 1992, new products are expected to travel more easily throughout Europe, creating greater problems of monitoring quality and competition for exporters. International Information Services Ltd (IIS) is an imaginative, service-oriented business that shops for major corporations. The company has a network of 400 shoppers that monitor product quality, competitors, and new products. According to IIS, some of the more innovative products include body deodorant from Israel that promises to keep the body odor-free for five to eight months and a four-in-one detergent from Germany. Most products that carry the "new" claim are really enhancements or modifications of existing products.

6.1.3

Bodur, Muzaffer and S. Tamer Cavusgil (1985), "Export Market Research Orientations of Turkish Firms," *European Journal of Marketing,* 19(2), 5-16.

This article provides a comparative analysis of export information needs and marketing research orientations of 88 Turkish exporters selling to two different regions. Firms exporting to the Middle East and North Africa are compared to their OECD (Organization for Economic Cooperation and Development) counterparts in terms of: (1) organizational and resource-related characteristics, (2) extent of information sought and kinds of information channels used, (3) nature of evaluative criteria employed in assessing export potential, and (4) level of involvement in export marketing research. In general, there appears to be a lack of a planned, systematic approach to exporting. Most exporters to the Middle East and North Africa studied deal in fresh or processed food products, while various textile products make up the product mix of those exporting to OECD nations. The former rely more heavily upon export market research.

6.1.4

Cavusgil, S. Tamer (1985), "Guidelines for Export Market Research," *Business Horizons,* 28(6), November-December, 27-33.

The author presents some practical guidelines to assess export market opportunities based on in-depth interviews with executives of 70 exporting companies in Wisconsin and Illinois. In most of the firms studied, such a process was fairly unstructured. Since the number of world markets to be considered by a firm is very large, a sequential screening process is most efficient and effective. A sequential process consists of: (1) a preliminary screening to select attractive countries, (2) an analysis of industry market potential for each country selected, and (3) an assessment of company sales potential in favorable countries. Firms have developed practical approaches for estimating foreign market potential. Five specific approaches are: (1) the use of distributor/agent contacts, (2) advertising directed to prospective distributors or other customers, (3) participation in trade fairs, (4) expansion of the supplier relationship with domestic customers to overseas markets, and (5) trade audits.

6.1.5

Cavusgil, S. Tamer (1985), "Factor Congruency Analysis: A Methodology for Cross-Cultural Research," *Journal of the Market Research Society,* 27(2), April, 147-155.

This paper introduces the factor comparison methodology as a tool for comparative or cross-cultural research efforts where the researcher is investigating similarities and differences in the responses of subjects from different samples. A factor congruency method, employing the Burt-Tucker-Wrigley-Neuhaus coefficient, is defined and illustrated using data from a comparative study of exporting firms from the United States, Canada and Norway. The congruency coefficient relates each factor of one factor matrix to each factor from another matrix. The coefficient ranges in value from +1 for perfect agreement to zero for no agreement.

6.1.6

Cavusgil, S. Tamer (1987), "Qualitative Insights into Company Experiences in

International Marketing Research,'' *Journal of Business and Industrial Marketing,* 2(3), Summer, 41-54.

The nature and scope of international marketing research activities were investigated. The primary focus of international marketing research was basically a function of the company's stage of internationalization. Compared with domestic marketing research, international marketing research in general was less formal and quantitative. Four levels of internationalization were identified: reactive/opportunistic, experimental, active, and committed. Multinational companies that have reached higher internationalization levels seem to have developed fairly formalized and sophisticated procedures for international marketing research. The research implies that companies should ensure a smooth transfer of knowledge from domestic market research staff to international marketing research professionals.

6.1.7

Douglas, Susan P., and C. Samuel Craig, and Warren J. Keegan (1982), "Approaches to Assessing International Marketing Opportunities for Small-and Medium-sized Companies," *Columbia Journal of World Business,* 17(3), Fall, 26-31.

For small- and medium-sized companies, primary or customized research that monitors the international business environment is complex and expensive. The authors present ways for these companies to make ambitious, creative use of secondary sources to investigate opportunities for international expansion. Secondary data can be used to decide which countries and product markets to enter, to develop initial estimates of market size, and to monitor environmental change.

6.1.8

Ehrman, Chaim Meyer and Morris Hamburg (1986), "Information Search for Foreign Direct Investment Using Two-Stage Country Selection Procedures: A New Procedure," *Journal of International Business Studies,* 17(2), 93-115.

This article reports the development and testing of normative model for determining how firms should select the countries to be used in the information search for foreign direct investment. After a subset of countries is selected in the first stage of the decision process, a final selection process chooses the country with the best score within the subset.

6.1.9

Green, Robert T. and Arthur W. Allaway (1985), "Identification of Export Opportunities: A Shift-share Approach," *Journal of Marketing,* 49(1), Winter, 83-88.

The search for new export markets is a high priority. This ariticle considers a technique that could be useful in screening markets and products for possible export opportunities. The technique is called shift-share analysis and has been employed primarily in regional analysis studies. The authors demonstrate the manner in which shift-share analysis can aid in the generation of product/market sets having high export potential.

6.1.10

Hutcheson, J.M. (1984), "International Marketing Techniques for Engineers," *International Marketing Review,* 1(4), Autumn/Winter, 51-59.

International marketing is founded on research in a similar way to domestic marketing. However, the process is seen to require a closer understanding of subjective as well as objective analysis. Otherwise service, design or product strategy will not produce plans which achieve the long term profits to warrant overseas operations.

6.1.11

Jobber, David and John Saunders (1988), "An Experimental Investigation into Cross-National Mail Survey Response Rates," *Journal of International Business Studies,* 19(3), Fall, 483-496.

The research focuses on the effects of foreign and domestic source manipulations on cross-national response rates of business people in the United States and Britain. Results suggest that foreign source effects do not raise response rates.

6.1.12

Johansson, Johny K. (1987), "Market Research the Japanese Way," *Harvard Business Review,* 65(3), May-June, 16-22.

The research methods adopted by many Japanese companies are illustrated. A major reason why Japanese corporations succeed in global markets is the informed, hands-on market research they practice. When Japanese managements want information on changes in customer needs or tastes or on how the market will respond to new products, they don't depend on market research professionals and the so-called scientific research methods favored by corporations in the U.S. and Europe. Instead, they meet and talk directly with retailers, wholesalers, distributors, and brokers so that they can gain deep knowledge of their channels.

6.1.13

Kazuaki, Katori (1990), "Recent Developments and Future Trends in Marketing Research in Japan Using New Electronic Media," *Journal of Advertising Research,* 30(2), April-May, 53-57.

Major changes in the marketing research environment in Japan include the decreasing accessibility to interviewees at home, the difficulty in recruiting high-quality interviewers, and the higher cost of marketing research. Among various new media being used in market research, facsimile is most widely used. NTT Telemarketing Inc. has contracts with 50 storekeepers where public facsimile is located and maintains a research panel of 500 households in the vicinity of each such machine. Speed and the capability to send pictures and graphs as well as words and figures are advantages that fax has over other research methods. Videotex is another new medium that is being used for marketing research applications in Japan. Nippon Telemedia Service Inc. is now conducting marketing research using the Captain Standard Videotex system on an experimental basis.

6.1.14

Kobayashi, Kazuo and Peter Draper (1990), "Reviews of Market Research in Japan," *Journal of Advertising Research,* 30(2), April-May, 13-18.

The Japan Marketing Association conducted a mail survey among major companies in 1988 in order to clarify current usage of marketing research and to determine attitudes toward research in general and research usage. Questionnaires were sent to 2,000 marketing research staff and users of research in major companies; 380 usable questionnaires were returned. Major findings include: (1) Responsibility for marketing research is scattered. (2) There is recognition of the need for marketing research. (3) Marketing research information is currently needed or is in use in areas that are expected to become more important in the future. (4) About 60% of respondents replied that the ability to analyze data and write a report and the ability for project planning were important. (5) The degree of satisfaction of respondents using research firms was fairly good. (6) A total of 72% of respondents' companies have a computerized database for business information. Respondents agreed that the marketing research department should become a strategic department.

6.1.15

Mahmoud, Essam and Gillian Rice (1988), "Use of Analytical Techniques in International Marketing," *International Marketing Review,* 5(3), Autumn, 7-13.

This article illustrates the importance of analytical techniques in international marketing. An overview of related research is given. The authors ask the question:"Which way will research on the subject go in the future?"

6.1.16

Nasif, Ercan G., Hamad Al-Daeaj, Bahman Ebrahimi, Mary Thibodeaux (1991), "Methodological Problems in Cross-Cultural Research: An Updated Review," *Management International Review,* 31(1), 79-91.

Methodology issues in cross-cultural research are discussed. These issues include criterion problem, methodological simplicity, sampling, instrumentation, data collection, and generalizability. The criterion problem arises from the fact that there is no widespread agreement in the field on an operational definition of culture. The problems in sampling include the number of cultures and subjects that should be used as well as their representativeness. To solve the problems in data collection, such as the equivalence of administration, response, and timing, researchers from different countries should collaborate.

6.1.17

Parameswaran, Ravi and Attila Yaprak (1987), "Cross-National Comparison of Consumer Research Measures," *Journal of International Business Studies,* 18(1), Spring, 35-49.

A study was conducted to examine the degree to which measure unreliability as a result of construct, country-of-origin, and market-induced differentials impair the comparability of cross-national research findings. Mail questionnaires were completed by 158 business executives in the Atlanta, Georgia, area and 202 business executives in the Istanbul, Turkey, area. Results indicate that the same scales may have different reliabilities in different cultures. In addition, the same scales may exhibit different reliabilities when used by the same individual in evaluating products from different cultures. Specifically, it was found that differing levels of awareness, knowledge, familiarity, and affect with the peoples, products in general, and specific brands from a chosen country of origin may result in differentials in the reliability of similar scales when used in multiple national markets.

6.1.18

Sarin, Sharad (1987), "Industrial Market Research in India," *Industrial Marketing Management,* 16(4), November, 257-264.

Some 50,000 organizations in India may be involved in industrial marketing. These firms can be categorized into four groups: (1) those committed and having internal arrangements, (2) those with some internal arrangements but basically indifferent, (3) the ad hoc users, and (4) the ignorant and suspicious. Most Indian firms used market research to examine supply and demand. Only recently organizations have started appreciating such things as competitive analysis and organizational buying behavior. However, the collection of secondary sources of information in India is difficult, and any project must have a provision for original field research. The best results in obtaining data in India have been through in-depth interviews, and mail surveys could not be substituted for direct field studies.

6.1.19

Schlegelmilch, Bodo B., K. Boyle, and S. Therivel (1986), "Marketing Research in

Medium-Sized U.K. and U.S. Firms,'' *Industrial Marketing Management,* 15(3), August, 177-182.

Concentrating on small- and medium-sized firms and comparing UK and US companies this study analyzes why so few industrial goods companies conduct marketing research. A questionnaire was sent to 300 engineering firms with 100-500 employees, equally divided between the US and UK. Of the 82 usable responses, only 10 from the US and 15 from the UK utilized marketing research. Differences were found between the user-nonuser and the US-UK subsamples. Among users, the mean number of employees was greater than among nonusers. There was a preponderance of in-house marketing research, indicating different research needs for engineering firms. On average, US companies spent nearly twice what UK companies did on marketing research, even though the US firms were much smaller. The lack of commitment to and understanding of marketing research may continue to hinder the performance of British engineering companies.

6.1.20

Walters, Peter G.P. (1983), ''Export Information Sources—A Study of Their Usage and Utility,'' *International Marketing Review,* 1(2), Winter, 34-43.

This article discusses the role of information in the export development process and identifies some recent findings regarding the utilization of export information sources. Propositions regarding patterns of information acquisition and the perceived utility of the input are then examined using data from a sample of forest products exporters.

6.1.21

Wheeler, David R. (1988), ''Content Analysis: An Analytical Technique for International Marketing Research,'' *International Marketing Review,* 5(4), Winter, 34-40.

Effective international marketing requires collection of large amounts of data from diverse sources and sensitive use of such information in marketing strategy. While marketing information systems help managers incorporate some kinds of data into their planning, content analysis offers a different set of insights into cultural concepts, themes and trends not usually captured by traditional data systems. Content analysis has evolved as a research technique since the 1920s, largely in social science applications. Today, aided by new analytical techniques and optical scanners, which can read huge volumes of material inexpensively; and state-of-the-art computer software, which can handle languages such as Chinese, Japanese, and Arabic, content analysis has great promise for international marketing applications.

6.1.22

Wood, Van R. and Jerry R. Goolsby (1987), ''Foreign Market Information

Preferences of Established U.S. Exporters,'' *International Marketing Review,* 4(4), Autumn,43-52.

Using a sample of more than 130 established exporters, this study empirically examines the information preferences of decision makers responsible for evaluating foreign markets. Export information preferences are analyzed across distinct industries, and implications for export facilitating agencies and foreign parties are explored.

6.1.23

Yong, Yeong Wee, Kau Ah Keng, and Tan Leng Leng (1989), ''A Delphi Forecast for the Singapore Tourism Industry: Future Scenario and Marketing Implications,'' *International Marketing Review,* 6(3), 35-46.

This article attempts to ascertain the future scenario of the Singapore tourism industry through the use of the Delphi technique. Two panels were established for the purpose of this study. The first panel consisted of key individuals in the local tourist industry. The second panel was comprised of an international group of executives participating in an executive development program in Singapore. Based on the findings, events with higher probability of occurrence and crucial to tourism development are identified.

6.2 Buyer Behavior

6.2.1

Banting, Peter M., Andrew C. Gross, and George Holmes (1985), ''Generalizations from a Cross-National Study of the industrial Buying Process,'' *International Marketing Review,* 2(4), 64-74.

This article focuses on one key aspect of industrial buying behavior, namely the buying process itself. Using a common questionnaire, a large sample of respondents in Australia, Canada, the UK and the US were interviewed by mail from two sectors, the paper and pulp and chemical and allied products industries. The similarity of results between the different industries and the countries—as well as similarities between this and previous surveys in the UK and US—allows generalizations to be made about the respective involvement of corporate departments in the purchase process for equipment, materials and components.

6.2.2

Barksdale, Hiram C. (1982), ''A Cross-National Survey of Consumer Attitudes Towards Marketing Practices, Consumerism and Government Regulations,'' *Columbia Journal of World Business,* 17(2), Summer, 71-85.

Consumer attitudes on the national marketing systems of six countries were examined. The theory that opinions might follow a "life cycle pattern," reflecting the development of national consumer movements was found unsupported. Wide cross-national agreement was observed on many topics.

6.2.3

Brown, Jacqueline, C. David Light, and Gregory M. Gazda (1987), "Attitudes Towards European, Japanese and US Cars," *European Journal of Marketing,* 21(5), 90-100.

The US is one of the most important marketplaces for cars in the world due to its market size and the discretionary income of its consumers. A study examined US consumer attitudes toward foreign and domestic cars to determine appropriate marketing strategies for foreign car manufacturers exporting to the US. A questionnaire asked 249 university students to rate their attitudes about cars produced in six countries on the basis of several attributes: safety, styling, fuel economy, price, reliability, acceleration, and workmanship. Results indicate the following ranking, from highest to lowest: (1) Germany, (2) Japan, (3) the US, (4) France, (5) the UK, and (6) Yugoslavia. Although German cars received the highest ratings on four of the six attributes selected, students selected Japanese cars as being the best value.

6.2.4

Cordell, Victor V. (1991), "Competitive Context and Price as Moderators of Country of Origin Preferences," *Journal of the Academy of Marketing Science,* 19(2), Spring, 123-128.

The findings are reported from an experiment setting where subjects made product choices and country of origin and other variables were manipulated. The findings suggest that buyers are more cautious about products from less developed countries when the financial risk is higher. However, within a given product class, manipulating the price did not produce interaction effects with country of origin. When buyers from a consumer segment is willing to purchase goods from less developed countries they usually expect something in return—either reduced price or some risk mitigant. The interaction of country of origin with competitive context suggests that country of origin is more important for upscale products within a class.

6.2.5

Darling, John R. and Van R. Wood (1990), "A Longitudinal Study Comparing Perceptions of U.S. and Japanese Consumer Products in a Third/Neutral Country: Finland 1975 to 1985," *Journal of International Business Studies,* 21(3), 427-450.

Changes in consumer perceptions of U.S. and Japanese products and marketing efforts in Finland are examined. The data were collected from consumers living in the Finnish metropolitan areas of Helsinki, Tampere, and Turku during 1975, 1980, and 1985. The results indicate that, while Finnish consumer perceptions of U.S. products and marketing efforts have improved over time, the corresponding perceptions of the Japanese alternative have improved substantially more. In areas where U.S. competitors had initial advantages, the results indicate that, by 1985, Japanese firms were able to overcome such advantages and were perceived as superior in all categories. While the US share of Finnish consumer imports remained relatively constant from 1970 through 1987, the corresponding Japanese share steadily increased.

6.2.6

Davis, Bonnie D., Sue Ann Kern, and Brenda J. Sternquist (1990), "The Influence of Country of Origin, the 'Buy American' Campaign, and Store Prestige on Consumers' Perceptions of Quality and Estimates of Price," *Advances in International Marketing,* Vol.4, 73-95.

To counteract foreign competition, the textile-apparel industry has developed that "Buy American" campaign. This study examines the influence of country of origin, store prestige, and "Buy American" campaign on consumers' quality perceptions and price estimates for two identical apparel products. Using an experimental design, three product information cues—country of origin, store prestige, and "Buy American" information—were manipulated. Only store prestige significantly influenced consumers' quality perceptions and price estimates.

6.2.7

Ford, David (1984), "Buyer/Seller Relationships in International Industrial Markets," *Industrial Marketing Management,* 13(2), May, 101-112.

Effective relationships and relationship management in international industrial marketing are crucial to supplier success in the foreign market. An examination was conducted of the relationship between industrial buyers' evaluations of the technical and commercial skills of suppliers and their evaluation of suppliers on other dimensions, which measure suppliers' ability to build a relationship with them. Analysis of 196 questionnaire responses from marketing and purchasing executives in five European countries was done using redundancy matrices and canonical analysis. Findings support the existence of a strong connection between buyers' assessments of suppliers' technical and commercial skills and the extent of the suppliers' commitment to them and the conflict level in their relationship. Suppliers must be willing to reduce the social, cultural, and technological distance between themselves and their buyers.

6.2.8

French, W.A., H.C. Barksdale, and W.D. Perreault, Jr. (1982), "Consumer Attitudes Toward Marketing in England and the United States," *European Journal of Marketing,* 16(6), 20-30.

Considering the uncertainties of the political-economic environment, what is the mood of English consumers? Do they accept market prices within the EEC competitive framework or would they opt for price controls? Are attitudes favorable to the range of products available or is there widespread suspicion about quality? More to the point, do the marketing system and its component activities win a general vote of confidence? Through answering these questions, this article presents a composite picture of public attitudes toward marketing, consumerism and related regulations at the beginning of the 1980s. Adapting a research instrument that has been used abroad, a study of consumers in England was undertaken for the purpose of uncovering attitudes toward the marketing system as well as the factors underlying those attitudes.

6.2.9

Green, Robert T., Jean-Paul Leonardi, Jean-Louis Chandon, Isabella C. M. Cunningham, Bronis Verhage, Alian Strazzieri (1983), "Societal Development and Family Purchasing Roles: A Cross-National Study," *Journal of Consumer Research,* 9(4), 436-442.

Rodman (1972) developed a cross-cultural framework for the analysis of the distribution of marital power in decision making. Rodman proposed that the allocation of decision authority between spouses is linked to stages of societal development, including patriarchy, modified patriarchy, transitional equalitarianism, and equalitarianism. The usefulness of Rodman's framework is illustrated in a cross-national study of marital decision making, using data from Gabon, Venezuela, France, the Netherlands, and the US. Data were analyzed using correspondence analysis, which visually maps the relationships among nominal data. The results support the relationship between marital decision roles and societal development. Decision making in Gabon and Venezuela is significantly more husband-dominated than in France, the Netherlands, or the US.

6.2.10

Hampton, Gerald M. (1987), "Comparing Dutch and U.S. Attitudes Toward Foreign Investments," *International Marketing Review,* 4(3), Summer, 54-62.

This article reports the results of a cross-national study designed to determine the attitudes that exist in the minds of American and Dutch citizens when they consider the possibility of investments being made in their country from a selected group of nations. The findings show U.S. respondents have a more positive attitude toward domestic and foreign investments than do the Dutch. Overall there were few significant differences between American and Dutch attitudes toward foreign investment.

6.2.11

Han, C. Min and Vern Terpstra (1988), "Country-of-Origin Effects for Uni-National and Bi-National Products," *Journal of International Business Studies,* 19(2), Summer, 235-255.

The effects of country-of-origin and brand name cues on consumer evaluations of uninational and binational products and estimates of the perceived values of such cues are examined by way of personal interviews of a quota sample of household residents in a midwestern city. Participants are 18 years of age or older; non-US residents and residents of group living quarters are excluded from the sample. Color televisions and subcompact automobiles are targeted since they are often binational and their country images are expected to be considerably different. For the country stimuli, the following countries were selected: U.S, Japan, Germany, and Korea. Quota sampling was used to select the population elements. Results indicate that consumer perceptions of product quality, at the level of individual product dimensions as well as the overall level, vary across product modes, and sourcing country stimuli are found to have greater effects than brand name on consumer attitudes toward binational products.

6.2.12

Ho, Suk-ching and Yat-ming Sin (1988), "Consumer Protection in China: The Current State of the Art," *European Journal of Marketing,* 22(1), 41-46.

In the past, consumer protection was unheard of in the Peoples' Republic of China. However, with the recent efforts to revitalize the country's economy, the consumer market has flourished. At the same time, malpractices on the part of enterprises at the expense of consumers also have surfaced. The malpractices have included deceptive advertising, trademark violations, and other unethical business practices. In response to this problem, the China Consumer Council was established in December 1984. Measures have been taken to counter profiteering producers and tradespeople. Although the Chinese have developed a consumer consciousness, it will take a long time for the concept to reach the level of importance it has in the West. For example, shortages of some consumer goods and the fact that better quality products are being exported to earn hard currency have sometimes forced unfair terms on Chinese consumers.

6.2.13

Hooley, Graham J., David Shipley and Nathalie Krieger (1988), "A Method for

Modelling Consumer Perceptions of Country of Origin," *International Marketing Review,* 5(3), Autumn, 67-76.

The influence of country of origin on consumer attitudes and evaluations of product and service offerings is becoming increasingly important as competition in the international marketplace intensifies. This paper proposes a methodological approach to uncover and better understand the effects of country of origin images. Two distinct product categories are examined to illustrate the use of such an approach followed by a brief discussion of managerial implications.

6.2.14

Huszagh, Sandra M. and Arthur Murphy (1984), "Third World Markets Demand Household Data for Successful Consumer Goods Marketing: Mexico as a Case Example," *International Marketing Review,* 1(3), Spring/Summer, 66-72.

Influence in husband/wife purchasing decisions for durable goods among Mexican consumers is investigated. Results indicate traditional husband dominance in less affluent households, and female participation through joint decision making in middle class households.

6.2.15

Jacobs, Laurence, Charles Keown, Reginald Worthley, and Kyung-Il Ghymn (1991), "Cross-cultural Color Comparisons: Global Marketers Beware!" *International Marketing Review,* 8(3), 21-30.

The Luscher color test is used to compare color associations in China, South Korea, Japan and the United States. Respondents were asked which color they associate with words such as expensive, happy, love and dependable. They were also asked to relate the colors to countries, such as Italy and France: institutions, such as restaurants and theaters; and product packages, such as a soft drink label and a box of headache remedy. The finding show that, while some colors seem to show cross-cultural consistency, other colors such as purple and grey, hold opposite meanings in different cultures.

6.2.16

Johansson, Johny K., Susan P. Douglas, and Ikujiro Nonaka (1985), "Assessing the Impact of Country of Origin on Product Evaluations: A New Methodological Perspective," *Journal of Marketing Research,* 22(4), November, 388-396.

A multiattribute attitudinal model is introduced as an effective approach to examining the impact of country of origin on product evaluations. A questionnaire was sent to two sample groups—72 graduate students from the US and 82 students from Japan. The resulting data are analyzed to eliminate problems caused by differences in response set bias and to specify the final variables and the formulation of the simultaneous equations model. Results suggest that the impact of country of origin may be substantially more complex than has been previously assumed and that other information besides nationality should be considered in product evaluations. There is little evidence of stereotyping based on country of origin.

6.2.17

Kaynak, Erdener (1985), "Some Thoughts on Consumerism in Developed and Less Developed Countries," *International Marketing Review,* 2(2), Summer, 15-30.

In marketing literature, consumerism is often treated as a developed country phenomenon. The reason for this is partially attributable to a complete lack of appropriate conceptual and methodological frameworks to study consumerism issues across cultures and nations, specifically in less-developed countries. This article develops working propositions to study consumerism in multiple environments. Consumerism issues in developed countries versus LDC environments are discussed and their implications for international trade and marketing are elucidated.

6.2.18

Kaynak, Erdener and Solveig Wikstrom (1985), "Methodological Framework for a Cross-National Comparison of Consumerism Issues in Multiple Environments," *European Journal of Marketing,* 19(1) 31-46.

This study focuses on conceptualization of consumerism activity across countries—specifically, Sweden, Canada, and Turkey—and on probable consumer-related problems international firms may encounter in marketing their products in these nations. In addition, a framework is developed for analyzing the consumerism issues. Specific areas of discussion include (1) developed versus less-developed country (LDC) practices, (2) macro-environmental factors affecting the development of consumerism, (3) concept development for cross-national consumerism activity, and (4) managerial implications. Consumerism demands a healthy macroeconomic environment that is clearly lacking in most LDCs. As a result, consumerist attention in such countries focuses on micro issues (e.g., package sizes and product safety), whereas in developed nations, consumerists attempt to deal with major macro issues such as poverty.

6.2.19

Kaynak, Erdener (1989), "How Chinese Buyers Rate Foreign Suppliers," *Industrial Marketing Management,* 18(3), August, 187-198.

The author examines the attitudes of industrial purchasers from the Peoples' Republic of China toward a variety of products from 11 major foreign sourcing countries. Data for this study were collected through self-administered questionnaires distributed to a group of 2nd- and 3rd-level government officials attending an executive training program. The results of this research show that Chinese industrial purchasers' perceptions of foreign products have changed dramatically in the recent past. With the exception of electronics and telecommunications equipment, German products were rated as best by most respondents. US products were viewed as equal or similar to those of Japan on a product quality basis, with the exception of vehicles and motorcycles.

6.2.20

Keown, Charles F. (1985), "Asian Importers' Perceptions of American Manufacturers," *International Marketing Review,* 2(4), Winter, 48-54.

Twenty-eight importers from the five "dragons" in Asia (Japan, South Korea, Taiwan, Singapore and Hong Kong) were interviewed about their problems in doing business with American manufacturers and their suggestions for increasing future imports from the United States. Findings are presented in a marketing framework: product, price, distribution, promotion, regulations and interactions. Overall, American firms were perceived to apply the selling concept, to use short-term planning, and to provide little support to their Asian agents. By contrast, Japanese and European firms used the marketing concept, did long-range planning, and provided substantially more promotional assistance.

6.2.21

Kostecki, M. M. (1985), "The Consumer in a Socialist Economy," *European Journal of Marketing*, 19(1), 20-29.

Some of the practical issues that confront the consumer in a socialist economy are reviewed. The author argues that the theoretical primacy of the production principle and social interests under socialism is considerably challenged by the primacy of the bureaucracy and elitist political interests. Consumer choice under socialism is indeterminate, and consumer influence on production is very limited. The only realistic way to increase consumer sovereignty is to reduce economic centralism through the enhanced role of voluntary exchanges and the granting of increasing competence to the person in the line in front of a shop. Whether this reform will be acceptable politically is a vital issue for the future development of the East European socialist economies where consumers, workers, and managers are likely to increase aggressively their political pressure on the existing establishment and force economic decentralization.

6.2.22

Lee, Chol and Robert T. Green (1991), "Cross-cultural Examination of the Fishbein Behavioral Intentions Model," *Journal of International Business Studies,* 22(2), 289-305.

Most of the principal theories associated with consumer behavior have been developed and tested in the United States. A question that has been posed by some consumer researchers concerns the applicability of these theories outside of the United States. The study reported in this paper is a cross-cultural examination of the applicability of the Fishbein behavioral intentions model in Korea and the United States. Korea can be characterized as a collectivist culture that is different from the individualist culture dominant in the United States. The findings suggest that the Fishbein model can be employed to explain consumers' behavioral intentions formation in a Confucian culture, as well as in the United States.

6.2.23

Malhotra, Naresh K. (1988), ''A Methodology for Measuring Consumer Preferences in Developing Countries,'' *International Marketing Review,* 5(3), Autumn, 52-66.

An approach for measuring consumer preferences in developing countries is presented. The role of marketing research in developing countries and the salient factors which have an impact on how marketing research should be conducted in these countries are briefly discussed. The popular preference measurement procedures developed in the advanced nations are briefly reviewed and found to be unsuitable for use in developing countries. Hence, an alternative approach is proposed which reduces the data collection demands imposed on the respondents.

6.2.24

McGee, Lynn W. and Rosann L. Spiro (1991), ''Salesperson and Product Country-of-Origin Effects on Attitudes and Intentions to Purchase,'' *Journal of Business Research,* 22(1), January, 21-32.

The effect of salesperson's nationality on buyer attitudes is examined. Salesperson ethnic background and product country of origin were manipulated, and their effect on buyers' evaluations of the salesperson, sales presentation, product, company, and intentions to purchase were analyzed. In one experiment, Indian salespeople were rated as more professional and more likable than US salespeople. Japanese salespeople were seen as more friendly and more likable than US salespeople. This was the first reported attempt to evaluate the impact of national stereotyping on the industrial purchasing process.

6.2.25

Mitchell, Ivor S. and Tom O. Amioku (1985), ''Brand preference Factors in Patronage and Consumption of Nigerian Beer,'' *Columbia Journal of World Business,* 20(1), Spring, 55-67.

Until recently, Nigerian beer consumption grew although prices continually increased. Now that the beer industry has reached the mature stage of the product life cycle, the survival of individual companies will depend on how their brands meet the characteristics of target markets. In this paper, the authors explore what factors influence beer consumers' brand preferences. They recommend that the industry must pay more attention to the consumer while increasing product research and improving product features.

6.2.26

Morganosky, Michelle A. and Michelle M. Lazarde (1987), "Foreign-Made Apparel: Influences on Consumers' Perceptions of Brand and Store Quality," *International Journal of Advertising*, 6(4), 339-346.

Using a congruity theory approach, this article reports findings from telephone interviews of 100 US consumers who were asked to evaluate the quality of apparel for three brand types (name, designer, and store), four store types (department, discount, national chain, and off-price), and imported versus US-made apparel. Designer brands made in the US were viewed as having the best quality, while imports sold in discount stores received the lowest quality ratings. Department stores were rated the highest and discount stores were rated the lowest of the four store types. Regarding brand types, name brands received the highest quality ratings, and store brands received the lowest quality ratings. The US-made association did not increase or decrease the perception of name-brand quality, but store brands were perceived as significantly higher in quality if they were made in the US.

6.2.27

Muller, Thomas E. and Christopher Bolger (1985), "Search Behavior of French and English Canadians in Automobile Purchase," *International Marketing Review*, 2(4), Winter, 21-30.

To determine whether French and English Canadians had different information search patterns prior to automobile purchase, 210 buyers of 1983 and 1984 Ford and Toyota automobiles in two Ontario and two Quebec cities were surveyed. The result shows that compared to their English counterparts, French Canadians evaluated ten per cent fewer alternative car makes, spent 30 per cent fewer days in the search process, took 67 per cent fewer test drives, and scored eight per cent lower on a measure of overall depth of search.

6.2.28

Muller, Thomas E. (1991), "Using Personal Values to Define Segments in an International Tourism Market," *International Marketing Review*, 8(1), 57-70.

Value-based research can be applied to the segmentation of international tourism markets. US residents planning a pleasure trip to metropolitan Toronto and Ontario were surveyed at home about a week before their departure. The relative importance attached by the visitors to 16 attributes that describe the touristic attractiveness of a foreign city were used as clustering variables. Three major segments were found with each segment possessing a unique personal-value profile. These value profiles were meaningful and distinctive enough to offer international tourism marketers actionable portraits on which to base product development and marketing communication strategies that match a segment's personal-value orientations.

6.2.29

Murray, J. Alex and David L. Blenkhorn (1985), "Organizational Buying Process in North America and Japan," *International Marketing Review,* 2(4), Winter, 55-63.

Organizational buyer behavior in North America and Japan is compared. As North American firms become suppliers to the Japanese, knowledge of this behavior becomes increasingly important. Implications are presented for understanding Japanese influences in the organizational buying process through utilizing a generalized model from the marketing literature.

6.2.30

Ofir, Chezy and Donald R. Lehmann (1986), "Measuring Images of Foreign Products," *Columbia Journal of World Business,* 21(2), Summer, 105-108.

This paper presents a method for measuring country-level images for products. The method, which requires only ordinally sealed data and produces more efficient estimates than simple averages, is applied to American skier' images of European ski-vacations. The results indicate that the images of Switzerland, Austria, and France are relatively homogeneous with Switzerland more positively viewed than of France.

6.2.31

Papadopoulos, Nicolas, Louise A. Heslop, and Jozsef Beracs (1990), "National Stereotypes and Product Evaluations in a Socialist Country," *International Marketing Review,* 7(1), 32-47.

This paper reports findings of a cross-national consumer survey conducted in the US, Canada, the UK, the Netherlands, France, West Germany, Greece, and Hungary. The study's main purpose was to investigate the country-of-origin effect in depth. The factor analyses suggest some consistency in the underlying dimensions used by consumers to assess products and their origins. The respondents' views were found to be neither the same for various Western-origin products nor universally positive. The study provides some tentative evidence that product images may influence, or may be influenced by, country images. The study's findings suggest that the direction of causality between these two constructs is less clear than was previously thought.

6.2.32

Ryans, John K. , Saeed Samiee and James Wills (1985), "Consumerist Movement

and Advertising Regulation in the International Environment: Today and Future,''
European Journal of Marketing, 19(1), 5-11.

Given the growing power of consumer organizations and the increased world-wide
efforts to regulate advertising, how has this phenomenon been viewed by advertising
and marketing executives? Do they feel that consumer organizations accurately
reflect consumer views? And what changes in regulatory climate and consumerist
effort do they perceive for the future? This paper intends to answer these questions
through the findings of two studies—one conducted overseas among German and
Swiss advertising and marketing leaders and the other among the U.S. business
community. Generally, European and U.S. executives alike see these consumer
organizations as being non-representative of consumers and as being anti-
advertising. They feel that the consumer organizations are self-interested and using
government legislations to achieve their ends. At the same time, the consumerists are
viewed as misunderstanding the consumer and underestimating his or her
intelligence.

6.2.33

Sadafumi, Nishina (1990), ''Japanese Consumers: Introducing Foreign Products/
Brands into the Japanese Market,'' *Journal of Advertising Research,* 30(2),
April-May, 35-45.

Research was conducted on the attitude of Japanese consumers toward foreign
countries and products. Their perceptions were examined via two surveys. The first
was conducted in Tokyo and in Osaka, Japan, in 1986 on 1,420 men and women. The
second was conducted in Tokyo in 1987 on 700 women. A general comparison with
domestic products shows that foreign products are thought to be appealing in terms
of design and individuality. However, their function and quality are rated as reliable.
The European image is represented by traditional goods, such as Mercedes Benz and
Wedgewood, and the US image by cola, jeans, cigarettes, and chain restaurants. As
a result of a cluster analysis based on the eight items of image data, four types were
recognized—brands with images based on international images, country of origin,
country of entry, and function-quality.

6.2.34

Samli, A. Coskun, Dhruv Grewal, and Sanjeev K. Mathur (1988), ''International
Industrial Buyer Behavior: An Exploration and a Proposed Model,'' *Journal of
the Academy of Marketing Science,* 16(2), Summer, 19-29.

The authors analyzed models of organizational buying behavior by Webster and
Wind, Sheth, and Anderson and Chambers and found that these models have many
factors that affect their credibility and reliability in the international arena. Then the
authors proposed an international industrial buyer behavior model which has four
distinctive features: (1) an input-output format, (2) the buying decision resulting in

certain outcomes of extrinsic or intrinsic value, (3) identification and prioritization of factors influencing the international industrial buying behavior and a composite index of international industrial buyer behavior developed using a multiattribute technique, and (4) depiction of the international industrial buying process and the internal working of the buying unit. The total index scores provided by the model may allow international industrial marketers to cluster the world markets and match product features accordingly.

6.2.35

Shamdasani, Prem N. and Dennis W. Rook (1989), ''An Exploratory Study of Inpulse Buying in an Oriental Culture: the Case of Singapore,'' *Singapore Marketing Review,* Vol.4, 7-20.

This study represents a first, in-depth exploration of impulse buying in an oriental culture. It is a replication and extension of Rook's study of impulse buying in the U.S. Prepurchase influences, decision-making processes, and postpurchase aspects of Singapore consumers' impulse buying experience are analyzed. Together, these two studies provide the necessary background to conduct a more extensive cross-cultural study of impluse buying in the U.S. and Singapore.

6.2.36

Shimp, Terence A. and Subhash Sharma(1987), ''Consumer Ethnocentrism: Construction and Validation of the CETSCALE,'' *Journal of Marketing Research,* 24(3), August, 280-289.

The concept of consumer ethnocentrism is used to represent the beliefs of American consumers about the appropriateness or morality of buying foreign-made products. The CETSCALE was developed to measure ethnocentric tendencies, and a preliminary study of 800 consumers provided data. The scale was purified through judgmental panel screening and two purification studies. In order to test the reliability and construct validity of the 17-item scale, four separate studies were performed. Results show that the scale's internal consistency reliability was quite high, and the scale's convergent and discriminant validity were supported. The concept was also held to be nomologically valid. The effect of the threat of competition of foreign products upon individuals' quality of life and economic livelihood was also found to be significant.

6.2.37

Steinberg, Howard M. (1987), ''Detecting Consumer Attribute Shifts: A Technique for Monitoring International Marketing Strategies,'' *Columbia Journal of World Business,* 22(4), Winter, 3-7.

The author intends to explain why psychological meaning cannot help answer the standardization versus adaptation debate for international marketing strategies. The first section of this article uses current psychological theory to expose the vulnerability of the proposed psychological meaning approach. In the second section, an experiment which makes use of a simple nonparametric test affirms the hypothesis put forth in the first section. The study concludes with the implications of these findings and suggests a potential restriction for the technique and a more appropriate use for the psychological meaning technique in conjunction with conjoint analysis.

6.2.38

Tan, Chin Tiong and Catherine Ngui (1985), "Ethnic Differences in Reactions to Children's Advertising," *International Marketing Review,* 2(4), Winter, 31-37.

A printed advertisement was shown to dyads of mother-child subjects of Chinese, Malay and Caucasian origins. The analysis showed that after seeing the advertisement the groups differ on several dimensions such as awareness and understanding of the advertisement, reasons for liking the advertisement, and mother-child interaction on product request.

6.2.39

Thorelli, Hans B. (1985), "Product Information: Search and Satisfaction The PRC, Overseas Chinese and Thailand," *International Marketing Review,* 2(4), Winter, 12-20.

Confined to samples of middle-class consumers in the PRC and Thailand this comparative study included questions concerning awareness, attitudes and experiences of PRC Chinese, Thai-Chinese and Thais in the area of perceived risk and search for and satisfaction with product information. A major finding is that in these regards the Thai-Chinese are clearly closer to the Thai than to the Chinese consumers.

6.2.40

Vandermerwe, Sandra; L'Huillier and Marc-Andre (1989), "Euro-Consumers in 1992," *Business Horizons,* 32(1), January/February, 34-40.

In 1992, the European Community will create a single internal market. Euro-Consumers are a potentially new market which may become more lucrative and more stable than the US and Japan. Europe will convert itself into the largest single market in the industrialized world, 30% larger than the US by 1990. Within the EC, age groups will be more evenly distributed than in Japan or the US, making it a more stable market. The EC market will be both large and rich. The latest estimate for the 12-member EC shows a gross domestic product of $4,263.7 billion at current exchange rates. However, the average Euro-Consumer's purchasing power is less than that of average Americans or Japanese. Though a complex market,

Euro-Consumers are likely to become more similar in their needs for products and services.

6.2.41

Wall, Marjorie, John Liefeld, and Louise A. Heslop (1991), "Impact of Country-of-Origin Cues on Consumer Judgments in Multi-Cue Situations: A Covariance Analysis," *Journal of the Academy of Marketing Science,* 19(2), Spring, 105-113.

The effect of country-of-origin on buyers' evaluation of product quality, risk to purchase, perceived value, and likelihood of purchasing was tested. Country-of-origin information was found to be more important in affecting product quality assessments than price and brand information. While price was important in value assessment, brand was significant in a few product-specific cases. Age, education, sex, and perceptions of ability to judge products were variously related to consumers' ratings of quality, risk, value, and likelihood of purchase. However, much of the variation in consumer judgments was not accounted for by the variables employed.

6.2.42

Yavas, Ugur and Secil Tuncalp (1984), "Exporting to Saudi-Arabia: the Power of the 'Made-in' Label," *International Marketing Review,* 1(4), Autumn/Winter, 40-50.

This study examines Saudi consumers' attitudes toward a "made-in UK" label. The authors also discuss several strategies that can be used to promote the "made-in UK" label in Saudi Arabia.

6.2.43

Yavas, Ugur and Secil Tuncalp (1984), "Perceived Risk in Grocery Outlet Selection: A Case Study in Saudi Arabia," *European Journal of Marketing,* 18(3), 13-25.

The purpose of this study is to assess if perceived risk is a determinant of supermarket patronage by using Saudi Arabia as a case in point. The findings illustrate that a Saudi consumer's decision to patronize supermarkets is inversely affected by the level of risk associated with shopping at supermarkets: the higher the risk perception, the less likely it is that a consumer will patronize supermarkets. It appears that a combination of risks causes some consumers to prefer other shopping places more familiar to them. These potential risks include: (1) consumers' perceptions that shopping at supermarkets may negatively affect the way others think of them; (2) products purchased at supermarkets may turn out to be contaminated or adulterated thus leading to a waste of their efforts in getting them exchanged/returned; and (3) altogether waste of their money.

6.2.44

Zaichkowsky, Judith L. and James H. Sood (1989), "A Global Look at Consumer Involvement and Use of Products," *International Marketing Review,* 6(1), Spring, 20-34.

Respondents from 15 countries reported their level of use and involvement with 8 products and services. The results indicated that country accounted for 8% to 45% of the variation in product and service usage. Among regular product users, country accounts for 1% to 20% of the variation in involvement levels across products and services.

Author Index